WRITING IN THE KITCHEN

Writing in the Kitchen

ESSAYS ON SOUTHERN LITERATURE AND FOODWAYS

EDITED BY DAVID A. DAVIS AND TARA POWELL

UNIVERSITY PRESS OF MISSISSIPPI / JACKSON

www.upress.state.ms.us

The University Press of Mississippi is a member
of the Association of American University Presses.

Copyright © 2014 by University Press of Mississippi
All rights reserved
Manufactured in the United States of America

First printing 2014
∞
Library of Congress Cataloging-in-Publication Data

Writing in the kitchen : essays on Southern literature and
foodways / edited by David A. Davis, Tara Powell ; foreword
by Jessica B. Harris.
    pages cm
    Includes bibliographical references and index.
    ISBN 978-1-62846-023-0 (hardback) — ISBN 978-1-62846-024-7
(ebook) 1. American literature—Southern States—History
and criticism. 2. Food in literature. 3. Food—Southern States.
I. Davis, David A. (David Alexander), 1975– editor of compilation.
II. Powell, Tara, 1976–
    PS261.W75 2014
    810.9′975—dc23   2014005433

British Library Cataloging-in-Publication Data available

TO OUR MUTUAL TEACHER AND FRIEND, FRED HOBSON

CONTENTS

FOREWORD

JESSICA B. HARRIS

Writing in the Kitchen: Essays on Southern Literature and Foodways was conceived at a meeting of the Society for the Study of Southern Literature in New Orleans in 2010. David A. Davis of Mercer University and Tara Powell of the University of South Carolina had crafted a panel on Food and Southern Literature, which they asked me to moderate. Following the successful panel, ideas perking away, we moved on to that city's Southern Food and Beverage Museum and after that to dinner. There, after some wine and some discussion, we began to focus our discussion and to think of transforming the panel into a collection of essays on the subject using some of the presentations as the basis. David and Tara took on the formidable task of crafting the volume and soliciting essays from fellow scholars across multiple disciplines who were working at the intersection of the study of food and foodways and the study of the American South. It took some fits and false starts, but after about four years, the result of that evening is now the volume that you hold in your hands. I'd always known that the work would be a filling meal of thoughtful musings on food as it is shown in the literature of the South. *Writing in the Kitchen: Essays on Southern Literature and Foodways*, though, is not a simple meal but a thirteen-course banquet that is hugely satisfying.

Writing in the Kitchen: Essays on Southern Literature and Foodways is a varied compilation that is at the same time scholarly and approachable and covers all aspects of food from production through consumption. It deals with such classically southern issues as agriculture and urbanization, as well as race, gender, and ethnicity, in new and innovative ways. To paraphrase African American author and anthropologist Zora Neale Hurston, *Writing in the Kitchen: Essays on Southern Literature and Foodways* examines the literature of the South and indeed the South itself through the spyglass of food. Containing works by not only some of the leading scholars in the area but by newer scholars as well, it is a worthy entry into the growing bibliography of works examining the food and culture of America's iconic South. As such, *Writing in the Kitchen: Essays on Southern Literature and Foodways* sets a high bar indeed and offers ample fodder for future investigations by the growing numbers of food studies students. Voila!

Recipe for a Food Studies Classic

Ingredients

1 David Davis
1 Tara Powell
12 scholars of various disciplines

Assemble 4 scholars in New Orleans to discuss food in southern literature. Mix well at the annual conference of the Society for the Study of Southern Literature. Marinate well with oysters and wine until idea for a book is formed. Then continue discussion at the Southern Food and Beverage Museum. Allow to mature, then add the remaining scholars to the mix. Season with humor and scholarship and let simmer for 3 years. Finally, assemble into a well-curated collection. When done, serve it up proudly to an awaiting audience. The results can be savored in one sitting or in small bites.

    SAVOR!

ACKNOWLEDGMENTS

A host of generous people have helped us in shaping this collection of essays. We appreciate the enthusiasm of Jessica Harris and Leila Salisbury for the project, as well as the hard work of the scholars who have contributed the essays collected here. We also thank the organizers of the Society for the Study of Southern Literature meeting in New Orleans, at which the notion for this collection was cooked up, and the curators of the Southern Food and Beverage Museum for inviting us and our colleagues into their space to talk about food and southern literature. The interest and good ideas of our literature and southern studies students at the University of South Carolina and Mercer University have also been important to us as we thought about how to put together a rigorous, readable study that would be useful to a range of scholars and students. Last, but never least, we are grateful to our spouses, Kris Davis and Mike Mareska, and our families, with whom we so often set the table and then sit down to enjoy these foods, to talk about writing, and to connect new memories to old through foodways. This is your book, too.

WRITING IN THE KITCHEN

Chapter One

READING SOUTHERN FOOD

DAVID A. DAVIS AND TARA POWELL

This book began in New Orleans. We put together a panel on southern literature and foodways for the biennial meeting of the Society for the Study of Southern Literature in 2010. Because we were meeting in a city famous for its collision of ethnicities, its culture of excess, and its profusion of distinctive foodways, we felt a session to discuss the role of food in southern literature was appropriate, and the conversation in that session was heady and exciting. We moved a group of interested parties to the Southern Food and Beverage Museum to expand the discussion, and we soon knew from the energy in the ensuing dialogue that food had a special resonance in southern literature. It seems obvious. Examples of food abound in southern writing, lending their sweet, smoky, greasy redolence to stories about life in the South. Later, as we enjoyed oysters and bourbon at a restaurant in the French Quarter, Jessica Harris suggested that the time would be right for a collection of essays that formally opened a conversation about southern literature and foodways, and she asked us if we might be interested in putting one together. With our mouths full, we nodded our heads to agree.

We are both native southerners, raised on grits and greens. We have participated in many of the rituals of southern food—pig pickins, dinner on the grounds, fish fries, and funeral potlucks. We have both become scholars of southern literature and taught in interdisciplinary southern studies programs. David has taught courses about southern food, and Tara has written poems about southern food, so we both have a personal, vested interest in this topic. We understand that the phrase "southern food" covers a complex of microregional and ethnic identities, historical problems and contradictions, and disparities of poverty and plenty. The prevailing trend in American popular culture, extending from nineteenth-century accounts of plantation groaning tables overloaded with regional delicacies to Paula Deen's much-mocked obsession with butter, has been to associate southern food with abundance and extravagance, but the reality of southern food is that it is based more on ingenuity born of privation and necessity. Southern foodways originated through the use of available ingredients, typically whatever could grow locally, prepared with simple, sometimes primitive, techniques. It has these characteristics of locality, simplicity, and necessity in common with many of the great ethnic cuisines of the world.

Southern foodways have figured in American popular culture for a long time, but they have become the subject of increasing scholarly attention recently. John Egerton's pioneering 1987 book *Southern Food* established a baseline of traditions, recipes, and restaurants, and a special edition of *Southern Quarterly* Peggy Prenshaw edited in 1992 focused attention on southern food and literature with classic essays by Minrose Gwin, Patricia Yaeger, and others. The Southern Foodways Alliance, directed by John T. Edge, was founded in 1999 to connect chefs and scholars with vernacular traditions and create a vibrant forum for discussion of both traditions and innovations. Southern foodways scholarship has expanded quickly in the past few years with the publication of such books as *Building Houses Out of Chicken Legs: Black Women, Food, and Power* (2006) by Psyche Williams-Forson, *The New Encyclopedia of Southern Culture: Volume 7: Foodways* (2007), edited by John T. Edge, *Stirring the Pot: The Kitchen and Domesticity in the Fiction of Southern Women* (2008) by Laura Sloan Patterson, *Hog and Hominy: Soul Food from Africa to America* (2008) by Frederick Douglass Opie, *Savage Barbecue: Race, Culture, and the Invention of America's First Food* (2008) by Andrew Warnes, *Cooking in Other Women's Kitchens: Domestic Workers in the South, 1865–1960* (2010) by Rebecca Sharpless, *High on the Hog: A Culinary Journey from Africa to America* (2011) by Jessica Harris, and *A Mess of Greens: Southern Gender and Southern Food* (2011) by Elizabeth S. D. Engelhardt.

This outpouring of scholarly interest in southern food signals that southern food is a revealing area of inquiry. Food is a text upon which the history and values of the southern people are written. Foodways reveal, for example, how Native American, African, and European cultures blended to yield a distinctive, synthetic culture. Cornbread is made from maize, a native New World ingredient, and it has developed a totemic significance as the food on which southerners survived for centuries. This coarse, humble bread, which can be baked directly over a fire, signifies the defining characteristics of southern food: blending of cultures, resourcefulness in the face of poverty, and the persistence of tradition. In the past generation, however, modern advances in global food distribution, industrialized agriculture, and international flows of population have threatened to displace southern food traditions, leading some people to fear that southern food will become a cultural atavism. This worry may be valid, but southern food has so far proved to be highly dynamic. It has absorbed even more cultural influences, penetrated popular culture, and retained its reputation as America's major contribution to global cuisine.

Reading southern literature with an awareness of food reveals how integral it is across a broad range of texts, new and old. It is seemingly everywhere. Food in southern literature often has a symbolic value: food in kitchens often signifies domesticity, the struggle for food symbolizes poverty, abundance of food indicates wealth, preparation of food may reflect gender roles, food labor can mark racial hierarchy, sharing food often represents social or community bonds, raising food can symbolize agrarianism or connection to land, and eating traditional southern food reinforces southern identity. Although food can be highly significant in a text, it is often inconspicuous. Yet, if we consider the number of texts depicting poverty near the point of starvation, such as *Tobacco Road* or *Let Us Now Praise Famous Men*; novels that feature the kitchen as a crucial setting, such as *To Kill a Mockingbird* or *The Member of the Wedding*; and books that focus on a major social event centered on food, such as *Delta Wedding*, then the vital role that food plays in these texts becomes more evident.

We do not mean to suggest, though, that food has an established or defined set of meanings in a text. Often, it is delightfully ambiguous, nuanced, or subtle, and sometimes food can unlock a critical reading of a text. At the end of William Faulkner's *As I Lay Dying*, for example, Vardaman and Dewey Dell, both of whom had been disappointed by not getting what they wanted from their arduous journey to Jefferson, console themselves by eating bananas while they wait for the father to join them. Their "mouths half open and half-et bananas in their hands" indicate their surprise at meeting the new Mrs. Bundren, but the bananas signify more than just surprise (260). Bananas are a perishable tropical fruit that, while commonplace in grocery stores now, were difficult to acquire in the rural South during the Great Depression. The bananas, which were grown on plantations owned by Americans in quasi-colonial states—banana republics of Central America—demonstrate both America's imperialism in the early twentieth century and the development of modern systems of transportation and distribution. United Fruit Company, headquartered in New Orleans, dominated the international banana trade and, in a paradigm that spans from colonialism through globalism, exploited workers in one country and created millionaires in another. This reference to bananas in Jefferson indirectly connects Faulkner's novel to the works of many Latin American writers who depicted the labor of banana workers, such as Pablo Neruda's poem "United Fruit Co.," which indicates the hemispheric connections of southern culture.

Not all southern food references are this subtle, though. One of the most obvious examples of food in southern literature is the image of Scarlett O'Hara in Margaret Mitchell's *Gone with the Wind* ravenously devouring a radish, the only food remaining on the devastated Tara plantation after Sherman's soldiers marched through. After she eats it, "her empty stomach revolted and she lay in the soft dirt and vomited tiredly" (592). This moment is her nadir, but she heroically gathers her strength and vows, "As God is my witness, I'm never going to be hungry again" (593). This scene, which in the film version takes place just before intermission, resonated in the imaginations of Depression-era southerners, many of whom had gone hungry, who may have seen the fact that Scarlett embraced industrialization to rebuild her family's fortunes as a model for revitalizing the southern economy, which, like Reconstruction-era Tara, still depended on cotton production. In this case, the humble radish symbolizes the depths of destitution and privation southerners suffered both during Reconstruction and during the Great Depression.

While this is one of the most famous examples of food in southern literature, perhaps the most important example is in Ralph Ellison's *Invisible Man*. Finding a yam vendor on the streets of Harlem selling bubbly baked sweet potatoes leads the Invisible Man to reflect on southern food and black identity. He notes that the black bourgeoisie in the South would be ashamed to be seen eating chitterlings, mustard greens, pigs' ears, pork chops, and black-eyed peas in public (265). In the city, however, he enjoys the freedom to eat yams on the street without shame. "But not yams," he thinks, "I had no problem concerning them and I would eat them whenever and wherever I took the notion. Continue on the yam level and life would be sweet—though somewhat yellowish. Yet the freedom to eat yams on the street was far less than I had expected upon coming to the city" (267). His disillusionment over the limits of his freedom indicates the false promise of social equality in the North that propelled the Great Migration, but this scene also demonstrates the power of food to excite memory and to reinforce identity. As African Americans left the South, they transported traditional foodways with them. Food is one of the most resilient markers of ethnicity, which is why immigrant communities often maintain food traditions even as other practices assimilate into the mainstream.

Eating is a means of performing identity, so eating traditional southern foods allows people to perform southern identity, whether they are southern or not. This has led to a concern about the future of traditional southern foodways that may be called the fried chicken paradox. Since the emergence of the interstate highway system and the networks of fast food franchises that feed America's long-distance drivers and daily commuters, fried chicken has surpassed cornbread in popular culture as the totemic southern food. Served at Kentucky Fried Chicken, Popeyes, Church's, and Chick-fil-A, mass-produced chicken has been exported out of the South, even globally, as a commodified version of traditional southern food. The result is a version of southern foodways based on marketing hokum that worries traditionalists who lament the inauthenticity of culinary exports. The ascendency of mass-marketed southern food in popular culture has sent many southern chefs back into the pantry to recover presumably authentic recipes and ingredients, partly as a means of preserving southern identity. While this preservation is good for both scholars and gourmands, it also creates its own false condition of consumption. Southern foodways, like all vernacular cuisines, developed from the use of available ingredients prepared with available methods, so in the conditions of modern life, fast-food fried chicken—in addition to the enormous influx of ethnic foods and mass-marketed products available in modern grocery stores—is southern food. The self-conscious act of preparing or eating traditional southern food, therefore, is a deliberate act of performing southern identity.

Let us not, though, dismiss southern foodways as an imaginary construct. Southern foodways constitute a distinctive cuisine, and their development mirrors southern history. The earliest southern foodways were Native American foods, which blended elements of village agriculture, growing primarily corn with some other indigenous vegetables, with hunting and gathering. European colonists introduced new ingredients, including the essential pig, along with new techniques, a preference for baking, and a palate for heavily salted food. The African slave trade brought ingredients from Africa, such as okra, and from the New World tropics, particularly sugarcane in its botanical form and as processed products—sugar, molasses, and rum. African slaves added more techniques and tastes, especially an affinity for rice, and incorporated new spices and peppers. The blending of these cultures and methods over several decades produced a recognizable cuisine, and that system of foodways has continued to develop into the twentieth century, yielding some famous dishes, such as smoked pork barbecue, black-eyed peas simmered with hog jowl, cracklin' cornbread, and sweet potatoes candied with molasses, plus modern industrial foods such as heavily sweetened carbonated beverages, including Coca-Cola, Pepsi, a rainbow of fruit-inspired drinks, and manufactured treats such as MoonPies and pecan logs.

Southern food is often a revealing lens into southern history, but one could legitimately worry that the image of southern food in contemporary popular culture distorts the long history of food as a social problem in the South. Recent cookbooks such as *The Lee Bros. Southern Cookbook* by Matt and Ted Lee, *Screen Doors and Sweet Tea* by Martha Foose, and *A New Turn in the South* by Hugh Acheson celebrate and reinvent vernacular southern foodways, but one could come away from these books assuming that food has always been abundant and delicious in the South. This is a myth that needs to be debunked. In truth, for many southerners, food security has been and continues to be a serious issue. For most of the South's history, its laborers working in the plantation system, including slaves and sharecroppers, survived on the famous three Ms: small rations of meat, meal, and molasses. Small farmers who depended on cotton and tobacco, inedible staple crops, for their income, could often not afford to raise enough of their own food for subsistence. Ironically, although the South had a primarily agricultural economy through the second half of the twentieth century, it imported a significant percentage of its food, and serious issues of food inequality continue to reflect the region's troubling history of race and class divisions.

The southern diet has also led to multiple epidemics of nutritional diseases. Hunger and starvation have followed periods of drought, flood, and economic instability, and outbreaks of cholera and other food-borne illnesses have occurred. Perhaps the most unsettling nutritional disorder in southern history is the epidemic of pellagra, a niacin deficiency, that affected thousands of southerners in the early twentieth century. Poor southerners ate a diet heavily based in corn, but the corn was often ground. It was not treated with lye in the process called nixtamalization developed by the Aztecs to create hominy. Corn contains niacin, but it is not nutritionally available in unprocessed corn, and many poor southerners did not have access to other vegetable sources of niacin. Pellagra sufferers developed dermatitis, diarrhea, and dementia, and, if untreated, could die; the problem was so pervasive that Congress established a hospital for pellagra in Spartanburg, South Carolina, in 1914. The epidemic subsided by the late 1930s, and resulted in an increased use of hominy, often ground as grits, in the southern diet. But the southern diet continues to be a nutritional problem. Now, more than 30 percent of the population of most southern states is obese, and diabetes, heart disease, and hypertension rates have increased, prompting public health officials to propose changes in the way southerners eat.

Southern food involves a mass of contradictions. One of the clearest illustrations of the historical and cultural paradoxes of southern food is the rise and fall of Paula Deen. Divorced and broke with two small children in 1989, Deen began preparing sack lunches for businesses in Savannah—a venture she would eventually parlay into a successful restaurant. With entrepreneurial zeal and infectious charisma, she grew a southern food empire with several shows on the Food Network, a popular restaurant in Savannah, a chain of buffets at Harrah's casinos, and multiple endorsement deals with culinary products such as cooking pans, ham, and butter. She became America's surrogate southern grandmother, embodying comfort and a bit of naughty self-indulgence. This stage of her meteoric career appeared to come to a public end in 2013, when a deposition in which she admitted to making racist comments was released to the press. In the subsequent fallout, she lost her contract with Food Network and most of her endorsements. She shifted quickly into a symbol for the South's latent, casual racism, and a poorly coordinated public relations response made matters worse, leaving some people to defend her as a victim of persecution and others to denounce her as a fraud. Either way, her public persona signifies the inherent contradictions of southern food, in which a legacy of racism and exploitation lingers just beneath a veneer of hospitality and nostalgia.

◆ ◆ ◆

The way southerners eat is a text. Southern food reveals history, social values, and social problems; it maintains community and identity; and it contributes to the development and maintenance of southern culture. We can read and interpret southern food in several modes—as artifact, as ritual, as daily practice, as representation, and as symbol. The essays in this collection offer interpretations of southern foodways that employ all of these methods to focus attention on the role food plays in southern literature and to broaden the discourse about foodways. Literal food has meaning, and literary food does, too: often in ways that decipher the complex cultural coding embedded in literal foodways. The following essays cover a long period of history to represent several microregions and distinct ethnicities, and they draw on multiple critical methodologies to examine different textual forms and discuss a cross-section of specific foodways. Variety is one of the features of this collection as a whole, but within this variety we identify a set of important themes that are crucial to the study of southern literature and foodways, including looking at how a consideration of foodways illuminates literary qualities in nontraditional texts, complicates the imaginative representation of domestic spaces, destabilizes the constricting notion of binary black and white Souths, and enriches the special symbolic possibilities in foods across a range of familiar and unfamiliar literary texts.

Some of the essays in this collection expand our notions of texts about food by offering interpretations of food as a signifier in works that are outside the literary mainstream. David Shields explains that print culture in the early republic focused primarily on agriculture because growing crops was crucial to the young nation's economic viability. America's foremost thinkers, including Thomas Jefferson, obsessed over the development of new farming methods and the introduction of new crops, and the southern plantation before the invention of the cotton gin tended to be a highly diversified, innovative agricultural laboratory. The advent of the cotton plantation divided the southern economy from the northern economy, and Marcie Cohen Ferris analyzes the descriptions of distinctively southern food in the personal writings of northern visitors and of some southerners. She reveals that the traditions of southern food developed in a dynamic, sometimes contentious, social milieu, and that southern food was not universally appreciated or consistently appetizing. Sarah Walden discusses the racial tension in southern cookbooks from 1880 to 1930 to expose the role African American women played in establishing southern foodways and to explore the relationship between domesticity and literacy in the segregated South. Cookbooks are the texts that most obviously record food traditions, so they are essential for the study of foodways, but Elizabeth Engelhardt challenges the boundaries between cookbooks and fiction in her interpretation of Landonia Dashiell's story "Aunt Sanna Terry," finding that the conventional boundaries between fiction and cooking are porous in instructional texts by club women about cooking and domesticity.

Another approach to considering food's role in southern literature explores how books about food often take place within domestic spaces. Many such books portray everyday life in the home as a site of racial and gender conflict. In the segregated South, for example, African American women performed the cooking and domestic labor in the homes of many white families. Ann Romines's essay analyzes Willa Cather's imaginary account of her grandmother's kitchen in Virginia and the slave women who prepared the family's meals. Cather's novel *Sapphira and the Slave Girl* critiques the complex racial mores that operated within the plantation household. David A. Davis examines the depiction of the intimate interracial domestic relationships in three novels by white women writers set during the Civil Rights Movement, when the system of domestic racial division that had been largely unchanged since the antebellum period finally collapsed. Another of the essays argues that Ann Allen Shockley explodes the conventional boundaries of interracial domestic intimacy in *Loving Her*, her unheralded novel about an interracial, interclass lesbian relationship. Psyche Williams-Forson demonstrates in this essay that Shockley's novel, in which the black working-class partner takes on domestic tasks for her wealthier white partner, reinforces the established paradigms of race and gender at the same time that it challenges them.

The paradigms of southern culture, however, become much less stable beyond the black-white binary that has historically dominated mainstream social relations. The South is, and seemingly always has been, both highly diverse and socially rigid, and microregional populations and ethnic minorities contribute distinctive food traditions to southern cuisine. As southern foodways blended Native American, African, and European foods together, Native American populations were systematically and ruthlessly displaced, but in the same way that Native Americans have continued to maintain an identity within the South, their foodways endure. Melanie Benson Taylor finds that traditional Native American foodways resonate in contemporary Native American literature in ways that mark the painful history of Removal. Erica Abrams Locklear focuses on the microregional foodways of the Appalachian South, another cuisine that endures in the contemporary South. Taking the recent cultural ascendency of Appalachian foods as her point of departure, she argues that Appalachian writers have been reacting against negative perceptions of their culture and promoting local foodways for decades. The influx of Asian immigrants into the South in the past generation has incorporated a new range of flavors into southern food as well, but Lisa Hinrichsen contends that the move to the South has been difficult, creating fragmented identities she discusses in two novels by Vietnamese American authors. For members of these immigrant communities, food functions as a mnemonic bridge connecting the southeastern United States to Southeast Asia.

Finally, images of food in literature spark memories and fuel the imagination, so writers often use food for its symbolic value. References to southern food can signify the region's painful past, can represent southern identity, and can indicate the trajectory of the South's future. Tara Powell finds these meanings and more in the use of food symbolism by contemporary southern poets. Nikky Finney, for example, titled her recent collection *Head Off and Split*, using the images of preparing and eating fish to represent the complications, contradictions, and rewards of maintaining a black southern identity in general and a connection to her childhood home and her family in particular. Ruth Salvaggio explores the inherent poetry of southern food, specifically the cuisine of her native New Orleans, as a place where food infuses language, history, music, and geography, and where centuries of settlement by dozens of immigrant populations have both demonstrated the development of southern food as a process of cultural blending and created a unique cuisine that amplifies the mixture of cosmopolitan cultures. She finds in the language of sweet potatoes, artichokes, and mirlitons the tastes and smells that feed her memory.

We hope this collection whets readers' appetites for more considerations of foodways in southern literature. The scholarly attention focused on southern foodways recently has touched on the periphery of southern literature, but we feel that food can open a vital field of discourse, leading to new readings of southern writing, as well as to a better critical understanding of regional foodways. We are convinced that literature tells us things about foodways that history, sociology, and anthropology cannot and, conversely, that analyzing depictions of food unlocks new interpretations of southern literature. Our session at the Society for the Study of Southern Literature conference in New Orleans inspired us to think more critically about food and southern literature, and the provocative essays in this collection set the metaphorical table for a literary feast.

Works Cited

Ellison, Ralph. *Invisible Man*. 1952. New York: Vintage, 1995.
Faulkner, William. *As I Lay Dying*. 1930. New York: Vintage, 1991.
Mitchell, Margaret. *Gone with the Wind*. 1936. New York: Warner Books, 1993.

Chapter Two

BOOK FARMING
Thomas Jefferson and the Necessity of Reading in the Agrarian South

DAVID S. SHIELDS

ometime during the first three decades of the nineteenth century, the old customary instruction in agriculture, the rote imitation of the practices of one's parents and grandparents in the fields and garden, no longer insured success. Only print provided a sure pathway to sustenance and surplus. One either became a book farmer or endured a life of risk, subsistence, and privation. The turn toward letters reflected no dawning of scientific enlightenment or spread of agricultural gentility. Terror impelled it. A generation of agricultural prophets arose, proclaiming woe—men like John Taylor of Caroline County, Virginia, and George W. Jeffreys of North Carolina—but even the dullest dirt pusher did not need an oracle to read the signs: topsoil washing into streams, infestations of weeds, declining productivity, and an unending stream of young men moving west toward new land rather than farm the family acres. The crisis that birthed agricultural literacy took place in different places at different times—first in the tobacco-exhausted Chesapeake Tidewater, then in erosion-prone corn lands of the Piedmont, then the cotton lands of Carolina.

The soil crisis of the early nineteenth century shaped the creation of a particular world of letters. It supplanted the book-centered transatlantic conversation of agricultural reformers and horticulturists (the world in which the "founding gardeners" grew to maturity in the eighteenth century) with a periodical culture, regional in focus, demotic in its exchanges, and organized in tension with a network of associations, nurseries, and fairs. The transformation can be witnessed in the engagements of the most conspicuous agricultural reformer of the early republic, Thomas Jefferson. Yet its fullness resided in the explosive expansion of an American world of agricultural letters in which the South articulated its sectional identity and addressed its peculiar challenges in terms of labor, trade, staple cultivation, and soil management. This essay will examine the circumstances that compelled farmers to read, to experiment, and to pick up the pen. It will also remind twenty-first-century readers that agricultural letters during the antebellum period was the most robust literature in the nation, generating the most titles, printing the greatest number of contributing authors, and having the most consequential influence upon the conduct of ordinary life. Yet it remains the least studied of any significant body of writing generated in nineteenth-century America.

In 1819, Maryland lawyer and sportsman John Stuart Skinner launched *The American Farmer*, the first magazine in the United States devoted to agriculture.[1] Its success ignited the explosion of the agricultural press, a periodical literature so vast by the Civil War that only religion, in all its denominational multitude and contentiousness, approached having a commensurate number titles and pages.[2] Thomas Jefferson recognized the transformation afoot and marshaled his great authority to compound writing's influence upon agricultural practice. Within a year after Skinner commenced his magazine, Jefferson used *The American Farmer* in 1820 to advocate the keeping of personal farm journals and to promote the formation of personal libraries on agriculture. Jefferson believed, as did most classical republicans, that writing enabled reflection upon practice and therefore its emendation. He had witnessed the consolidation of an experimental class of farmers in France and England and had educated himself on their findings. He anticipated, but would not live to see, a more demotic world of experimental farmers called into being by *The American Farmer* and its many imitators in America.

How did Jefferson know that the moment for the transformation of agriculture had come? Why was 1820 the year that the word would overturn the tradition of farming practice and inaugurate a new enlightened way? We have to look to Jefferson's closest intellectual comrade, James Madison, for context. In August and September of 1819, *The American Farmer* serially published Madison's address as the first president of the Albemarle Agricultural Society of Virginia upon the state of the art. This address, made famous by Andrea Wulf's appreciation in *Founding Gardeners* of its nascent environmentalism, is a complex and fascinating document, displaying a global and historical sense of his subject, while simultaneously attending to local conditions. It mixed confidence in the enlightened march of civilization with trepidation about the economic and environmental forces troubling farming in the Old Dominion. He saw with particular clarity the continental dimensions of his subject, noting with a Malthusian sensibility how agricultural organization put into place the conditions for population growth, and how the Louisiana Purchase invited that swelling population to surge westward in search of new lands to cultivate. The lure of the west put pressure on eastern farming, particularly in drawing the ambitious and talented from eastern holdings. He noted that the price of labor had increased in recent years fourfold, while the price of land had increased tenfold. "It might be profitable, therefore, now to contract the surface over which labour is spread even if the soil retained its freshness and fertility. But this is not the case. Much of the fertile soil is exhausted, and unfertile soils are brought into cultivation" (Madison 170). Traditional agriculture in Virginia in 1820 was in crisis because of declining productivity, caused by farmers year after year planting the same cash crops, tobacco and corn, until the soil had been leached of nutriment. Madison also noted that in South Carolina the unremitting cultivation of cotton performed the same damage. The widespread impoverishment of the land demanded change and the imposition of some system to make agriculture viable.[3] "The evil of pressing too hard on the land has also been much increased by the bad mode in ploughing it" (170). Shallow plowing up and down hilly land occasioned the erosion of topsoil. Madison championed horizontal (i.e., contour) deep plowing, the regular employment of manures to restore land, crop rotation, and the periodic resting of land for a fallow season.

Throughout the address Madison criticized the neglect of soil replenishment by "some farmers"—an unenlightened cohort that includes men "of distinction." No doubt these were latter day believers in the colonial doctrine of the inexhaustible fecundity of American land. When settlers first came to Virginia, they found natives planting maize, squash, and beans in untreated soil and enjoying enormous yields. Colonists abandoned the field rotations that their European forebears had undertaken for generations.[4] At best, colonists had their livestock graze and dung a field. They did not intercrop like the Native Americans. In places, the practice of letting fields lie fallow periodically was abandoned. Season followed season until exploiting the topsoil became an American farming tradition that even the declining yields in tobacco fields did not shake, at least until newly opened, freshly fertile lands to the west began outproducing and underselling Virginia's commodities, even with the costs of transport. In 1817, the year of The Albemarle Agricultural Society's founding, construction began on the Erie Canal, threatening the eclipse of southern commerce by goods brought through New York from the upper Midwest. In 1820, projectors first planned the Chesapeake and Ohio Canal along the Potomac River. For the established planters of Virginia, the prospect of competing in the corn and wheat markets with Ohio farmers inspired anxiety.

In certain respects, John Taylor of Caroline's *Arator* (1813) activated the agrarian anxiety over the soil.[5] The canal projects and commodities market exacerbated it. By 1819 and 1820, a full-blown agrarian apocalypse haunted the imaginations of southern agriculturists.[6] The second wave of agricultural society formation among farmers in the 1810s and '20s more closely approximated a codependency of gatherings than the sociable and patriotic rural projectors, who made up the societies formed at the end of the eighteenth century. It was to this anxiety that Madison and Jefferson offered systematic agriculture as a consolation and the illuminating word of the agricultural book and magazine as an anodyne.

The linkage between the soil crisis and the work of agricultural print can be seen in Jefferson's 1817 letter to George W. Jeffreys, which was published in the June 9, 1820, issue of *The American Farmer*. Jeffreys, a North Carolina planter, wrote to several American luminaries requesting information on plowing and also on the ideal agricultural library.[7] Among those who responded were John Taylor of Caroline, John Adams, John Esten Cooke, and Jefferson, who wrote: "The horizontal ploughing, after which you inquire, has been practiced here by Col. Randolph, my son-in-law, who first introduced it about a dozen or fifteen years since. Its advantages were so soon observed, that it has already become very general and has entirely changed and renovated the face of our country. Every rain before that, while it did a temporary good, did greater permanent evil, by carrying off our soil; and fields were no sooner cleared than wasted. At present we may say that we lose none of our soil" (Jeffreys 93). Indeed, Jefferson's own farms had suffered extraordinary erosion damage in the 1790s prior to the adoption of horizontal plowing.

Jefferson's missive communicated his faith in the power of emulation among farmers, observing how Thomas Mann Randolph, Jr.'s[8] practices spread throughout a region because of their evident benefits. Agricultural societies enabled such emulation, putting members in contact with model planters and directly informing them of successful experiments. Jefferson later in the letter showed that even he, a savant and ex-president, could imitate the actions of a younger cultivator. Jefferson noted that he had adopted Randolph's method for a hilly farm he owned near Lynchburg: "It is spreading rapidly, and will be the salvation of that, as it confessedly has been of this part of the country. Horizontal and deep plowing, with the use of plaster and clover, which are but beginning to be used here, we believe will restore this part of our country to its original fertility."

Jefferson climaxed his letter to Jeffreys with an apology that he had lacked the time to master the theory of planting, followed by a catalogue of titles comprising an agricultural library so daunting it would have made any reader wonder whether agricultural theory could be mastered. It contained fifty-four titles. Adams, in contrast, provided no titles, and offered names of only three authorities: John Taylor, Jethro Tull, and M. Duhamel Du Monceau. (See appendix.) Jefferson organized his list to give predominance to the cultures whose climate and location most closely approximated that of Virginia: Italy and France. The Italians appeared first, with pride of place being allotted the classical Roman writers on geoponics—the study of plant development in natural soils—then moderns. The French titles were dominated by three names—Duhamel, Abbe Rozier, and Lastayrie—all systematizers strongly influenced by enlightenment encyclopedics. No Spanish or Ibero-American works appeared on the list. The English agronomists and horticulturists appeared next, with philosophical and scientific works first in order, several volumes of the older sort of polite ruralia, then four titles by the prolific Arthur Young, including his *Experimental Agriculture*. Jefferson's catalogue concluded with eight American titles on agriculture, eight international titles on gardening, and five English and French volumes on pomology. Subject matter ranged from the new chemical analysis of soil and food to statistical agronomy to the latest methods for processing apples and pears into cider and perry.

What does the list convey? The order speaks a very plain truth. Despite the fact that the twenty-first century celebrates Jefferson as the experimental gardener and pomologist—the man whom Peter Hatch reminds us tirelessly introduced novel cultivars into his kitchen gardens and fruit trees into his orchards[9]—he viewed work in geoponics as the most important thing to be mastered in agriculture. His contributions to *The American Farmer* bear this out: an essay on Italian clover as a green manure, explication of the design for a mouldboard plow that slices soil deeper and easier than current models, and a letter on horizontal plowing. Only his dissertation on Parmesan cheese departed from soil-centered agriculture. Perhaps we can understand the emphasis when we recall that corn, tobacco, and wheat were the plants that kept Jefferson's household solvent, the staples that dominated the fields of Monticello, Tufton, Shadwell, Lego, Poplar Forest, Tomahawk, and Bear Creek. Madison pungently observed in his "Address," "Tobacco and Indian Corn, which for a long time on the east side of the Blue Mountains were the articles almost exclusively cultivated, and which continue to be cultivated, the former extensively, the latter universally, are known to be great impoverishers of the soil. Wheat, which has for a number of years, formed a large portion of the general crop, is also an exhausting crop" (171). To keep solvent, Jefferson had to counter the degradation of the soil caused by planting his triad of staples, a difficult task given his frequent absences from home, his bad judgment in overseers, and his willingness to experiment with manures and crop rotations that sometimes failed to improve the soil. This experimental approach to farming imperiled his finances, for as Edwin Morris Betts observes in his edition of *Thomas Jefferson's Farm Book,* many initiatives proved to be "unprofitable ventures" (viii). One thinks particularly of his frustrated attempt to plant the hillsides of Albemarle County with muscat grapes. Not a single glass of vintage issued from that area, which now makes the finest vigonier wines in the world.[10]

Jefferson's misadventure with wine reveals the principal liability of books as guides to growing. Despite being possessed of exhaustive accounts of French viticulture—treatises by Maupin, Duhamel, and Rozier—and despite the experiences of his Italian grape-growing neighbor Philip Mazzei, Jefferson's vines failed, done in by phylloxera, raccoons, birds, and black rot. He was not alone. Everyone trying to use *Vitis vinifera* and a European handbook in North America suffered a similar fate, until Nicholas Herbemont, John James Dufour, and Colonel Adlum devised a viticulture suited to the climate, pathogens, and soil conditions of the United States in the 1820s.[11] As Col. John Taylor observed, when asked to name the book titles he would recommend in a farmer's library, "Of the agricultural books I have, most have been compounded from theory, and have tended to chiefly prove that fine writers make bad farmers" (Taylor 93). The volumes most useful to Virginia readers would be the various transactions of the Agricultural Society of Philadelphia[12] which were "[p]articularly valuable being better adapted to our soil and climate, than most foreign books; and as treating miscellaneously, of a great variety of subjects. . . . This objection however exists to most books extant upon the subject of agriculture, as the great variety of soils and climates" prevents pertinence in many cases.

The lesson of geoponics is that understanding local conditions of soil, climate, and environment determine success or failure of farming. Single-author books, even by well-traveled writers, cannot attain this level of particularity. But periodicals, edited by practical men of letters, incorporating the contributions of an array of correspondents reporting on local experiences and experiments, could make matters more germane to American farmers. The year 1820 would be the moment when farmers throughout the United States would take pen to paper to exchange views on manures, plant diseases, insect pests, and new cultivars. Each would participate in a mobile conversation, posing immediate replies, challenges, supplementations to the reports and addresses published in previous issues. The desire for a fount of information attuned to local conditions would shape the history of these periodicals after the founding of *The American Farmer*; the great majority announced a regional, state, or local focus: *The New England Farmer, The Genesee Farmer, The Southern Agriculturist, The Southern Planter, The Maine Farmer,* and

The Tennessee Farmer. Their inscription of broader national or international concerns—or their engagement in abstract principles of botany, biology, nutrition, or technology—took the form of reprinting of articles from other journals and extracts from important books.

In 1832, when Dan Bradley of New York reflected on "The Origin and Progress of Agricultural Journals," he noted the primary benefit of the periodicals: "I consider agricultural publications, especially those that are periodical, as the cheapest, the most efficient, and the most sure means, like to be resorted to, of encouraging and promoting improvements in this pre-eminently important branch of Industry" (6). Unlike southern agriculturalists who defined the cultural other of their project of rural improvements as the manufacturing interest, Bradley saw the enemy as the unthinking drones of traditional farming—the rural idiots: "It is known that when farmers read nothing on the subject of their occupations, and are operated upon by no other exciting cause, their minds become torpid as to projects of improvements, and they seldom indulge thoughts of deviation from the old and beaten track of business" (6). Reading the agricultural press would "break up this mental torpidity" and instill an ambition for improvement and a will to compete with fellow farmers in the contest of the field and market. It would also habituate farmers to the practices of the world of letters.

The vibrancy of a periodical conversation presupposed that a farmer have some facility with a pen and some hard matter to report. The eighteenth century had seen the large-scale planters become trenchant epistolary communicators, as farmers instructed or responded to merchants, overseers, seedsmen, and fellow agriculturists on business and the art of growing. The large-scale farmers kept ledger books of revenues and payouts. Surprisingly few maintained records of plants grown, laborers employed, or any concrete aspect of planting aside from weather. A half-dozen diaries are cited insistently in accounts of eighteenth-century agriculture: the diaries of John Grave, Col. Landon Carter, Benjamin Hawley, Ebenezer Parkman, and Mary Cooper. All are life records in which agricultural notices appear and are not exclusively records of farming, treating field usage, crops, labor use, and yield—the information that would become the grist of periodical exchange in the age of experimentation. Jefferson's records—his garden book and his farm book—are perhaps the very first that survive in that form. Upper-class Virginia planters knew of their existence and looked to them as models. When Thomas Marshall of Facquier County, Virginia, wrote to *The American Farmer* about crop rotations, he concluded his letter with the following observation: "I cannot forbear recommending to you, if the plant be not already adopted, to keep a regular journal of your agricultural proceedings. It will enable you to correct errors into which you may have formerly been seduced; to compare the state of forwardness in which your business may be at any given time, with what it was in preceding years; to account for many phenomenon by being able to recur to the state of the earth or of the atmosphere at some preceding period; and will prove a source at once of instruction and delight" (262). Journals of personal agricultural proceedings became commonplace in the 1820s and '30s, cited repeatedly in the agricultural press from all parts of the country.

Thomas Jefferson's farm book was an untitled manuscript record composed on 174 pages of 6-x-8-inch paper, most of which now resides in the Coolidge Collection of the Massachusetts Historical Society. It contains diaries, inventories, and a collection of pithy sentences on practical matters entitled "Aphorisms, Observations, Facts in Husbandry." It treats the years 1774 to 1805 and 1809 to 1824, remarking horse pedigrees, slaves and their locations, disbursements of beds, blankets, clothes, shoes and food to slaves, slave births and deaths, his land roll of livestock, a bill of building expenses, records of orchard plantings, calculations on labor value and building materials, livestock, plantings, and harvests on his several farms, summaries of meat production for 1794, and diaries of agricultural work for 1795 and other years. For historians of slavery and farm labor, these records provide valuable insight. For a historian of the relation of writing to agriculture, the most telling material appears in the collection "Aphorisms, Observations, Facts in Husbandry." It is interesting as much for what it is not as what it is. It is not a gathering of proverbial wisdom about farming practice; no homey sentiments of the "[t]ickle the soil with your hoe and you will laugh a large harvest" variety. Such proverbs would appear regularly as filler in the agricultural journals, but Jefferson has no use for such received wisdom because of its generality. He preferred, instead, empirical findings or rules. So his collection aggregates facta bruta, isolated facts, and maxims: "Goats: kids are fit for the table from 3. Weeks to 3. Months old" (75) or "Overseers: not to share till seed-grain is taken out, & then of what is sold or eaten by measure only" (76). Frequently, he gleaned facts from the experiences of planters in his social network: "green pork when made into bacon loses one fourth. C. H. Harrison" (78) and "Buckwheat: it rots in the ground completely in a fortnight. G. Washington" (81). Sometimes, he excerpted a resonant observation from an author in his agricultural library: "[Arthur] Young's experiments shew that ploughing in fall gives from one to three bushels per acre produce more than ploughing in the spring. 4. Exp. agr. 206–211" (79). The richest moments in the collection occurred when he synthesized the information provided by his own experience with those of his neighbors into a program of cultivation,

VIII. Rotation of crops.									
	1.	2.	3.	4.	5.	6.	7.	8.	9.
G. Washington's Rotation is	wheat	buck-wheat	wheat	clover	clover	clover	potatoes corn		
Dr. Logan's	wheat	barley	corn	potatoes flax	wheat	barley clover	clover	clover	*
a good one	corn & oats in halves	peas	wheat	clover	clover				

such as his plan for crop rotation, referencing those used by George Washington and Dr. George Logan of Stenton in Pennsylvania (97) (see table). The myriad findings and facts appeared under a scatter of headings, like a commonplace book, except that the order was intuitive rather than alphabetical. In sum, they reveal agricultural practice to have been an ameliorative set of performances and processes constructed inductively out of findings drawn from experience, from the experiences of capable fellow farmers, and from a library of authoritative farmer-writers from both sides of the Atlantic.

If Jefferson's farm book confronts a reader with the brute matter of tilling, hog killing, building, and managing slave labor, then his garden book presents a more evocative and overtly experimental view of farming. The sixty-six manuscript pages supply calendars of plantings, crop varieties, and yields dating from 1769 to 1824. The earliest entries treat his gardens and orchards at Shadwell, the remainder, gardening at Monticello.

Jefferson grew flowers, herbs, and vegetables in his gardens, reflecting that pre-twentieth-century tendency to intermingle practical and aesthetic rationales for planting. Flowers were beautiful, but were understood to have been medicinal as well. While Jefferson had moved beyond the old humoral picture of health, he retained the Galenic belief that nutrition had both corrective (invalid cuisine) and normative (regular fare) regimes of ingestion, both of which had to be supported in the kitchen beds, particularly on an estate where the health of many laborers mattered. His calendars announced at irregular intervals the planting, grafting, blooming, setting, and harvest dates of plants and trees. Consumption caused him to cast his notice beyond the bounds of Monticello: "May 8 eat peas at Barclay in Charles-City" and "May 15 eat strawberries at Dr. Richman's." By the frequency of mention, fresh spring peas meant as much to Jefferson as they did to any Englishman, as the first fruits of the season of plenty. The plantings were commonplace until 1774, when a host of Italian vegetables, the benefaction of Philip Mazzei—radicchio, Tuscan garlic, Salvastrella di Pisa—appeared in the lists. Indeed the explosive expansion of vegetable varieties can be viewed directly as a function of Jefferson's connection with Mazzei, who had moved to Virginia in 1773 with a band of immigrants intent on introducing the olive to American culture. Jefferson's laconic record includes indications of quantities planted, notices of problems, such as insect infestation or diseases, that disrupted cultivation, and records of crop yields—all the gist of experimental investigation. But its interest lay in the variety of cultivars listed and their frequently transatlantic provenance.

Two similar kinds of listings appeared in early farm periodicals: the market price listing and the advertisements for nurseries. The former bore a date, a list of commodities' names, and prices current at a given market locale; the latter had a catalogue of plants available for purchase. The former tended to be restricted to the staple items available in a market at a season; the latter documented the variety of plants and seeds being vended. Of the two, Jefferson's notes more closely resemble the latter. Even before the American Revolution, Jefferson was aware of the creation of global gardens, plantings incorporating an extensive range of plant material. He had seen the Bartram garden in Philadelphia firsthand and knew about Alexander Garden's "Otranto" in South Carolina. He had read about Kew and knew the French royal gardens. In the nineteenth century, a new model of master garden emerged, combining experimental, educational, and commercial dimensions: William Prince's Linnean Garden, Parmentier's orchard in Brooklyn, Jesse Buel's nursery near Albany, and Nicholas Herbemont's and James Guignard's mirror gardens in Columbia, South Carolina. The exceptional, exemplary character of these sources of plant material figured in print and writing by lists of what they contained. Certain of the journals, particularly those associated with agricultural societies in the 1820s, established nurseries so that subscribers could obtain seed and cuttings of the plants they read about in contributions to the journals. This tendency to link horticultural collections expressed itself in books, such as William Robert Prince's pomological manuals tied to his New York gardens, as well as periodicals, including Jesse Buel's *The Cultivator*, which linked both his Albany nursery and the New York Agricultural Society for which he was chief plant curator.[13]

American nurseries could not have come into existence without the aid of print. Print established a more than local clientele for unusual seeds and plants, it stimulated the ethic of improvement among farmers, and it inspired anxiety that inherited habits of soil treatment and growing would lead to ruin that only crop diversification and rotation could forestall. Print also spread a spirit of emulation and competition among farmers by publishing the winners of the cattle shows or the recipients of society premiums for grains and vegetables.

In the year Jefferson died, 1826, Rev. Charles Goodrich of Hartford, Connecticut, surveyed the transformations wrought in American farming since the American Revolution. He noted that since 1806, "agricultural societies have increased from a single one to between fifty and sixty" (Goodrich 68). He noted how their "Shows and honorary rewards" had proved a stimulus to innovation. The agricultural fair, like the model farm, provided the agricultural spectator with fodder for imagination and desire. "Is the farmer an admirer of the animal creation? He here sees domestic animals, both native and imported, of the finest forms and choicest qualities. Is he an admirer of the vegetable productions of the earth? Here are exhibited specimens, which shew, that if in the sweat of his brow, man must toil, a munificent Providence does not let him toil in vain." He noted print's important role in renovation of American farming. Indeed, the success of the agricultural revolution under way depended upon "our farmers, as a body, becoming men of more *reading and information in their profession.*" What had the exchange of information in print, through fairs, and the proceedings of agricultural societies wrought? "At the commencement of this period, the highest crops of potatoes were state at 200 bushels to the acre—now, crops of this vegetable are not unfrequently made of from 400 to 700 bushels. Then the highest quantity of corn gathered from an acre was from 40 to 50 bushels—now, we read of numerous crops of from 60 to 120 bushels. . . . Many valuable roots and plants, such as the mangel wurtzel,[14] the Swedish turnip, the carrot, the common beet, the cabbage, some of which were before scarcely known, have been introduced as general crops, and yield hundreds of bushels to the acres. . . . Our farms are better ploughed, better manured, better seeded, better drained, and better fenced" (68).

Jefferson was as much a beneficiary as a maker of the transformation of American agriculture. We tend, perhaps, to make him too much an exceptional figure, advancing extravagant claims about the priority of certain of his practices, the unprecedented character of his plantings at Monticello, or the influence of his actions. The truth of the matter is that agricultural history is so underdeveloped an area that we lack the information to judge who introduced a plant or practice into America in most instances. Who could tell that Susanna Wright on the Susquehanna River in Pennsylvania grew and ate eggplant twenty years before Jefferson planted Mazzei's seeds in his Monticello garden? It is a fact unmentioned in any horticultural or agricultural chronicle. What we can say with certainty is that he did view himself as a participant in a society of agricultural experimenters, intent on reforming planting because of the peril of continued extractive use of the soil, who looked to conversation, the exchange of plant materials, and print as a means of replenishing soil, diversifying plantings, and constructing a system of practices. He attended to his local network of experimental planters for ideas about practice and soil treatment. He read letters and books for a transatlantic community of agriculturists to learn about principles of botany, biology, and geology and to discover cultivars that might be suited to the circumstance of the Virginia Piedmont. In the person of Philip Mazzei, he found a neighbor, friend, and model planter possessed of cosmopolitan knowledge and a shrewd grasp of local conditions. Because of his frequent absorption in public affairs, Jefferson was often not present at Monticello to supervise farming directly, so he could not exchange in the sort of systematic investigation of growth and production that he wished. Nevertheless, he revered the art and read about it constantly. His greatest contributions to agriculture were as a publicist, recommending new cultivars to citizens, alerting the public to the looming crisis of the soil, devising practices that replenish fertility and promote sustainability, and conspicuously participating in the new periodical world of agricultural letters. He did not claim that autodynamic power of an agricultural auteur. Indeed, exceptional individualism on the part of a farmer would have seemed to Jefferson inimical to success as a cultivator.

The spirit of the experimental age of farming expressed itself precisely in the same manner as the spirit of the earlier republic of letters did and the spirit of academic scientific inquiry does now—through collaboration, conversation, and exchange.[15] Perhaps this truth was expressed no more eloquently or bluntly than by the editor of *The New England Farmer*: "the cheapest way to gain knowledge is to take advantage of the experience of others; and he who refuses to be taught by the experience of others, if not a fool, is certainly not so wise as he might be" (Editor 126). Jefferson was no fool. He tried to be as wise as he could be. And he tried to share in his letters, in *Notes on the State of Virginia*, in his conversations with his society of farmers, and in his contributions to *The American Farmer* what wisdom he had gleaned making things grow in the Virginia hill country.

Appendix: Jefferson's Recommendations for an Agricultural Library as published in *The American Farmer* 2.12 (June 16, 1820):

Geoponica Bessi, Niclasii Lipsiae, 1781, or Lat. 2 vols. 8vo.
Scriptores rei rusticate veteres, (Cato, Barro, Columella, Palladius,) the edition published at
    Leipsie by Schneider, about 1790–9 vols. 8vo.
Oeconomie rulale de Saboureux, 6 vols. 8vo. [*A translation of Cato, Barro, Columella,*
    Palladius.]
Dickson's Husbandry of the Ancients, 2 vols. 8vo.
L'Agricultore del Trinci, 2 vols. 12 mo. Or 1 vol. 8vo.

Dizzionario D' Agricultura dal Ronconi, 2 vols. 8vo.

Reflexions su L'agriculture de Naples, par Tuppruti, 8vo.

Corso di Agricultura dal Proposito Lastri, 5 vols. 12 mo.

Istruzzione elementary di Agricultura del Fabbroni, 8vo.

Della Coltivazione degli ulivi del vettori, é degli agrunic, 8vo.

Theatre D'Agriculture de De Serres, 2 vols. 4to. [*The late edition with modern learned notes.*]

Duhamel's Husbandry.

Rozier. [*There is a body of French Husbandry published by the Abbe Rozier and others, of high reputation, in 10 or 12 vols, 4to. Titles not recollected.*]

Traité de la vigne de Bidet et Duhamel, 2 vols. 12 mo.

Maupin sur la vigne, 8vo.

Traité sur la vigne, par Chaptal Rozier, Parmentier et Dussieux, 2 vols. 8vo.

Lasteyrie du Cotonnier et de sa culture, 8vo.

Daubenton's advice to Shepherds, 8vo. [*Translated and published in Boston.*]

Lasteyrie sur les bêtes à laine d'Espagne, 8vo.

Home's Principles of Agriculture and Vegetation, 8vo.

Mill's Chemical Elements of Agriculture, 12mo.

Kirwan on Manures, 12mo.

Hale's Statical Essays, 2 vols. 8vo.

Tull's Horse-hoeing Husbandry, 8vo.

Evelyn's Terra, by Hunter, 4to.

Hale's Body of Husbandry, 4 vols. 8vo.

Home's Gentleman Farmer, 8vo.

Young's Rural Economy, 8vo.

Young's Farmer's Guide, 8vo.

Young's Experimental Agriculture, 3 vols. 8vo.

Young's Travels in France. [*Young's Annals of Agriculture, and many other works, written merely for money, are scarcely worth buying.—Those here named contain whatever of his is worth having.*]

Brown's Rural Affairs.

The Rural Socrates.

Boardley's Essays and Notes on Husbandry, 8vo.

Taylor's Arator, 12mo.

Peters' Agricultural Inquiries on Gypsum, 8vo.

Livingston's Essay on Sheep, 8vo.

Memoirs of the Philadelphia Agricultural Society, 2 vols. 8vo. [now 4]

Transactions of the Agricultural Society of New York, 4to. [*There are some good works published in the eastern states, titles unknown.*]

Millar's Gardener's Dictionary, folio.

Millar's Gardener's Calendar, 8vo.

Abercrombie's Gardener's pocket Dictionary, 3 vols. 12 mo.]

Every Man his own Gardener, by Mawe, 12 mo.

MacMahon's American Gardener's Calendar, 8vo. [*Philadelphia.*]

American Gardener by Gardiner and Hepburn, 12mo. [*Washington.*]

A Treatise on Gardening, by John Randolph, 16's. [*Richmond.*]

Culture de la Grosse Asperge de Hollande par Filassier, 12mo.

De la Brosse de la culture du figuier, 12mo.

Langley's Pomona, folio.

Knight on the Apple and Pear, on Cider and Perry, 12mo.

Forsythe on the culture and management of Fruit Trees, 8vo.

Evelyn's Sylva.

Traité sur les Abeitles par della Bocca, 3 vols. 8vo.

Notes

1. See Harold T. Pinkett, "*The American Farmer*, A Pioneer Agricultural Journal, 1819–1934."

2. For a history of agricultural publication, see A. L. Demaree, *The American Agricultural Press, 1819–1860.*

3. The crisis of the land was not restricted to the southern states. It was perceived as inevitable in every part of the country that had practiced extractive farming from the mid-eighteenth century onward. A "Northern Farmer" remarked that the old belief that acreage and skill were all that was needed for farming success was "ruinous to the country." Only the "diffusion of knowledge and practical skill" would enable cultivators to "restore" land "to its original fertility" (411).

4. Trudy Eden explains this in *The Early American Table: Food and Society in the New World* (40-41).

5. Steven Stoll in *Larding the Lean Earth* counterposes Taylor and Madison on political grounds, with Taylor's plantation autonomy serving as a libertarian counterposition to Madision's nationalized nature. When one turns to Madison's own agricultural writings, however, one finds them in total agreement on the crisis of the soil and the need for a system of replenishment and rational cultivation (71).

6. Perhaps no topic in agrarian studies has had a richer historical exposition. The founding work of the expository literature is Avery Odelle Craven and Louis A. Ferleger's 1926 classic *Soil Exhaustion as a Factor in the Agricultural History of Virginia and Maryland, 1606–1860.*

7. Jeffreys, perhaps the greatest agricultural savant of his generation in North Carolina, would publish his own thoughts on plowing, manures, and soil conservation under the cognomen "Agricola," *A Series of Essays on Agriculture and Rural Affairs* (Raleigh: Gales, 1819). The book contained vivid moments of agrarian apocalyptic, including the observation that the agriculture of his day was a "land-killing system."

8. At the time of the letter's publication, Jefferson's son-in-law was governor of Virginia and vice president of the Albemarle Agricultural Society.

9. See Peter J. Hatch, *The Fruits and Fruit Trees of Monticello; Thomas Jefferson and the Origins of American Horticulture*, and Peter J. Hatch and Edwin M. Betts, *Thomas Jefferson's Garden Book.*

10. John Hailman explains this point in *Thomas Jefferson on Wine* (371–96).

11. For an account of early American viticulture, see David S. Shields, *Pioneering American Wine: The Writings of Nicholas Herbemont, Master Viticulturist* (4–14).

12. For the history, projections, and publications of the society, see Stevenson Whitcomb Fletcher, *The Philadelphia Society for Promoting Agriculture, 1785–1955*.

13. William Robert Prince's books include *Pomological Manual; or, a treatise on fruits: containing descriptions of a great number of the most valuable varieties for the orchard and garden* ([New York], 1831), *A Treatise on the Vine* (New York, 1830), and *A Short Treatise on Horticulture* (New York, 1828). Buel's many contributions to American agriculture are surveyed and his writings excerpted in *Jesse Buel, Agricultural Reformer* (New York: Ayer Publishing, 1977). He was assistant editor of *The Genesee Farmer* before founding *The Cultivator* in 1835.

14. The mangel wurtzel was the celebrity root of the early republic, generating dozens of articles in the agricultural press about its efficacy as livestock feed. Tolerant to cold, this yellow-orange member of the beet family was grown as a winter crop in the South, and a summer crop well north into Canada. Its leaves could be eaten as well as the root.

15. If Jefferson was exceptional in anything, it was the extent of his connectedness in this world.

Works Cited

Betts, Edwin Morris, ed. *Thomas Jefferson's Farm Book*. Chapel Hill: U of North Carolina P, 2002.

Bradley, Dan. "The Origin and Progress of Agricultural Journals; their Utility, and Great Importance exhibited." *The Genesee Farmer* 2.1 (January 7, 1832, January 14, 1832): 6.

Craven, Avery Odelle, and Louis A. Ferleger. *Soil Exhaustion as a Factor in the Agricultural History of Virginia and Maryland, 1606–1860*. 1926. Columbia: U of South Carolina P, 2006.

Demaree, A. L. *The American Agricultural Press, 1819–1860*. New York: Columbia UP, 1941.

Eden, Trudy. *The Early American Table: Food and Society in the New World*. DeKalb: Northern Illinois UP, 2008.

Editor. "Advantages of Taking and Patronizing the New England Farmer." *New England Farmer* 1.16 (November 16, 1822): 126.

Fletcher, Stevenson Whitcomb. *The Philadelphia Society for Promoting Agriculture, 1785–1955*. Philadelphia: Philadelphia Society for Promoting Agriculture, 1976.

Goodrich, Charles. "Extracts from an Address Delivered before the Harford Country Agricultural Society, October 12, 1826." *New England Farmer* 6.9 (September 21, 1827): 68.

Hailman, John. *Thomas Jefferson on Wine*. Jackson: UP of Mississippi, 2006.

Hatch, Peter J. *The Fruits and Fruit Trees of Monticello; Thomas Jefferson and the Origins of American Horticulture*. Charlottesville: UP of Virginia, 2007.

——, and Edwin M. Betts. *Thomas Jefferson's Garden Book*. Chapel Hill: U of North Carolina P, 2001.

Jefferson, Thomas. *Thomas Jefferson's Farm Book*. Thomas Jefferson Papers, an Electronic
    Archive. http://www.thomasjeffersonpapers.org/farm/. Accessed March 15, 2009.

———. *Thomas Jefferson's Garden Book*. Thomas Jefferson Papers, an Electronic Archive.
    http://www.thomasjeffersonpapers.org/garden/. Accessed March 15, 2009.

Jeffreys, George W. Letter. *American Farmer* 2.12 (June 16, 1820): 93.

Madison, James. "An Address Delivered before the Agricultural Society of Albemarle, [Virg.]
    on Tuesday, May 12, 1819. By Mr. Madison, President of the Society." *American Farmer*
    1.21–23 (August 20, 27, September 3, 1819): 170.

Marshall, Thomas. *American Farmer* 2.33 (November 11, 1820): 262.

Northern Farmer. "Obstacles to the Diffusion of Agricultural Science." *Genesee Farmer* 3.52
    (December 28, 1833): 411.

Pinkett, Harold T. "*The American Farmer*, A Pioneer Agricultural Journal, 1819–1934." *Agri-
    cultural History* 24.3 (July 1950): 146–51.

Shields, David S. *Pioneering American Wine: The Writings of Nicholas Herbemont, Master
    Viticulturist*. Athens: U of Georgia P, 2009.

Stoll, Steven. *Larding the Lean Earth*. New York: Macmillan, 2002.

Taylor, John. Letter (Caroline, Port Royal, August 16, 1816) to George W. Jeffreys. *American
    Farmer* 2.12 (June 16, 1820): 93.

Chapter Three

CULINARY CONVERSATIONS OF THE PLANTATION SOUTH

MARCIE COHEN FERRIS

Southern cuisine is the result of a four-century-long "cultural conversation" among African Americans, Europeans, and Native Americans (Ownby ix). As their lives intertwined in the early South, a convergence of cultures took place, and nowhere is this better expressed than in foodways (Breen 195, 197). The voices of several literary communities in the plantation South reflect the process of acculturation that happened as natives and newcomers produced and consumed food. This essay cannot encompass the complete chorus of voices that speak of southern food, but it will sample the four following distinctive nineteenth-century "conversations": travelers and visitors in the antebellum era whose correspondence is filled with accounts of how "locals" ate, from enslaved African Americans to Charleston's white elite; literate white southerners who wrote diaries and letters that described their southern worlds from the antebellum era through Reconstruction; the autobiographies of former enslaved African Americans; and the voices of northern-born teachers and governesses who came South and witnessed the exploitive worlds of plantation slavery. These diverse resources reveal the abundant food landscape of the early South, the core ingredients and methods of southern foodways, and the negotiation of food production and access in the slaveholding household.[1] By listening to these voices, we discover an expressive language of food that expands our understanding of race and region in the American South.

A Southern World of Travelers

From the first exploratory expeditions along the Carolina coast by Europeans in the late sixteenth century to temporary settlements of the seventeenth-century

Chesapeake to sturdy farm houses and plantations of the colonial and antebellum South, European and American travelers and naturalists wrote about food they observed and consumed in the American South. How could one best describe the exotic South to families living an ocean away, to overseas investors and stockholders who backed early exploratory voyages, and to individuals considering making the journey themselves? Thick descriptions of climate, topography, rivers, fauna, and foliage interested readers, but accounts of food were particularly compelling. Detailed accounts and illustrations of southern food connected distant cultures with the region.

Mark Catesby, the early eighteenth-century British naturalist distinguished by his careful observations and evocative illustrations of the flora and fauna of the colonial southeast coast and the West Indies, provided one of the best early descriptions of the staple grain of southern foodways in the 1730s and 1740s: "Frumentum Indicum, Maiz Dictum: Indian Corn." Catesby noted that everyone—including enslaved African Americans and white settlers in Virginia and Carolina—ate corn. They prepared it in ways that are familiar to any southerner who enjoys cornbread, grits, and hominy: "the first is baking it in little round loaves, which is heavy, though very sweet and pleasant, while it is new. This is called pone. The second is called mush, and is made of the meal, in the manner of hasty-pudding; this is eat by the Negroes with cider, hog's-lard, or molasses. [. . .] The third preparation is homony, which is the grain boiled whole, with a mixture of bonavis, till they are tender, which requires eight or ten hours; to his homony is usually added milk or butter, and is generally more in esteem than any other preparation of this grain" (Catesby 86, 98–99).[2] Catesby also described "common European culinary plants" and fruits that grew well in the Carolina climate, including carrots, parsnips, turnips, peas, beans, cabbage, "colliflowers," apples, blackberries, figs, peaches, pears, thyme, savory, and "all aromatik herbs" (102). This list indicates the English influence in southern gardens.

Food and the bounty of the southern colonies also feature prominently in seventeenth- and eighteenth-century promotional literature written to encourage European immigration and settlement. John Martin Bolzius, a German pastor who came to coastal Georgia with a group of his coreligionists in 1734, wrote a primer on the core foods of the Georgia Lowcountry for colleagues in Europe: "Peanuts and potatoes are not the same thing" (Loewald, Starika, and Taylor 234). He recommended sweet potatoes for heavy laborers: "it is a good, tasty, quickly prepared and nutritious food" (235). "The best and most profitable crop is rice," he wrote, "which is planted to great advantage by those who have Negroes" (239). Bolzius criticized slaveholders for their inhumane treatment of enslaved people and for failing to "keep them in a Christian way regarding *food*, clothing, work, and marriage" (239).

Janet Schaw, a self-described "Lady of Quality," kept a journal of her travels with a small party of friends and family who sailed from their native Scotland to the West Indies, North Carolina, and Portugal in 1774 (Schaw). They enjoyed a sumptuous "family dinner" at the Antigua sugar plantation of a "Mr. Halliday," a meal Miss Schaw described in detail to "her eating friends" back home in Scotland (95–100). The dining table was laid with three rows of dishes, six dishes in a row in the high-style manner of "courtly" eating influenced by continental manners (95–96).[3] Turtle soup was dramatically displayed at the head of the middle row of fish, including local varieties such as "king fish," grouper, mullet, and snapper (96). While Schaw does not mention the enslaved West African cooks who prepared the meal, their presence is reflected in every dish on the table, including the red pepper–flavored sauce served with the fish, and "[a] little pod laid by every plate" (96).

Drawn by both professional interests and a desire to observe the plantation South and the institution of slavery, the number of European travelers grew to its apogee in the antebellum era (White 160). They included both anonymous travelers and well-known chroniclers such as Harriet Martineau (England), Alexis de Tocqueville (France), and Frederika Bremer (Sweden), as well as Americans, including the most recognized documentarian of antebellum life, Frederick Law Olmsted (Connecticut) (White 161; de Tocqueville; Martineau; *Homes of the New World*; *Seaboard Slave States*; *A Journey in the Back Country*; *The Cotton Kingdom*). These visitors came to the South on horseback, by train, and by steamboats down the Ohio and Mississippi rivers, following a route, or "grand tour" that was popular in the 1830s (White 160).[4]

The "grand tour" brought travelers like Davis Thacher—a young man seeking adventure and employment as a tutor in the South—down the east coast to Georgia and the Carolinas, across Alabama to Mobile and New Orleans, and then up the Mississippi and Ohio rivers into Tennessee and Kentucky (Toten 389, 547).[5] Thacher left his home in Appongansett, a small bayside town in southeastern Massachusetts, in 1816. His brothers accompanied him to nearby New Bedford, where he took a sloop to New York City and continued by boat to Charleston. Thacher found work as a tutor for a doctor and his family on a plantation near Charleston. He described fishing one night with a companion, "by the light of torch," and returning just before sunrise. "I caught 62 sea crabs, twelve stone crabs, and 7 cooters, both species of crabs are eaten here. They are … delicious … the stone crabs have claws as large as our largest lobsters—the cooters are a species of sea turtle—they are not large, from 16 to 18 inches long—esteemed by the natives—make excellent soup" (Thacher Diary).

What distinguished the writing of travelers to the antebellum South was their perspective as white, middle-class and upper-class outsiders. Slavery historian John Blassingame explains that "much of what the traveler saw was new to him. Consequently, he was much more likely to comment on things which resident whites accepted as commonplace" (379). And what was more commonplace than food? In nineteenth-century southern travel literature, writers described what we would refer to today as *terroir*, the sense of place embodied in everyday life, such as Davis Thacher's rich description of nocturnal spear fishing. As Bernie Herman explains, "[M]ore than the taste of place . . . [*terroir*] defines the particular attributes of place embodied in cuisine and narrated through words, actions, and objects. It captures a consciousness of association and belonging" (37). Thacher's exotic fishing adventure in the Carolina Lowcountry was an initiation—a food-centered ritual of place—that made him feel the same sense of belonging.

The "big eating" events included in the descriptions of southern meals were central to "southern hospitality." In 1828, a Maryland traveler described the white citizens of Natchez, Mississippi, as "peculiarly hospitable" (*The Rambler).* "It seems to be their chief delight to entertain strangers," he wrote, "and the greatest harmony and social intercourse exists among them" (*The Rambler).* Rogene "Genie" Scott, a young teacher from Vermont, came to work for a slave-holding family in Kentucky in 1858. "The people of the South justly deserve the appellation of 'hospitable,'" wrote Scott, "for though uneducated and unrefined, they are the most *kind-hearted* people I ever became acquainted with, and I have no doubt I shall love them next to my *Yankee friends.* They have the faculty of making one feel so perfectly at ease as soon as you enter their dwellings which is not always the case in my own loved New England" (Scott). Susan Dabney Smedes, daughter of a Mississippi planter, attributed the hospitality of her father's Virginia family to their "cavalier" ancestry, a mythic narrative of the white antebellum South. "The younger sons of noble houses, and other men of standing," wrote Smedes, "brought to their homes in the New World the customs and manners of the Old. The tone of society has always been truly English in Lower Virginia, the 'tide-water country,' as the people love to call it. Everybody kept open house; entertaining was a matter of course, anything and everything was made the occasion of a dinner-party" (Smedes 35).

Aspiring and well-to-do white women of the South expressed this longing for gentility through their displays of domestic hospitality. "Hospitality rituals dramatized the disparity of power between donor and recipient," explains Cynthia Kierner, "establishing a hierarchical relationship between the donor, who displayed wealth and benevolence, and the recipient, who enjoyed the bounty of patronage at the cost of independence" (37). This "culture of gentility" was crucial to the identity of elite, white southerners in the early nineteenth century (37).

Swedish travel writer Fredrika Bremer found southern hospitality overbearing and tedious. She felt like a captive at the table of her Macon, Georgia, hosts in May of 1850. Bremer noted that in Sweden guests paid more attention to conversation than to manners. At the table of elite white southerners, she was annoyed that guests could not help themselves, but had to depend on other guests and servants. "You seldom get just what you wish for, or as much or as little as you want, and not on the part of the plate where you wish to have it" (*America of the Fifties* 128–29). Bremer described a scene of "pickle persecution." A guest is offered and declines pickles. Another guest observes her neighbor's plate is pickle-less. Pickles are offered again, and once more refused. Just when the guest is "waiting for some reply interesting to you," a servant appears, "and with horror you behold pickles ready to be put upon your plate . . . thus goes on the meal—one incessant bustle of serving, which takes away all enjoyment of the food" (128-129).

Vermont native Jeremiah Evarts described plantation meals near Savannah and the Sea Islands during his southern travels in the 1820s (Evarts).[6] In Daufuskie, a Sea Island located between Savannah and Hilton Head Island, he stayed at Bloody Point, David John Mongin's cotton plantation, and was "entertained in the true style of southern hospitality" (Apr. 5, 1822). Food was abundant and of great variety, "no fewer than ten or twelve hot dishes for breakfast and supper, besides many cold ones" (Apr. 5, 1822).

Like many travelers from the North, Evarts critized slavery when he witnessed the treatment of enslaved workers during elaborate plantation meals. "The state of the slaves, as physical, intellectual, and moral beings, is abject beyond my powers of description," wrote Evarts. "Slaves have few conveniences for any kind of labor. They are obliged to every thing by the hardest" (Apr. 5, 1822). Referencing the abundance of the master's table, Evarts commented on the irony that "while such unlimited profusion reigned on the table of the master, a large portion of his slaves rarely tasted flesh. At Christmas, indeed, all are feasted, but generally the fare of the plantation slaves is coarse and scanty" (Apr. 5, 1822).

Mary Reed Eastman, a young bride from Massachusetts on a "wedding journey" with her minister husband, arrived in Charleston by ship in 1832, where they enjoyed the hospitality of their New England friends, Dr. and Mrs. Porter (Eastman).[7] Her account of a formal meal at the Porter home echoes the words of diarist Timothy Ford (1785), who described another Charleston dinner where enslaved servants surrounded the table like "a cohort of black guards" (Webber). Mary Reed Eastman was clearly stunned by these rituals of race and service. "While we sat at dinner, a slave stood behind us with a long whisk of peacock's feathers, to keep away the flies," wrote Eastman. "There were 12 at the table, and 4 slaves in attendance, who were constant in offering to us all the table afforded, with hardly a look from the mistress—one black man who seemed the head of the department, was handsomely dressed and had his gold watch chain and seal" (Eastman).

Private travel letters and journals written for family and friends, like those of Mary Reed Eastman, and travel literature directed at readers in America and Europe, such as that of Jane Schaw, revealed both everyday and extraordinary food worlds of the American South. Descriptions of food caught the attention of travelers as they visited the South, but the world at the heart of southern life—the home—was best described by southern diarists and correspondents in the antebellum period. South Carolina's white plantation elite is well represented through diarists Eliza Lucas Pinckney, Mary Motte Alston Pringle, John Berkeley Grimball, and the famous British actress-turned-plantation mistress, Fanny Kemble.

A Community of Letters

To help us understand the landscape of the antebellum southern household and the relationships that linked white and black southerners, Elizabeth Fox-Genovese describes the "overlapping communities" of plantation and farms, slave quarters, the church, and villages. For literate white southerners, another important community—"the community of letters"—reached across great distances to connect disparate worlds of home, family, the academy, summertime resorts, and the battlefront. Diaries and letters are the literary artifacts of this community, a tiny slice of the southern population characterized by educated, slaveholding white men and women, rather than the illiterate working-class people (68–69). These white southerners had both the status and the leisure that allowed them to write, as Drew Gilpin Faust states, to "create an extensive record of self-justification as well as introspection and self-doubt" (xii).

Plantation mistresses oversaw the burden of daily and seasonal work for the southern household. Far from the stereotypical image of the white "southern lady," mistresses were "overtly productive" (Lesbock 148). Growing, preserving, preparing, and controlling the distribution of food lay at the heart of this southern economic system. With the keys to the storehouse in hand—the symbol of their authority—white slaveholding women both excelled in and chafed at the responsibility of feeding their "families" (Fox-Genovese 110). Their relationships with enslaved household staff were defined by an "explosive intimacy" (98). As mistresses of the southern household, white slaveholding women wrote about food, the table, and the garden, assuming different voices as dutiful and neglectful mothers, as accomplished and awkward hostesses, as skillful and frustrated housekeepers, and as willing and resentful managers of enslaved workers.

Eliza Lucas Pinckney (1722–1793) was raised between England and her birthplace in Antigua, where she was part of the same elite, slaveholding world that Jane Schaw described on her visit to the West Indies from Scotland.[8] Pinckney was seventeen years old when her father left her in charge of the family's three Lowcountry plantations in South Carolina in the early 1740s. She managed over five thousand acres and many enslaved laborers and overseers who worked the land. After her marriage in 1744 to Charles Pinckney, she continued to experiment with plants, seeds, and crops that were new to South Carolina. Characterized by intellectual curiosity and a strong interest in science and reason, Pinckney was a woman of the Enlightenment. Pinckney's daughter, Harriott Pinckney Horry, inherited her mother's passion for agriculture and botany. She began a journal of her own favorite recipes in 1770, as her mother had done twenty years earlier.[9]

In a letter written to her brother in England, Eliza Lucas Pinckney described how eighteenth-century South Carolina looked and tasted. "The Country abounds with wild fowl, Venison and fish. Beef, veal and motton are here in much greater perfection than in the Islands, tho' not equal to that in England; but their pork exceeds any I ever tasted any where" (Pinckney 39–40). Pigs arrived with the earliest European explorers, including Christopher Columbus in 1493 and Hernando de Soto in 1539, who brought livestock respectively to the Caribbean and the early South. The exceptional taste of the pigs that Pinckney describes was a result of acorns and other nuts that free-range pigs foraged on in the southern woods, as well as peaches, corn, pumpkins, and other food crops given hogs to fatten them before slaughter. In the closing lines of her letter, she noted that "the staple commodity here is rice and the only thing they export to Europe" (39–40).

Harriott Horry's cousin, Mary Motte Alston Pringle, was the mistress of the Miles Brewster home in Charleston, a large household in which twenty-two enslaved African Americans cared for the twelve white members of the Pringle household in 1850 (*Politics of Taste* 251–52; Pringle "Household Inventory").[10] Like her cousin Harriott and her great-aunt Eliza Lucas Pinckney, Pringle kept a journal of recipes and household remedies that includes typical Lowcountry recipes for "rice cakes for breakfast," oyster soup, "shrimps in vinegar," the "Baltimore method for cooking terrapin," and in a home full of finely crafted furniture, the important directions for how "to polish mahogany" (Pringle "Receipt Book" Oct. 2, 1826). More revealing of the complicated domestic relationships of power, status, and race in a slaveholding household is Pringle's "Household Inventory Book," which she kept between 1834 and 1865. Mary Pringle oversaw her household with "an almost scientific precision," as seen in her daily and annual accounts of domestic artifacts, ranging from those of great value—the family silver—to the weekly piece of soap and "onsaburgs" or linen towels dispensed to the enslaved household workers (*Politics of Place* 251; Pringle "Household Inventory"). From her locked storeroom, Pringle gave her cook daily supplies of "1½ quarts of whole rice, 1 pint corn grist, 1 pint rice flour, a spoonful of lard," and for the washing of household linen, "1 quart of rice *every Monday* for starch" (Pringle "Household Inventory"). Pringle, or an enslaved servant in her stead, purchased other fresh food supplies, such as fruit, vegetables, poultry, meat, and fish each day at Charleston's Market Hall (Pringle "Household Inventory" 252).

John Berkley Grimball's 1832 diary reveals another side of the planter mind. Grimball was as concerned with his family's position and status among the wealthy, white elite of Charleston as Mary Pringle was with counting her tea towels and "kitchen things." Both John Berkley Grimball and his wife, Margaret Ann "Meta" Morris Grimball, kept extensive diaries in which they described their social, economic, and political worlds in Charleston and on their rice plantation located in the Colleton District in the southeast part of the state (J. Grimball, M. Grimball). Like the Pinckneys and other white Lowcountry planters, they spent their summer months in Charleston, away from the malarial conditions of their Lowcountry plantation.

Writing almost thirty years before the Civil War at the age of thirty-two, Grimball described the active social scene of Charleston in the summer and fall of 1832, before he returned to Grove Plantation. Grimball carefully recorded details of elegant dinner parties he attended "to guide him in the performance of his own" ("Raphaelle Peale's Still Life" 315–17; *Politics of Taste* 286; J. Grimball Oct. 16, 1832). He drew small diagrams of the dinner table and placement of dishes so he could re-create a similar style when he returned the hospitality of his hosts. Grimball wrote, "I put down these dinners because they are given by men of acknowledged Taste—and will afford hints, should I undertake to give one myself" (*Politics of Taste* 285–86). The weekly round of dinners hosted by a group of white gentlemen friends began around three or four o'clock in the afternoon and continued until nine or ten in the evening—an evolving performance of dining, conversation, business, politics, and enslaved service (*Politics of Taste* 285–86).

English-born Fanny Kemble was one of the most illustrious diarists of the antebellum Lowcountry (Kemble). Born into a noted family of British actors,

Kemble met her husband-to-be, Pierce Mease Butler, while she was touring in Philadelphia in 1832. Despite their different worlds and backgrounds, the couple married in 1834. In 1838, Butler took his wife and two young daughters to visit the Georgia cotton and rice plantations he had inherited from his grandfather.

Kemble viewed Pierce Butler's plantations through the eyes of an outsider—an Englishwoman, a nonsoutherner, and an abolitionist. She paid close attention to the substandard conditions that enslaved African Americans endured. The food patterns of the enslaved community were often at the center of Kemble's observations. "It was between eleven o'clock and noon," wrote Kemble, "and the people were taking their first meal in the day ... how do you think Berkshire county farmers would relish laboring hard all day upon two meals of Indian corn or hominy? ... They go to the fields at daybreak, carrying with them their allowance of food for the day, which toward noon, and *not till then*, they eat, cooking it over a fire, which they kindle as best they can, where they are working. Their second meal in the day is at night, after their labor is over, having worked, at the *very least*, six hours without intermission of rest or refreshment since their noonday meal (properly so called, for it is meal, and nothing else)" (Kemble Jan. 1839, 99). She noted the enslaved people's lack of proper chairs, tables, dishware, and utensils. They ate from "cedar tubs or an iron pot, some few with broken iron spoons, more with pieces of wood, and all the children with their fingers" (100).

Kemble's description of slave rations closely resembles those of other travelers to the South. Some masters provided more and others even less than Butler allotted his enslaved laborers each week. In Virginia, Frederick Law Olmsted observed, "The general allowance of food was thought to be a peck and a half of meal, and three pounds of bacon a week ... It is distributed to them on Saturday nights" (*Seaboard Slave States* 89–90). Where Kemble was horrified by the inadequate rations, Olmsted and Fredrika Bremer found the rations to be sufficient, or even generous (89–90). After observing enslaved fieldhands taking a midday break in a South Carolina rice field in the spring of 1850, Bremer asked if she could taste their meal of beans and corn cakes. "They seem contented, but were very silent," wrote Bremer. "I told them that the poor working people in the country from which I came seldom had such food as they had here" (*America of the Fifties* 107–8). Despite the race-tinged views of white travelers, there is no question that food supplied to enslaved people throughout the plantation South was grossly inadequate (Hilliard 56). "The lack of food was egregious," explains historic archaeologist Anne Yentsch, "the inhumanity staggering" ("Excavating the South" 67).

A Community of Memory

Slave autobiographies, such as Frederick Douglass's *Narrative of the Life of Frederick Douglass, An American Slave, Written By Himself* (1845) and Harriet Jacobs's *Incidents in the Life of a Slave Girl* (1861), include powerful accounts of food that underscore the depravity of slavery and the ugly underbelly of "southern hospitality."[11] Douglass described the savage appetites of slaveholders like his own master, Colonel Lloyd, whose dining table "groaned" under an uncivilized display of gluttony. "Here, appetite, not food, is the great desideratum ... The teeming riches of the Chesapeake bay, its rock, perch, drums, crocus, trout, oysters, crabs, and terrapin, are drawn hither to adorn the glittering table of the great house. The dairy, too, probably the finest on the Eastern Shore of Maryland—supplied by cattle of the best English stock, imported for the purpose, pours its rich donations of fragrant cheese, golden butter, and delicious cream, to heighten the attraction of the gorgeous, unending round of feasting ... all conspired to swell the tide of high life, where pride and indolence rolled and lounged in magnificence and satiety" (*My Bondage* 107).

In Harriet Jacobs's autobiography, the slave master, Dr. Flint—modeled on her North Carolina master, Dr. James Norcross—was a vindictive "epicure," who intimidated the slave cook at every meal (12). "If there happened to be a dish not to his liking, he would either order her to be whipped, or compel her to eat every mouthful of it in his presence. The poor, hungry creature might not have objected to eating it; but she did object to having her master cram it down her throat till she choked" (12).

Enslaved domestic workers, like the cook in Jacobs's narrative, often suffered worse exploitation than others because they were so closely observed by white slaveholders. Mistresses frequently accused cooks and household servants of any number of misdemeanors, from purposely ruining a recipe out of spite or lack of attention to stealing silverware and other valuables. Masters were equally hard on enslaved household staff. Frank Bates recalled his Alabama master whipping his mother "for leaving her finger print in the pone bread when she patted it down before she put it into the oven" (Bates). Leon Litwak writes, "To live in close day-to-day contact with his master, to know his capacity for deceit and cunning, to know him as few of the field hands could, enabled some slaves to hate him that much more, with an intensity and fervor that only intimate knowledge could have produced" (Litwak 158–59). Litwak recounts the narrative of "Aunt Delia," a former enslaved cook in North Carolina, that turns the defilement of food back onto the slaveholder, rather than the enslaved: "How many times I spit in the biscuits and peed in the coffee just to get back at them mean white folks" (158–59).

These iconic works are part of the narratives, memoirs, and autobiographies written by fugitive slaves before the Civil War and by former enslaved people in the postbellum era. William Andrews suggests that these resources provide "the invaluable perspective of first-hand experience" in the historical documentation of slavery in America (803–7). In shocking detail, African American voices challenged stories of the alleged gentility and mannered world of the white plantation table.

"Often have I thanked Heaven for the blessings which the pen affords": Food in the Correspondence of Northern-Born Governesses[12]

Perhaps no diaries and letters of the antebellum South reveal the region's pathologies and pleasures more clearly than those of young, northern-born, working-class, white women who were employed as governesses and teachers by white, slaveholding families. These women were liminal figures in the plantocracy—part professional, part hired help, part servant, part trusted family member—and, always, dispensable. If the situation was not considered "agreeable" to the family, it ended as abruptly as it began. As enslaved household workers knew, and white nannies quickly learned, these roles could change maddeningly and as quickly as shifting sand. Placed in the heart of the plantation household, white governesses were privy to intimate family life and exchanges between slaveholders and the enslaved. Descriptions of food—distinct tastes, rituals of daily meals, special occasions, and holidays, challenges of food supply and preparation in the southern heat, and most importantly, racial codes of slavery in the kitchen and at the table—were central to the worlds governesses observed (Plaag 27).

In the strange and alien plantation South, governesses Ruth Newcomb Hastings (b. 1831, Massachusetts), Tryphena Blanche Holder (b. 1834, Massachusetts), and Rogene "Genie" Scott (b. 1840, Vermont) kept detailed records of local customs in letters and diaries as a means to make sense of their experience, to stave off loneliness, and to share life-changing adventures with distant friends and family. Historian Wilma King said of eighteen-year-old Tryphena Holder, a teacher and nanny who worked for the Messenger family in Vicksburg, Mississippi, in 1852, "she fought rural isolation with approved weapons: ink, pen, and paper" (King xiii). Less than four years after she arrived in Mississippi, Tryphena Holder married David Raymond Fox, a Vicksburg native and physician. The couple moved into a small plantation home called Hygiene in the community of Jesuit's Bend, Louisiana, and began their family (1, 8). The same year Tryphena Holder arrived in Mississippi, 1852, Ruth

Hastings, age twenty-one, accepted a position as governess at Colonel John Nicholas Williams's home in Society Hill, South Carolina (Hastings "Biography"). And in 1860, nineteen-year-old Rogene Scott began her work as a tutor at Peter Tanner's plantation in Cheneyville, Louisiana (Scott Family Papers).

Tryphena Holder Fox had been wed just over a month and was setting up housekeeping in Louisiana, when she described the chief responsibilities of a "southern lady" to her mother. Fox modeled her behavior on Sophia Messenger, her former employer and the wealthy mistress of Baconham, one of the largest cotton plantations in Warren County, Mississippi (King 4–5). "In this country," Tryphena wrote her mother, "all provisions are kept under lock and key and one of the principal duties of a southern lady's housekeeping is to carry the key and give out the proper quantities of groceries for each meal, otherwise the cook would waste twice as much as was needed and pilfer as much more" (Fox July 7, 1856; Fox-Genovese 110; "Excavating" 66–68). Fox noted that with the help of "servants," "a Southern lady does not do much manual labor, [but] she had head-work enough to keep her busy" (July 14, 1856). By "head-work," she meant the management of her household, but it was the management of her enslaved labor that was the greatest challenge to Fox. Like most young, white women of her class and position, she was trained in household skills, but lacked the authority and experience to control enslaved labor (King 5; Fox-Genovese 110). Frustrated by her slave cook, Fox wrote her mother that "it is not pleasant to live on the same place & in as close proximity as one is obliged to do with the cook & be all the time at enmity with her & feel angry, whether I say anything or not" (Fox Dec. 16, 1860; Fox-Genovese 144). The behavior of enslaved people—from daily recalcitrance to attempts to escape—were constant expressions of resistance and rebellion, particularly with the growing talk of war and freedom (Faust 54). Drew Gilpin Faust argues that slaveholding women put in the position of managing increasingly rebellious enslaved workers were "in a significant sense garrisoning a second front in the South's war against Yankee domination" (54).

As tutor to the young daughters of Colonel John Nicholas Williams and Sarah Canty Witherspoon Williams, Ruth Hastings had a view of southern slavery shaped at the dining table and in the family's South Carolina home, "The Factory," named for the large cotton mill that stood nearby (Gill 296; Faust 54). Colonel Williams inherited one of the largest cotton plantations and fortunes in Darlington County, South Carolina. Mealtime practices at the Williams table reinforced Ruth Hastings's sense of alienation from the foreign world of the elite white southerners. "You can't imagine how strange it looks to me to see the children and Serena give the negroes about the house a biscuit or a wafer, or piece of gingerbread half eaten or a piece of melon from which all that I call good had been eaten," wrote Hastings. "They give the [slave] children Amy, Ellen, and even to Nelly, bones half picked and bits of meat or anything they happen to eat at lunch. I haven't learned yet how to give my leavings with a good grace. I am trying to learn" (Hastings July 13, 1852).

Curious about what his daughter was eating in South Carolina, Hastings's father asked if she lived on "hog and hominy" (Hastings May 26, 1852). Ruth responded to her father with a description of a typical day of eating at the plantation, which mirrored the culinary patterns of white, elite families throughout the antebellum South—a core cuisine of pork, cornmeal, local vegetables, and fruits. The Williamses, like other wealthy, white slaveholding families, had their own hogs, poultry, dairy cows for butter and milk, cattle for beef, rice from the nearby Lowcountry, corn, sweet potatoes, and store-bought food stuffs, such as wheat flour, sugar, salt, coffee, and spices. Most meals included many dishes. At breakfast, cold meats from the previous evening meal were often served with hot breads. During the school week, Hastings went downstairs a little before seven each morning for breakfast. "I do eat hominy every morning, though no one else does," she wrote. "It is always on the table then besides, some cold meat (Boiled ham or fish, and waffles made of sweet potatoes, very nice, *wafers* [,] a very thin cake to eat from your hand, biscuit, like butter crackers somewhat, only thicker, these hot, and sometimes cold bread. Since I have been here [,] strawberries. Mr. W[illiams] has besides what they call clabber. (bonny clapper) I have it for tea sometimes" (May 26, 1852). Clabber was a curdled or sour milk dish, typically eaten with fruit, sugar, and spices.

After completing morning school lessons with the Williams children, Hastings stopped at noon, ate a cold biscuit for a snack, and rested until the family ate dinner at two o'clock, or sometimes as late as half past three in the afternoon. The bells of the nearby cotton mill kept Hastings on schedule, and they woke her in time to dress for the midday meal. Dinner was the largest, most elaborate meal of the day for slaveholding families. The meal began with a first course of soup, followed by entrees and side dishes of seasonal vegetables, a salad course, and dessert. Hastings described the meal to her sister Mary Anne: "For dinner, always first some kind of soup, then two or three kinds of meat, always some fresh meat. Today chicken pie, ham, new potatoes, beets, onions, peas, rice, which they eat with meat as we do potatoes, often sweet potatoes, lettuce, then for dessert today what Mrs. W[illiams] called a Cherry Charlotte" (Hastings May 26, 1852). After an evening of reading or a quiet game, Hastings and the Williams children ate a light supper before bedtime, such as sponge cake and clabber (Aug. 28, 1852).

Rogene Scott enjoyed the French- and African American–influenced dishes of Rapides Parish, which lies to the west of the Atchafalay River in

Louisiana. Today this culturally rich region is known for its Cajun cuisine, shaped by displaced eighteenth-century French-speaking Catholics, who made their way from Canada to the ethnically and racially diverse worlds of southern Louisiana. Their rustic cuisine reflects how settlers incorporated local fish and critters of the bayous, marshes, and rice fields into food traditions they brought from Acadia.[13] "Oh let me tell you what a fine dish I partook of the other day," wrote Scott. "It was a mess of bullfrog. I could not have distinguished it from chicken if I had tried. Turtle soup I have also become very fond of, eels also. This Bayou Boeuf produces the very finest fish I ever saw and many a nice meal have I eaten from its contents. These southern creeks are very prolific, for they produce everything from Alligator, Garfish etc. down to the smallest *minnow*" (Scott May 23, 1859). Scott noted that though the Tanners' home and school were not grand—not unlike "our very old houses at home"—the family lived well given her observations of their daily food and clothing. She wrote that "the Southerner feels differently; if he has a plenty to eat and drink and wear he scarcely thinks of anything else" (Scott Mar. 14, 1859).

When Tryphena Fox left teaching, she married into white, slaveholding, southern society. Fox never questioned the morality of slavery, but instead became a slaveholding southerner herself, quickly adopting the racial attitudes of her employers, her husband, and the neighboring plantation families in Louisiana. Hastings, however, a single, homesick teacher, was troubled by the inhumanity of slavery and could not shed her feelings of being a northern outsider, all of which affected her stomach. When a letter arrived from her family, the Williamses hid it from Ruth until after she had eaten breakfast, "lest it should take away all my appetite, as letters do sometimes" (Hastings Oct. 9, 1852). Rogene Scott arrived in Louisiana with strong antislavery feelings. Peter Tanner, the master of the plantation, enjoyed teasing Scott about her opinions. "Nearly every evening we get out the checker board and try our skill," wrote Scott. "He calls me 'the North'—I call him 'the South'—so we 'the North' and 'the South' engage in a miniature battle and sometimes he whips the Abolitionist soundly and sometimes *vice versa*" (Scott Feb. 27, 1859).

By the time the first shots of the Civil War were fired at Fort Sumter in April 1861, Rogene Scott had moved from Louisiana to a teaching position in Nashville, Tennesee. She eventually returned to Vermont where she married and continued to teach. Ruth Hastings went home to New England in 1853, and observed the war from a distance as a young bride after her marriage in 1860. Tryphena Fox was caught up in the thick of the war. To avoid the conflict, she and her husband left their home in Jesuit's Bend soon after the fall of New Orleans on April 25, 1862, to live with Dr. Fox's family on their plantation,

Woodburne, near Vicksburg (King 16). In Mississippi, Tryphena Fox faced the same plight as other white, southern wives and mothers who attempted to provide for their families despite food shortages and raids from Union soldiers who confiscated livestock, crops, and food supplies.

Conclusion

On the home front and the battlefront, southerners captured their experiences during the Civil War through personal diaries, letters to family, and memoirs published after the war. From 1861 through 1865, food was central to these stories, as shortages plagued the South and Confederate troops (Smith).[14] Whether it was a famished soldier on the battlefront, a family seeking refuge in the city, women activists in the Richmond Bread Riots, or planters and Confederate officers paying exorbitant prices to obtain scarce luxury items, all shared the experience of want. Food was the universal language that all understood. Narratives described starvation of black and white soldiers and civilians, the cruelty of mercenary slaveholders, and futile attempts to protect southern food supplies and livestock. As the war continued, frustration and deep resentment over losing household enslaved labor, especially cooks, was a frequent theme in Confederate women's diaries as their families ate burned biscuits and sodden loaves of unrisen bread. Thousands of Civil War letters, journals, drawings of camp life, and notes scribbled into military field guides describe the food-related struggles of both men at battle and families on the homefront.

After the war's end, Reconstruction marked the beginning of a long, difficult journey as "slaves stepped into freedom and tried to define its dimensions" (Litwak 257). The most benign activities, including cooking and housekeeping, became expressions of independence as newly freed ex-slaves tested their new status. Enslaved cooks, now free, who continued to work for whites as paid servants demonstrated their independence in a variety of ways. With so little "hired help" available, whites began to recognize a shift in power as black servants requested fair working conditions as free labor. Many "mammies" transformed from the beloved, docile "pets" of white families into newly empowered laborers. "Emeline" was the much-admired cook on the Pine Hill Plantation in Leon County, Florida. When she went missing from the kitchen and guests were expected for dinner one day in May 1865, the mistress's daughter was sent to find her. Emeline was in her house, dressed in her Sunday best, readying herself for an emancipation picnic hosted by three regiments of black soldiers stationed near the plantation. "Take dem [storeroom and pantry] keys back ter yer Mother," said Emeline, "an' tell her I don't never 'spects ter cook no more, not while I lives—tell her I'se free, bless de Lord! Tell her if she want any dinner she kin cook it herself" (Litwak 347).

Acknowledgments

I am deeply grateful to Professor Wilma King, Arvarh E. Strickland Distinguished Professor, Department of History at the University of Missouri, for her insight and generous use of unpublished letters in the Tryphena Blanche Holder Fox collection at the Mississippi Department of Archives and History. A special thanks to archivist Laura Clark Brown at the University of North Carolina's Southern Historical Collection, research librarian Jacqueline Solis at the University of North Carolina's Davis Library, curators Barbara DeWolfe and Janice Longone at the William L. Clements Library, University of Michigan, the Clements' director emeritus John Dann, who donated the Ruth Newcomb Hastings collection to the library, archivist Dale Rosengarten at the Addlestone Library at the College of Charleston, and archivists at the South Caroliniana Library at the University of South Carolina and the South Carolina Historical Society in Charleston. I am also indebted to culinary historians Sandy Oliver and Damon Fowler. Finally, many thanks to former graduate students in the master's program in folklore, University of North Carolina at Chapel Hill—Marwa Yousif, for her research assistance, and Emily Wallace, for her editorial skills.

Notes

1. Food-related discussion and innovation focused on crops, seed varieties, and planting practices was another critical conversation in the nineteenth-century American South, shared in regional agricultural journals of the educated, white planter elite. Historian David Shields describes this period as the "age of experiment in American agriculture," which gave rise to the distinctive ingredients of Lowcountry cuisine. See Shields.

2. The *Oxford English Dictionary* defines "bonavist" as a "species of tropical pulse; a species of kidney beans."

3. See Yentsch, *A Chesapeake Family and Their Slaves*, 151.

4. See Alexis de Tocqueville, *Democracy in America* (1835); Harriet Martineau, *Society in America* (1837); Fredrika Bremer, *The Homes of the New World: Impressions of America* (1835); Frederick Law Olmsted, *A Journey in the Seaboard Slave States* (1856), *A Journey in the Back Country in the Winter of 1853–4* (1860), and *The Cotton Kingdom* (1861).

5. Born in Yarmouth, Massachusetts, on August 4, 1793, Davis Thacher was twenty-three years old when he began his journey to the American South. He returned to New England by 1819 to marry Mary Sellars Nye, with whom he had six children. Thacher, a deacon, died in Fairhaven, Massachusetts, on April 11, 1873, at the age of eighty.

6. Evarts, a Yale graduate, became a Christian missionary and activist for Cherokee rights. He vehemently opposed the Indian removal policies of President Andrew Jackson in the 1830s, and traveled throughout the Southeast to meet with Indian leaders and support their case against forced immigration to the West.

7. Mary Reed Eastman was born in 1806 in Marblehead, Massachusetts, and lived in New York City after her marriage to a Yale-educated minister, Ornan Eastman, in 1832. The couple traveled over five thousand miles on their wedding journey from Marblehead down the east coast to Augusta, Georgia, west to New Orleans, and back home via the Mississippi and Ohio rivers.

8. See Pinckney 34–35; Hooker 2–3.

9. See Schulz 105; Egerton 17–18; Hooker 18–33.

10. McInnis notes that by 1860, thirty-two slaves served the six Pringle family members living in the Miles Brewton home.

11. See also Titus, Warner, and Gwin.

12. "Catherine W.B" boarded with "Esquire Rucker" and his wife in Murfreesboro, Tennessee, where she was employed as a teacher for a small school. Her letter to Mrs. Greene begins, "It is among my chief sources of pleasure to be able to communicate with my absent friends. Often have I thanked Heaven for the blessings which the pen affords."

13. See C. Page Gutierrez for more on Cajun foodways.

14. See Smith's important work for a detailed exploration of how food, and the lack of it, was a central factor in the defeat of the Confederacy from the first shots fired on Fort Sumter to Lee's surrender at Appomattox. See also Taylor, "Long Years and Short Rations: The Civil War," in *Eating, Drinking, and Visiting in the Old South*, 95–104. For an excellent discussion of the Union army's attack on southern salt works during the Civil War, see Kurlansky, "The War Between the Salts," in *Salt: A World History*, 257–75.

Works Cited

Andrews, William L. "Slave Narratives." *The Companion to Southern Literature*. Eds. Joseph M. Flora and Lucinda H. MacKethan. Baton Rouge: Louisiana State UP, 2002. 803–7.

Bates, Frank. WPA Slave Narrative Project, Florida Narratives, Vol. 3, Federal Writers' Project, US Work Projects Administration. Manuscript Division, Library of Congress.

Blassingame, John W. *The Slave Community: Plantation Life in the Antebellum South*. New York: Oxford UP, 1979.

Breen, T. H. "Creative Adaptations: People and Cultures." *Colonial British America: Essays in the New History of the Early Modern Era*. Eds. Jack P. Greene and J. R. Pole. Baltimore: Johns Hopkins UP, 1984. 195–232.

Bremer, Fredrika. *America of the Fifties: Letters of Fredrika Bremer*. Eds. Adolph Benson and Carrie Catt. Carlisle, MA: Applewood Books, 2007.

Catesby, Mark. "Of the Agriculture of Carolina." *The Colonial South Carolina Scene: Contemporary Views 1697–1774*. Ed. H. Roy Merrens. Columbia: U of South Carolina P, 1997. 87–109.

Douglass, Frederick. *My Bondage and My Freedom*. New York: Miller, Orton, & Mulligan, 1855.

———. *Narrative of the Life of Frederick Douglass, An American Slave, Written By Himself. Slave Narratives*. Eds. William L. Andrews and Henry Louis Gates, Jr. New York: The Library of America, 2000.

Eastman, Mary Reed. Diary of Mary Reed Eastman, "Wedding Journey, Nov. 5, 1832–July 4, 1833." Mary Reed Eastman Papers, 1834–1987, South Carolina Historical Society, Charleston, SC.

Egerton, John. *Southern Food: At Home, on the Road, in History*. New York: Alfred A. Knopf, 1987.

Evarts, Jeremiah. Jeremiah Evarts Diary, MS 240, March 13–May 4, 1822. Georgia Historical Society, Savannah, GA.

Faust, Drew Gilpin. *Mothers of Invention: Women of the Slaveholding South in the American Civil War*. New York: Vintage Books, 1996.

Fox, Tryphena Blanche Holder to Anna Rose Clevand Holder. *A Northern Woman in the Plantation South*. Ed. Wilma King. Columbia: U of South Carolina P.

Fox-Genovese, Elizabeth. *Within the Plantation Household: Black and White Women of the Old South*. Chapel Hill: U of North Carolina P, 1988.

Gill, Christopher J. "A Year of Residence in the Household of a South Carolina Planter: Teacher, Daughter, Mistress, and Slaves." *The South Carolina Historical Magazine*, 97.4 (1996). 293–309.

Grimball, John Berkley. Diary of John Berkley Grimball, 1832–1883. Southern Historical Collection, Wilson Library, University of North Carolina at Chapel Hill. University Library, The University of North Carolina at Chapel Hill. 6 May 2012. http://www.lib.unc.edu/mss/inv/g/Grimball,John_Berkley.html.

Grimball, Margaret Ann "Meta" Morris. Diary of Margaret Ann "Meta" Morris Grimball, 1860–1866. Southern Historical Collection, Wilson Library, University of North Carolina at Chapel Hill. University Library, The University of North Carolina at Chapel Hill. 6 May 2012. http://www.lib.unc.edu/mss/inv/g/Grimball,Margaret_Ann_Meta_Morris.html.

Gutierrez, Page C. *Cajun Foodways*. Jackson: UP of Mississippi, 1992.

Gwin, Minrose. "Through the Autobiographical Glass Dimly: Mistress and Slave Woman as Obverse Images." *Black and White Women of the Old South: The Peculiar Sisterhood in American Literature*. Knoxville: U of Tennessee P, 1985. 45–109.

Hastings, Ruth. "Biography." Finding Aid, Ruth Newcomb Hastings Papers, William L. Clements Library, U of Michigan, Ann Arbor.

———, to her sister, Mary Anne Hastings, Oaky Hollow, SC, 13 July 1852. William L. Clements Library, University of Michigan, Ann Arbor.

———, to her sister, Mary Anne Hastings, Society Hill, SC, 26 May 1852. William L. Clements Library, University of Michigan, Ann Arbor.

———, to her sister, Mary Anne Hastings, Oaky Hollow, SC, 28 Aug. 1852. William L. Clements Library, University of Michigan, Ann Arbor.

———, to her sister, Mary Anne Hastings, and mother, Ruth Washburn Hastings, Society Hill, SC, 9 Oct. 1852. William L. Clements Library, University of Michigan, Ann Arbor.

Herman, Bernard L. "Drum Head Stew: The Power and Poetry of Terroir." *Southern Cultures*, 15.4 (2009): 36–49.

Hilliard, Sam Bowers. *Hog Meat and Hoecake: Food Supply in the Old South*. Carbondale: Southern Illinois UP, 1972.

Hooker, Richard J., ed. *A Colonial Plantation Cookbook: The Receipt Book of Harriott Pinckney Horry, 1770*. Columbia: U of South Carolina P, 1984.

Jacobs, Harriet A. *Incidents in the Life of a Slave Girl, Written by Herself*. Eds. L. Maria Child and Jean Fagan Yellin. Cambridge: Harvard UP, 1987.

Kemble, Fanny. *Journal of a Residence on a Georgian Plantation in 1838–1839*. Ed. John A. Scott. Athens, GA: U of Georgia P, 1984.

Kierner, Cynthia. *Beyond the Household: Women's Place in the Early South, 1700–1835*. Ithaca: Cornell UP, 1998.

King, Wilma, ed. *A Northern Woman in the Plantation South: Letters of Tryphena Blanche Holder Fox, 1856–1876*. Columbia: U of South Carolina P, 1993.

Kurlansky, Mark. *Salt: A World History*. New York: Penguin Books, 2002.

Lebsock, Suzanne. *The Free Women of Petersburg: Status and Culture in a Southern Town, 1784–1860*. New York: W. W. Norton and Company, 1984.

Litwak, Leon F. *Been in the Storm So Long: The Aftermath of Slavery*. New York: Vintage Books, 1979.

Loewald, Klaus G., Beverly Starika, and Paul S. Taylor. "John Martin Bolzius Answers a Questionnaire on Carolina and Georgia: Part II." *The William and Mary Quarterly*, 15.2 (1958). 228–52.

McInnis. *The Politics of Taste in Antebellum Charleston*. Chapel Hill: U of North Carolina P, 2005.

McInnis, Maurie D. "Raphaelle Peale's Still Life with Oranges: Status, Ritual, and the Illusion of Mastery." *Material Culture in Anglo-America: Regional Identity and Urbanity in the Tidewater, Lowcountry, and Caribbean*. Ed. David Shields. Columbia: The U of South Carolina P, 2009. 310–27.

Olmsted, Frederick Law. *A Journey in the Seaboard Slave States*. Ed. Harvey Wish. *The Slave States*. New York: G. P. Putnam's Sons, 1959.

Ownby, Ted. Introduction. *Black and White Cultural Interaction in the Antebellum South*. Ed. Ted Ownby. Jackson: UP of Mississippi, 1993.

Pinckney, Eliza Lucas. *The Letterbook of Eliza Lucas Pinckney, 1739–1762*. Eds. Elise Pinckney and Marvin R. Zahniser. Columbia: U of South Carolina P, 1997.

Plaag, Eric W. "'There is an Abundance of Those Which are Genuine': Northern Travelers and Souvenirs of the Antebellum South." *Dixie Emporium: Tourism, Foodways, and Consumer Culture in the American South*. Ed. Anthony J. Stanonis. Athens and London: U of Georgia P, 2008.

Pringle, Mary Motte Alston. Household Inventory Book, 1834–1865. Alston-Pringle-Frost Family Papers, South Carolina Historical Society, Charleston, SC.

———. Receipt Book, Oct. 2, 1826, Alston-Pringle-Frost Family Papers, South Carolina Historical Society, Charleston, SC.

Schaw, Janet. *Journal of a Lady of Quality: Being the Narrative of a Journey from Scotland to the West Indies, North Carolina, and Portugal, in the years 1774 to 1776*. Eds. Evangeline Walker Andrews and Charles McLean Andrews. Electronic.

Schulz, Constance B. "Eliza Lucas Pinckney and Harriott Pinckney Horry: A South Carolina Revolutionary-Era Mother and Daughter." *Carolina Women: Their Lives and Times*. Eds. Marjorie Julian Spruill, Valinda W. Littlefield, and Joan Marie Johnson. Athens: U of Georgia P, 2009. 79–108.

Scott Family Papers. Southern Historical Collection, Wilson Library, University of North Carolina at Chapel Hill.

Scott, Rogene A., to her brother Don, Cheneyville, Parish Rapides, LA. 27 Feb. 1859. Scott Family Papers, Southern Historical Collection, University of North Carolina, Chapel Hill.

———, to her mother, Cheneyville, LA. 23 May 1859. Scott Family Papers, Southern Historial Collection, Wilson Library, University of North Carolina at Chapel Hill.

———, to her mother, Cheneyville, Parish Rapides, LA. 14 Mar. 1859. Scott Family Papers, Southern Historical Collection, Wilson Library, University of North Carolina at Chapel Hill.

———, to her mother, Grayson, KY. 11 Mar. 1858. Scott Family Papers, Southern Historial Collection, Wilson Library, University of North Carolina at Chapel Hill.

Shields, David. *The Golden Seed: Writings on the History and Culture of Carolina Gold Rice*. Charleston: CRG Foundation, 2011.

Smedes, Susan Dabney. *Memorials of a Southern Planter*. Baltimore: Cushings and Bailey, 1888.

Smith, Andrew F. *Starving the South: How the North Won the Civil War*. New York: St. Martin's Press, 2011.

Taylor, Joe Gray. *Eating, Drinking, and Visiting in the Old South*. Baton Rouge: Louisiana State UP, 1982.

Thacher, Davis. Diary of Davis Thacher, 1816–1818. South Caroliniana Library, University of South Carolina, Columbia.

The Rambler, or, A tour through Virginia, Tennessee, Alabama, Mississippi and Louisiana; describing the climate, the manners, customs and religion, of the inhabitants. Interspersed with geographical and political sketches. By a Citizen of Maryland. Annapolis: J. Green, 1828. William L. Clements Library, University of Michigan, Ann Arbor.

Titus, Mary. "'Groaning Tables' and 'Spit in the Kettles': Food and Race in the Nineteenth-Century South." *Southern Quarterly*, Winter–Spring (1992). 13–21.

Toten, John R. *Thacher-Thatcher Genealogy*. New York: New York Genealogical and Biographical Society, 1910.

Warner, Anne Bradford. "Harriet Jacob's Modest Proposals: Revising Southern Hospitality." "The Texts of Southern Food." *The Southern Quarterly*. Ed. Peggy Whitman Prenshaw. Winter–Spring (1992): 13–19.

Webber, Mabel Louise, ed. "Diary of Timothy Ford, 1785–1786, with notes by Joseph W. Barnwell." *South Carolina Historical and Geealogical Magzine*, XIII.3 (1912): 142–43.

White, Robert. "Travel Writing." *The New Encyclopedia of Southern Culture: Volume 9: Litera-*
    ture. Ed. M. Thomas Inge. 2008. 159–62.

W. B., Catherine, Murfreesboro, TN, to Clarissa S. Greene, Salisbury, NH. 26 July 1841. Wil-
    liam L. Clements Library, U of Michigan, Ann Arbor.

Yentsch, Anne Elizabeth. *A Chesapeake Family and Their Slaves: A Study in Historical*
    Archaeology. NY: Cambridge UP, 1994.

———. "Excavating the South's African American Food History." *African American Food-*
    ways: Explorations of History and Culture. Ed. Anne L. Bower. Urbana: U of Illinois P,
    2007. 59–98.

Chapter Four

MARKETING THE MAMMY

Revisions of Labor and Middle-Class Identity in Southern Cookbooks,
1880–1930

SARAH WALDEN

T he struggle to determine the proper women's role in the 1893 World's
Columbian Exposition epitomized the role of domesticity in regional and
race relations at the turn of the century. The president of the fair's Board
of Lady Managers, Bertha Honoré Palmer, argued that the board spoke for all
women, though she neglected to appoint any African American representa-
tives. Instead, Palmer chose to publicize the all-white board's interregional
composition, thus promoting a narrative of postwar regional—rather than
racial—reconciliation.[1] Her vision for the fair was a Woman's Building—and
in particular a Model Kitchen—constructed to demonstrate advancements
in domestic technology and to elevate women's private roles as housewives
to the public standards of industrial efficiency and scientific progress. Visitors flocked to see demonstrations by popular cooking school experts such as
Juliet Corson and Maria Parloa and to witness the introduction of technologies such as the electric dishwasher. African American women, however, were
not permitted to play a leadership role in any portion of what was designed
to be a beacon of modern domesticity.

Meanwhile, in another part of the fair, the R. T. Davis Company had hired
Nancy Green to play the role of their newest marketing figure for boxed pancake mix, Aunt Jemima. This performance of the mammy stereotype epitomized the interregional romance suggested by the Board of Lady Managers.
Much of the African American presence at the fair could be found in similar exhibits. The Virginia Building, for example, was a replication of George
Washington's Mount Vernon, complete with black actors playing the roles of
plantation slaves. While white board members worked to promote domesticity as a public, intellectual pursuit, they actively omitted black women from

such exhibits, as southern women in particular viewed them as capable only of domestic service, not of intellectual thought (Wallace-Sanders 63). Thus black women at the World's Fair were only permitted to perform domestic tasks under the guise of slavery, reinforcing traditional assumptions of the American middle class as both white and native-born, and containing any threats to these increasingly tenuous borders.[2]

The decisions surrounding women's roles at the 1893 World's Fair demonstrate the tension among several competing categories of identification, particularly for women, in the late nineteenth and early twentieth centuries. The Progressive movement brought domestic work to the public sphere as white women gathered in reform clubs and aid societies, taught in cooking schools, and arranged safe, sanitary domestic spaces for the urban poor. The efforts of clubwomen and domestic scientists, who were primarily middle-class white women, demonstrate the emerging intellectual and economic power of the middle class. As the women's club movement emerged in the American South, the rhetoric of domestic reform became characterized by antebellum racial ideologies. Membership to the middle class was demonstrated through a performance of domestic acuity, yet this performance was complicated by the categories of identification engaged in women's participation in the World's Fair: race, class, and region. As domesticity became increasingly treated as an intellectual pursuit, African American women, often viewed by whites as "natural" or "instinctual" domestic laborers, became increasingly marginalized from middle-class identities.

African American women's clubs, however, which flourished alongside white women's clubs in the final decades of the nineteenth century, worked to contest the traditional cultural representation of black women as uneducated, unintelligent, and incapable of mental work beyond that demanded by domestic service in a white household (McHenry 190). Yet African American clubwomen also had to battle the reigning notion that a woman's power was found in the social application of her domestic abilities.[3] How could they claim middle-class identities while still distancing themselves from their previous domestic identities? The answer, as I will argue in this essay, can be found in domestic print culture. By examining several groups of cookbooks by southern authors, we can understand their complex domestic performances that attempted to define or lay claim to this source of power.

Two groups of cookbooks published between 1880 and 1930 illustrate the use of print publicly to define women's middle-class domestic identities: mammy cookbooks, or cookbooks written by white authors in the voice of an African American domestic servant, and cookbooks written by former African American domestic servants who sought to position themselves as independent individuals and businesswomen. These include cookbooks by clubwomen as well as those by women not directly associated with a women's club. As cookbooks throughout the nineteenth century established domestic literacy and expertise as the purview of the middle class, African American women used the cookbook as a rebuttal to their traditional representation as domestic laborers with instinctual and irreproducible domestic knowledge by using print to position themselves as middle-class Americans. In return, mammy cookbooks—written by white southern women as a response to clubwomen's activities, particularly in the north[4]—glorified the racial and class hierarchy of Old South plantation mythology, already popular in fiction and domestic literature as a reconciliation tool. These texts invoke a peaceful image of a contented society that stood in opposition to the often overwhelming, undefined, and contested project of reform in northern cities. They reveal a culture undergoing the dual processes of modernization and preservation, of promoting reunification and regional distinction. The juxtaposition of African American domestic servants in the Jim Crow South and the rise of an educated and intellectual black middle class informs both black- and white-authored southern cookbooks by challenging claims of cultural heritage and middle-class identity.

Competing Definitions of Middle-Class Identity

Large-scale women's participation in the Progressive movement grew out of their Civil War and Reconstruction activism (Smith-Rosenberg 173). The regional and racial ideologies that existed prior to the war, however, complicated the process of reform. Grace Elizabeth Hale writes that the political disputes following the Civil War, which institutionalized regionally integrated "economic trends toward centralization, standardization, urbanization, and mechanization" led to an uncomfortable lack of unity regarding the general representation of "American collective identity" (6). While "identity" is an ambiguous category, and "collective identity" is both superficial and inevitably exclusive, literary attempts at reconciliation demonstrate that, at least for some portions of the population, psychological unity by means of defined "American" identity was an important component of postwar culture. As a result, traditional hierarchies began to dissolve and race "became the crucial means of ordering the newly enlarged meaning of America" (7). While white Americans worked to strengthen middle-class collective identity and authority by reinforcing racial boundaries, southern white women's response to northern reform as well as the rise of a black intellectual middle class in both regions led to several competing definitions of middle-class American identity.

Cookbooks and domestic writing were important elements of this multifaceted movement to define middle-class domestic identity. By the final decades of the nineteenth century, advancements in print technology and increased literacy in all sectors of the population brought with them a heightened awareness of the cookbook as a literary genre as well as a tool of social reform. As a symbol of middle-class status, domestic expertise, and cultural ownership and authority, women authors embraced it as a means of cultural preservation and production.

The increasingly powerful white middle class often used food and its representation as a means to fortify boundaries during the Progressive era. The reform fervor that characterized Progressivism in northern cities also carried with it an emphasis on white racial superiority and race betterment, an indication of the simultaneous desire of Progressives to improve living and working conditions for the urban poor without creating economic or social competitors.[5] The discipline of domestic science emerged to address the perceived unsanitary living conditions of the working poor. Women such as Ellen Richards, early leader of the domestic science movement, promoted scientific approaches to nutrition as a type of cultural salve, arguing that one could improve one's living conditions by following diet guidelines based on the nutritional components of a food (carbohydrates, lipids, etc.). Yet the focus was not upward mobility but quality of life in one's current living and working conditions. In fact, according to founder Ellen Richards, the mission to improve the race of Americans could be accomplished by strengthening the middle class.[6] Domestic science was integrated into the curriculum of primary and secondary educations throughout the nation, and domestic scientists also promoted dietary standardization in historically black colleges such as Hampton and Tuskegee (Witt, *Black* 109). Thus Progressive domestic reform was characterized in part by its attempt to contain "foreign" threat, be it immigrant or African American.

By the turn of the century, the woman's club movement had begun to take root among emerging black and white middle classes in the American South. Yet devotion to a life of public reform presented unique complications for both groups of women. The white "southern lady" had to contend with the traditional perception of her role as a private bastion of moral purity, while black southern women's social and geographical mobility was limited due to the restrictions Jim Crow laws placed on racial progress and influence. While this structure is consistent with northern domestic reform in that it seeks to fortify social boundaries based on race and class, white southern women also sought to promote their region as the national ideal, using the stratified space of the antebellum home as an emblem of middle-class unity of purpose. Antebellum racial ideologies privileged the labor hierarchy of mistress and slave. Postbellum labor structures, in which black domestic servants were common in middle-class homes and cooking was often considered the lowest form of domestic labor, replicated this hierarchy by privileging the source of domestic ability: intellect for whites, instinct for blacks. To "[associate] African American women with food," writes Rebecca Sharpless, "branded them as being closer to nature, wilder, less refined than their white employers" (xv). When faced with the threat of rising immigrant and African American populations, many white middle-class Americans looked to the antebellum South as a means of bolstering what they believed to be the inherent superiority of white, native-born Americans.[7]

Reconstruction introduced sentimental representations of southern domesticity designed to promote psychological reunification. To remove northern fears of the South's continued violence or secession, southern women writers actively promoted a revised domesticity in their cooking texts. Cookbooks in particular utilized a careful rhetoric of reconciliation that included "Americanizing" southern recipes or instructing women to adopt a northern work ethic while at the same time proclaiming the distinctiveness of southern cuisine and character as necessary components for the future of the reunified nation.[8] Cookbooks such as Marion Tyree's *Housekeeping in Old Virginia* (1877) and M. E. Porter's *New Southern Cookery Book* (1871) emphasized the power of domestic spaces by emphasizing the "peaceful" hierarchy of the antebellum plantation home rather than what many considered to be the chaotic project of reform in northern cities. Southern domestic writers thus "created the culture of segregation in part by fusing the northern middle-class antebellum precedent of posing the 'home' as a symbolic counterweight to the expanding role of the market with a white southern sense of the inviolability of white supremacy" (Hale 93). Domestic discourse, particularly in the form of cookbooks, further established these romanticized sources of power by claiming its legacy in tangible southern food cultures.

Like white-authored domestic texts, African American clubwomen also emphasized the power of the home. In March 1894, Ellen Bartelle Deitrick opened her paper to the Boston Woman's Era Club with these words: "As the homes are so will the nation be, for the nation is nothing more than a collection of what is produced in the homes. The as it is oftener called, domestic science, is thus the very key-stone of the political arch" (6). Through club activities, black women worked to "represent themselves and expand their identities" to counter popular representations such as the mammy (McHenry

190). They emphasized working toward home ownership as the ultimate representation of freedom, as well as divisions of domestic labor that replicated business or factory structures, such as cooperative laundry services, to allow women more time for intellectual work and more money saved. Through intellectual management of one's domestic responsibilities, African American women could avoid the control of another; in other words, a woman could achieve self-possession. African American domestic texts thus threatened white southerners' preferred cultural narrative, as they challenged the labor hierarchy of the white home.

Domesticity as a form of social redemption emerged in conjunction with increased educational, career, and volunteer opportunities for southern white middle-class women, and decreased possibilities for southern blacks (Edwards 183). In essence, southern domesticity as a function of a white middle class was created to enforce the ideology of Jim Crow in the private sphere. While this is similar to the ultimate project of the northern domestic scientist, southern domesticity often rejected the standardization of cuisine and technique promoted by northern reformers. Instead, they promoted the distinction of southern cuisine—its superior taste, rather than its nutritive properties, indicated the superior cultural tastes of southerners as collective group. And physical taste, as an offshoot of physical labor, was the purview of the romanticized southern mammy. It was this growing sentiment that, at least in part, led to the proliferation of mammy rhetoric and advertising at the turn of the century.

"Neither could she write": Revising the Labor of Southern Cookery

In conjunction with the rise of race-based marketing techniques such as Aunt Jemima and Uncle Ben in the late nineteenth and early twentieth centuries, a new wave of cookbooks emerged. Mammy cookbooks, or cookbooks written primarily by white women to glorify the celebrated southern cuisine created by domestic slaves and servants, promoted a national food culture based on a strategic rejection of contemporary racial politics. Authors of mammy cookbooks worked to strike an effective balance between modern cookery and southern nostalgia. They emphasized the intellectual labor of recipe writing in order to de-emphasize the bodily labor of cooking. The mammy provided an effective centerpiece on which to base their arguments for the distinction of southern cuisine: as a racial type distinguished by her large bodily frame, she could represent domestic labor in its physical form, allowing the white women recording her recipes to perform the intellectual labor. The mammy cookbook performs several functions in the late Progressive Era. It constructs a nostalgic and romantic imagining of the Old South as a direct response to the domestic science standards of northeastern reformers, and it actively impedes racial progress and reconciliation by promoting a stereotype characterized by the recognition of her own racial inferiority. Finally, it defines a southern community based on print representation. "Mammy's" cooking may have distinguished regional cuisine and unified regional identity, they argue, but print is the only labor that lasts. And print, particularly in the American South, is a designation of white middle-class authority.

From her inception at the 1893 Chicago World's Fair as a character played by former Kentucky slave Nancy Green, Aunt Jemima came to represent antebellum romanticism. Her popularity as a consumer trademark virtually installed the racially nonthreatening mammy in every American household, further standardizing the stereotype. Her domestic space, however, is that of a plantation kitchen rather than a middle-class kitchen, thus symbolizing "slaveocracy as a positive, enriching experience shared by white Americans in the North and in the South" (Wallace-Sanders 62). Advertising, such as the story of Aunt Jemima or the covers or title pages of mammy cookbooks, combined print and picture to create a powerful image of black women as contentedly and gratefully subservient. Their dark skin color and domestic behaviors not only marked them as "different" from white consumers, but also indicated that these racial markers are easy to distinguish, reinforcing racial boundaries by removing qualities that might destabilize racial identity, such as literacy or intellectual activity. The mammy also represented a nonthreatening, desexualized female presence. In her cookbook, *Dishes and Beverages of the Old South* (1913), Martha McCulloch-Williams describes her as "an oblate spheroid" who "stood five feet, one inch high, weighed two hundred and fifty pounds, had a head so flat buckets sat on it as of right, [and] was light on her feet, in number twelve shoes" (15). Her caricatured physical presence distinguished her from the slight physical frame that designated white women as morally strong,[9] and this distinction suggested that she would be unable to challenge white women's moral dominance.

Domestic writers capitalized on the marketability of the southern mammy to unify not only regional identity, but also racial identity, around constructed cultural memory. The romanticized mystique of the "Old South" was intended to lead readers/consumers to believe that southern women also had a "special knowledge," and products such as pancake mix or cookbooks gave women commercial access to the very mammy who made it all possible. Concerning the project of reunification based on domestic identity, she was in effect "a mammy for the national household" (Wallace-Sanders 66). Thus the mammy suggests not only psychological reunification, but commercial reunification, a concept fully integrated with turn-of-the-century industrialism. Mammy cookbooks utilize the commercial imagery and rhetoric of the mammy that would resonate with a national audience while simultaneously claiming their origins in southern heritage, invoking what Wallace-Sanders calls a "blend of agrarian and industrialized idealism" that would come to characterize middle-class domestic performances (69).

While many postbellum southern cookbook authors wrote to preserve familiar recipes commonly prepared by slaves (Witt, "Intersections" 107), it is important to remember that they preserve not only the recipes, but also the racial ideologies that produced them. The prose introductions to mammy cookbooks clearly illustrate white women's use of labor imagery to reinforce a strategically constructed racial hierarchy. By attributing physical labor to African American women and intellectual management of labor to white women, these cookbook authors work to insert themselves into and control a food culture that has relied upon slaves and domestic workers for its history and distinction. Much as African American women worked to counter the image of the mammy through print representation of their middle-class intellect and skills, white southern women used print to reclaim a history based on the labor of others by reinstating the historical image of the mammy. They recognize that their ownership of their own intimate practices of consumption—to some extent, the basis of their very identities—are called into question when African American women begin writing cookbooks of their own. In order to reclaim possession of their collective history, white women begin a careful manipulation of the representation of labor practices, arguing that while the physical labor is performed instinctually by African American women, the intellectual control—manifested through manuscript and print—is the property of whites.

The first task of the mammy cookbook is to limit the black woman's social mobility by lamenting the vanishing figure of the mammy. Katharin Bell begins her cookbook, *Mammy's Cook Book* (1927), by memorializing her former servant: "With the dying out of the black mammies of the South, much that was good and beautiful has gone out of life, and in this little volume I have sought to preserve the memory and the culinary lore of my Mammy, Sallie Miller, who in her day was a famous cook" (x). Bell continues to broaden her memory to include all southern mammies, and thus unite her audience around a communal figure: "She possessed moreover, all those qualities of loyalty and devotion which have enshrined her and her kind, and in the loving hearts of their 'White Folks,' to whom they were faithful, through every vicissitude and change of fortune" (x). Mammies, in Bell's illustration, are revered as representations of a passing era of southern history. Bell firmly places the mammy, and by extension all black women, in the realm of memory, painting them as "dying out" rather than active members of society. She can be remembered only through her recipes, a task, Bell implies, that can only be accomplished through white women's literacy and generosity.

A second, related task of the mammy cookbook author involves positing racial unity among white readers. While it is highly likely that a majority of readers did not experience the antebellum pastoral idyll represented in these texts, they are included in the nostalgia for a separation of labor based on intellectual ability. Betty Benton Patterson's *Mammy Lou's Cook Book* (1931) presents the most self-consciously drawn portrait of this figure: "Mammy Lou's cook book had to be written, for Mammy Lou is a composite characterization of all the negro mammies we have known, loved, and lost awhile. These mammies are vanishing" (ix).[10] By grouping African American domestic servants in a "composite," Patterson likewise groups white middle-class readers as those mourning "her" passing. Patterson also demonstrates the characterization of the mammy as an instinctual cook, one whose kitchen was subject to circumstance and temperament; in other words, she was decidedly unscientific. This also sets her apart from white readers whose domestic performances are characterized by education and intellect.

Though they engage its emphasis on intellectual labor, white authors' representations of southern kitchens also serve to counter the rigidity of northern domestic science. McCulloch-Williams begins her text with an extended introduction common to domestic science texts, but hers is instead a detailed description of the domestic education she received in "mammy's" kitchen. She writes, "[T]he kitchen proper would give Domestic Science heart failure, yet it must have been altogether sanitary" (12). This depiction of the mammy demonstrates her difference from modern cookery methods that demand precision and consistency, and thus her racial distinction from white cooks who promote and publish these methods. Patterson also nods to the domestic science movement when she writes early in her introduction, "We wanted to tell the world about this cooking. But we knew that the recipes would have to be definite. And mammy's recipes were as secret as inventions to end war!" (ix). The term "definite" indicates both the emphasis on science in the recipe and the prevalent idea that black women were "natural" or improvisational cooks, and did not use recipes. These were, of course, ideas that had been disproven by several published African American cookbooks, but in an effort to reclaim authority over one's culture, Patterson reverts to the concept of inherent, mythical knowledge that created distinctive southern cuisine. Both texts romanticize southern food culture in opposition to the problems of poverty and sanitation that plagued northern industrial centers.

The most important task of the mammy cookbook was to revise the meaning of culinary "labor" from cooking to writing. Patterson suggests that the true praise for the translation of these recipes into text belongs to "generations of Southern ancestry from Virginia, North Carolina, Kentucky, Georgia, Alabama, Mississippi, Louisiana, and for two generations, Texas" (ix). She continues, "We cannot assume all credit for putting these recipes into definite form." Lest we believe she is going to give the southern mammy any agency in this discussion, Patterson quickly adds, "Grandmothers many times 'great,' as well as our own grandmother, mother, proud aunts and cousins, had done this before our day." So while she invokes the mammy as an authenticator of southern cuisine, she seems to argue that the real labor of southern food is making her "secret" recipes "definite," and for this arduous task she thanks generations of white southerners. Patterson further invokes this emphasis on a shared past by referring to white southerners first as a "clan," then as a "family": "But the cry of the clan had been, 'Keep them in the family.'" Patterson's juxtaposition of the terms "clan" and "family" suggests a further emphasis on the racial boundaries of southern heritage. She writes of the mammy that she reared "white 'chillun' to be kind and 'mannerly'" and fed them "nourishing food as well as catered to the family and the numerous 'cump'ny' that came to the Big House" (ix). In so doing, Patterson creates a community defined by race and gender, all thankful to their "mammies" for the inspiration, so to speak, to record their shared heritage through recipes. And in her text, the dying breed of the mammy is just that: an inspiration, a myth, not an individual who performed actual physical labor and upon whose labor this shared heritage rests.

The popularity of incorporating dialect into the introduction, headings, even the recipes themselves, also aided this revision of labor: "Most cookbooks that use African American recipes and voices identify the cooks only by first name, mirroring daily face-to-face practice in the Jim Crow South" (Sharpless xxiv). Dialect blurs the distinction between black cook and white author, finally rendering "[the cooks] and their work invisible, as only the author's labor is visible in the text" (xxv). What remains, then, is the intellectual labor of writing and the distinctive tastes of the recipes, both a variation of and a reaction to the standardization of domestic science.[11]

Mammy cookbooks can be read as a form of blackface entertainment, popular at the turn of the century, but when viewed in the context of a domestic era dominated by the "euthenics" principles that informed Richards's home economists,[12] their message becomes even more insidious. White authors suggested their racial supremacy by their sympathetic depictions of vanishing black mammies. Rather than highlighting whiteness, they emoted nostalgia for blackness, virtually erasing from their illustration its modern, intellectual forms. Mammy cookbooks hindered the process of racial uplift and education—in other words, social mobility—by lamenting the passing of "proper" forms of blackness. They took away the modern black woman's voice by speaking through her preferred predecessor, the domestic servant. During a time when black clubwomen understood the value placed on print and literacy and worked to use this form to establish themselves as part of the American middle class, white women used print to combat their agency by suggesting a set of criteria for exceptional black women—domestic, devoted, and secretive (i.e., illiterate)—and then concluding that exceptional black women no longer exist. Furthermore, they suggest that it is now the duty of literate white women to keep their memory alive through print, thus negating the efforts of middle-class black women, despite their rapidly increasing rate of print. Mammy cookbooks are thus a form of representational eugenics, defining blackness as a stagnant composite of stereotypical images while representing whiteness as intellectual, virtuous, sympathetic, and evolving. In a culture of increased segregation, mammy cookbooks represent spatial segregation in print. White women express their racial mobility by inhabiting the kitchens and recipes of black women as a way to obstruct their progress into middle-class modes of domesticity.

Written by Herself: African Americans and the Business of Domesticity

Several decades prior to the mammy trend in cookbook authorship, black women began to assert their middle-class domestic identities by entering the field of domestic publishing. Cookbooks by African American women complicate the narrative of white women as domestic authorities. White women worked to associate African American women with the physical labor of cooking rather than the intellectual activity of interpreting its importance to the nation. As white women worked to make domestic labor a cerebral process, black women still performed much of the actual labor, especially in the South. Employment opportunities for African American women were slim, and racial ideologies made it difficult for them to find work outside of the domestic sphere (Kleinberg 115). And yet, while white women worked to reinforce the characterization of black women as mammies by using rhetoric that emphasized physicality and instinct, by the 1860s black women had begun to write their own cookbooks, performing both the actual and intellectual labor of cooking.[13] Through the use of print technology, black women marketed their knowledge—rather than their labor—as a valuable commodity. By recording and publishing their own recipes, these women, most of them former slaves and/or domestic servants, were able to demonstrate ownership: of knowledge, of home, of self. Finally, they worked to rebut the representation of their abilities as instinctual by utilizing domestic science rhetoric of clarity and precision to emphasize the reproducibility of their recipes.

Middle-class African American women were somewhat divided in their opinions about the role of domesticity in racial progress. African Americans were already associated with domestic service. However, they also recognized that acceptance of their middle-class identity was in part reliant upon their abilities to demonstrate continuity with their contemporary domestic discourse. African American women writers worked to create a sense of a collective racial identity through their depictions of domestic spaces, similar to the project of white writers. By better defining these boundaries in print, they could help black women define them in practice. They recognized the potential of the cookbook as a means to claim traditional domestic identity while documenting distinct intellectual and cultural tastes.

Following a tradition of African American–authored domestic texts begun in the 1820s with Robert Roberts's *House Servant's Directory* (1827), African American women such as Abby Fisher, author of *What Mrs. Fisher Knows About Old Southern Cooking* (1881), and Emma Hayes, author of *The Kentucky Cook Book* (1912), used their experiences as paid cooks to promote their domestic authority as an intellectual commodity. Abby Fisher's text in particular is "significant because its existence undermines one of the key mythologies that white plantation-school writers and southern cookbook authors propagated about black women cooks—that they cooked 'by instinct' and knew not what they did" (Witt, "Intersections" 107). Even Fisher's text, which was transcribed rather than written by Fisher herself, emphasizes that her knowledge is printable and reproducible, rather than secret or irrational.

African American women participated in the intellectual labor of cookery by recording and publishing their own recipes, recipes that were often claimed by their white employers. African American women, as both slaves and servants, were often coerced into giving away recipes by owners or employers (Sharpless xxii), but print allowed them to claim the recipes, skills, and literacy for themselves. The act of publishing and distributing a cookbook indicates ownership of domestic knowledge and skill and of the home space that produces them. Home ownership, which was also an important theme in African American women's club publications, was a sign of both self-possession and security against invasion, a common image in African American literature during the time period (Bernardi 203). This also meant that the food resulting from a woman's practical and intellectual labor could define her home space and nourish her own family, rather than that of her white employer. Though many southern African American women found work as domestic servants and thus had to contend with post-Reconstruction nostalgia and Lost Cause mythology, two of the most important African American–authored domestic texts, Abby Fisher's 1881 cookbook and Bertha Turner's edited *Federation Cook Book* (1910),[14] were published in California, thus avoiding the complex power negotiations and conciliatory culture of the North/South regional antagonism.

Abby Fisher is the fourth African American person known to publish a cookbook, and only the second woman, the first being Malinda Russell in 1866. Fisher was likely a slave, though she does not discuss this status, explicitly or implicitly, in her text. She also does not mention her race within her book, and what little we know of her history comes primarily from historian Karen Hess. We know even less of Emma Hayes, and our knowledge of her comes only from her own brief introduction: "This book is the work of a colored cook of many years' experience, and who has had ample opportunity for experimenting and testing the recipes presented. They are simply and easily made, and have proved to be excellent. The book will be found a most useful addition to any kitchen." It is signed "Sincerely, MRS. W. T. HAYES, Author of the Kentucky Cook Book." Though several scholars have speculated as to her identity, inadequate birth and employment records have not yet led to a concrete conclusion.

Fisher's and Hayes's texts share specific rhetorical qualities. Each includes a short preface in which neither author gives personal background, but instead explains her conditions of authorship. She explains why she chose to publish a cookbook (usually requested by others), and her years of experience, giving her text—and thus herself—authority based on practice. Also, each author assures readers that they will find her text satisfactory and easy to follow. Though Abby Fisher and Emma Hayes avoid the extended introductions of science and nutrition common in cooking school texts, both emphasize precision and reproducibility in their cookbooks, as well as their success as professional cooks. Both women imply that they have had to earn their living based on their domestic abilities; they are neither an art nor a fashionable trend. By basing their authority on their domestic service, they complicate the hierarchy of the white kitchen. The authoritative body in the kitchen is a black body, a construct that both replicates the familiar paradigm of black domestic

servants common in many white households while at the same time alter-
ing the power structure through print and its accompanying assumptions of
authority, education, and intellect.

These texts challenge the inherency of white domestic superiority by giving "evidence of the invisible labor" that made white middle-class lifestyles
possible (Zafar 139–40). By destabilizing race and class boundaries, Debra
Bernardi argues, African American women writers were able to gain power
and fortify their own collective identity (210). Moreover, their texts challenged
the origins of the cuisine and cultural heritage claimed by generations of
white southern women, in whose minds the labors of cooking and writing
were rarely performed by the same individual. While Fisher and Hayes rely
on their domestic service for their authority, they also promote their middle-class identities by emphasizing their public roles. Fisher, for example, was
also a businesswoman. She is listed in the 1880 San Francisco city directory as
a manufacturer of pickles, preserves, etc., and her title, "Mrs. Abby Fisher &
Co.," along with an address of her residence/business, suggests that she used
domestic skills to begin her own business, rather than using them in the home
of another family (Hess 77). Her self-representation in print, as well as her
obvious business acumen (as she was well known and supported for her work)
contests boundaries of domesticity as the realm of the white middle class.

Due to their typical depiction as able but "mysterious" cooks, African
American cookbook authors were also careful to avoid distinction of their
food based on physical taste alone. Neither Fisher nor Hayes describes the
value of their recipes in terms of their distinctive flavors. Instead, they use
traditional print recipe formats to convey the intellectual work of their recipes: both appear in narrative form, incorporating the list of ingredients into
the instructions. Both include careful measurements, and suggest only that
readers season to taste, a ubiquitous instruction in published cooking texts.
Codifying recipes by recording clear measurements and careful instructions
implicitly claimed the level of authority of the domestic scientist, or the ability to own one's knowledge.

African American cookbook authors did not completely ignore the potential of the mammy as a social tool, however. Many writers carefully worked
to rebut her image within their texts. Witt argues that Fisher and Hayes likely
capitalized on the popularity of the mammy in American culture as a means
of marketing their own texts and achieving economic success: "[Abby Fisher]
might be understood to have distanced herself from the mammy stereotype
in stressing the transcribability of what she 'knows' while, paradoxically,
recuperating aspects of the mammy's emerging culinary aura to further her
own celebrity" ("Intersections" 107). By appropriating genre characteristics

of traditionally white-authored texts, black cooks elevate themselves rhetorically to the level of white cooking authorities, demonstrating the possibilities of racial uplift and critiquing readers' assumptions of race-based abilities through a familiar and popular genre.

Perhaps the best example of destabilizing mammy rhetoric can be found in Fisher's recipe "Pap for Infant Diet." In this most overt reference to her personal history, she boasts of raising eleven children on this diet. Both infant mortality rates and her possible slave past make this achievement particularly remarkable, and Zafar concludes, "Any prior reticence about her past . . . is subordinated to insuppressible pride in her success as a black mother" (143). Yet while Zafar rightly praises Fisher's celebratory remarks, her maternal success also supports popular rhetoric of the maternal mammy and her increasingly popular role in American culture. The mammy, however, is often depicted as caring for white children over her own. Fisher's recipe indicates care for her own children and effort at rebutting the mammy stereotype using its own rhetoric. Fisher, it seems, recognized that this was the context in which white readers would understand her maternal authority, and she worked within this framework to distinguish herself from it.

Fisher's "Preface and Apology" concludes, "The book will be found a complete instructor, so that a child can understand it and learn the art of cooking" (3). This choice of words is telling, and we wonder whether it was her choice or that of her transcriber. By invoking the image of a child learning to cook, she addresses her audience on several levels. First, she reminds them of time spent with their childhood mammies, of learning to cook by the hands and words of this magically wise old woman. Second, by suggesting that a child can learn such techniques, she avoids the accusation that she considers herself more of an authority than a white woman, and her authority on southern cooking is relegated to the collective southern imaginary. Her actual words, printed publicly, break the imaginative boundary and threaten white claims on southern culture. By referencing teaching a child rather than an adult, her remarks remain as nonthreatening as the mammy stereotype with which she will be associated. Finally, though, her remarks could contain a subtle critique, masked in the very plantation rhetoric to which her audience was accustomed. By infantilizing southern white women, Fisher rewrites the traditional comparison of blacks' intellectual capabilities with those of children, thus countering the romanticized representation of southern white women as gentle, nonlaboring, even weak, by calling it what it is: childlike. In this way, she uses their desire to construct a romantic southern memory to voice her own critique.

Of course, we must balance the rhetorical possibilities of her statement with its historical reality. Fisher could not write, and thus another person transcribed her text. Karen Hess points out several examples of recipe titles recorded phonetically, such as "Circuit Hash" instead of succotash and "Carolas" instead of crullers (84). This suggests a close transcription of her dictation, rather than a transcriber who actively revised the text, which could lead us to the conclusion that Fisher's words in her preface were also her own. Finally, her cookbook was published by the Women's Co-Operative Printing Office in San Francisco, and Fisher thanks the many friends and patrons who helped her compose and publish this text. Her transcriber, likely a member of this group, would have been a participant in the process of promoting racial and gender progress by breaking down ideological or romanticized barriers created by the mammy and its accompanying assumptions of illiteracy, childlike innocence, and subordinate contentment.

◆ ◆ ◆

Literature about cooking presented American women with a domestic paradox. In the hands of white domestic scientists, cooking was intellectual labor, best performed by those with careful and thorough educational training, preferably through domestic science principles or a reputable cooking school. In the hands of black women, however, cooking was instinctual, pleasurable, and individualized. Domestic scientists staked their reputations on standardization, or the reader's ability to reproduce their recipes and domestic advice exactly. Southern white writers presented black women cooks, on the other hand, as necessary precisely because their knowledge could not be reproduced, due to both their unscientific methods of cookery and their assumed illiteracy. These competing representations of late nineteenth-century cookery existed simultaneously in American society. These designations both reinforced cultural assumptions of racial identity and indicated, like reconciliation cookbooks before them, white America's preference for this uncomfortable partnership over the unfamiliar territory of racial equality.

In effect, the infamous 1893 World's Fair foreshadowed the conflicts of domesticity and race that would plague the nation well into the twentieth century. Nancy Green's performance as a southern mammy presented visitors with an emblem of the tensions in turn-of-the-century domestic discourse. Black women wished to distance themselves from a history of domestic service, though both domestic skills and authority were necessary to public perceptions of middle-class womanhood. Thus the domestic servants in their texts demonstrated the progress of African American domesticity, a recognition and rebuttal of the popular mammy mystique. White southern women, however, used the mammy as a way to limit racial progress, to commemorate black women's years of service while denying them a modern middle-class identity. The mammy in southern foodways thus exists as a means of both gauging and regulating racial progress, and this conflict shaped southern domestic discourse throughout the early twentieth century. A careful examination of southern cookbooks reveals that the battle for middle-class identity rested heavily on the region's struggle to define domestic authority.

Notes

1. For more on this, see Wallace-Sanders 63.

2. For more on the Model Kitchen, see Gail Lippincott 141–64. For more on Nancy Green's performance as Aunt Jemima, see Wallace-Sanders.

3. Jane Addams referred to this concept as "municipal housekeeping" (Gere and Robbins 643). Women Progressives often referred to their public duties as a "gospel of social motherhood" (Kleinberg 177).

4. Many cookbooks of this genre were published by northern publishing houses.

5. Glenna Matthews writes that the "very closeness between Progressives and home economists that gave the new discipline its social dimension . . . also meant that home economists would share in some of the less desirable characteristics of Progressives, such as their Anglo-Saxonism" (163).

6. Ellen Richards, founder of the domestic science movement, discussed this concept at length in *Euthenics, the Science of Controllable Environment* (1910).

7. Nina Silber writes, "[When] [c]onfronted with the haunting specters of class conflict, ethnic strife, and alienation that their own industrialized society had produced, many northerners remained unconvinced about the benefits of industrial progress and about obliterating whatever remained of the old southern legacy; in many ways, they were unconvinced as to the unqualified benefits of the Union victory. Sectional union could thus offer a bridge for northern ambivalence, between a modern and a premodern world" (5–6).

8. Marion Tyree's *Housekeeping in Old Virginia* (1877), for example, emphasizes the importance of Virginia's brand of domesticity throughout American history, while *Mrs. Porter's New Southern Cookery Book* (1871) demonstrates the revised role of the New South by including recipes that represent both northern and southern culinary traditions.

9. Nina Baym describes the competing roles of "spiritualized intellect" and gendered physicality, or the idea that "a weaker body equals less body, and less body equals more spirit" (*Feminism* 118).

10. Sharpless notes that Patterson attributed recipes to various cooks by (first) name, at least giving credit to the various women who made up her "composite" mammy (xxvii).

11. The mammy trend continued into the 1950s. White southern cookbook writers often attributed their cooking knowledge to their "mammies," even when the recipes themselves went unmarked. The civil rights movement marked the end of the prevalence of these stereotypes in much mainstream media, though they certainly remained in the minds of authors and cooks, both black and white.

12. In *Euthenics, the Science of Controllable Environment* (1910), Richards defines her term as "the betterment of living conditions, through conscious endeavor, for the purpose of securing efficient human beings" (vii).

13. Historian Janice Longone recently discovered an 1866 cooking text by Malinda Russell. Its content was primarily a record of European dishes cooked for a wealthy southern family, rather than those she had developed herself. It was also published several decades before the trends I explore emerged in African American domestic publishing. For these reasons, I do not include it here, though its existence is certainly significant.

14. Though Turner's text is an excellent example of a clubwomen's cookbook, it does not claim southern heritage, as it was compiled and edited entirely in California. For this reason, I do not include it in this essay.

Works Cited

Baym, Nina. *Feminism and American Literary History*. New Brunswick: Rutgers UP, 1992.

Bell, Katharin. *Mammy's Cook Book*. Los Angeles: Trade Printing Company, 1927.

Bernardi, Debra. "Narratives of Domestic Imperialism: The African-American Home in the *Colored Women's Magazine* and the Novels of Pauline Hopkins, 1900–1903." *Separate Spheres No More: Gender Convergence in American Literature, 1830–1930*. Ed. Monika M. Elbert. Tuscaloosa: U of Alabama P, 2000. 203–24.

Bryan, Lettice. *The Kentucky Housewife*. Cincinnati, 1839.

Deck, Alice A. "'Now Then—Who Said Biscuits?' The Black Woman Cook as Fetish in American Advertising, 1905–1953." *Kitchen Culture in America: Popular Representations of Food, Gender, and Race*. Ed. Sherrie A. Inness. Philadelphia: U of Pennsylvania P, 2001. 69–94.

Edwards, Laura F. *Scarlett Doesn't Live Here Anymore: Southern Women in the Civil War Era*. Urbana and Chicago: U of Illinois P, 2000.

Fisher, Abby. *What Mrs. Fisher Knows About Old Southern Cooking*. 1881. Bedford, MA: Applewood, 1995.

Gere, Anne Ruggles, and Sarah R. Robbins. "Gendered Literacy in Black and White: Turn-of-the-Century African-American and European-American Club Women's Printed Texts." *Signs* 21.3 (1996): 643–78.

Hale, Grace Elizabeth. *Making Whiteness: The Culture of Segregation in the South, 1890–1940*. New York: Vintage, 1998.

Hayes, Emma. *The Kentucky Cook Book*. St. Louis: J. H. Tompkins Printing Company, 1912.

Hess, Karen. "Afterword." *What Mrs. Fisher Knows About Old Southern Cooking*. 1881. Bedford, MA: Applewood, 1995. 75–90.

Kleinberg, S. J. *Women in the United States, 1830–1945*. New Brunswick: Rutgers UP, 1999.

Lippincott, Gail. "'Something in Motion and Something to Eat Attract the Crowd': Cooking with Science at the 1893 World's Fair." *Journal of Technical Writing and Communication* 33.2 (2003): 141–64.

McCulloch-Williams, Martha. *Dishes and Beverages of the Old South*. New York: McBride, Nast, & Company, 1913.

McHenry, Elizabeth. *Forgotten Readers: Recovering the Lost History of African American Literary Societies*. Durham: Duke UP, 2002.

Matthews, Glenna. *"Just a Housewife": The Rise and Fall of Domesticity in America*. New York: Oxford UP, 1987.

Montgomery, Rebecca. "Lost Cause Mythology in New South Reform: Gender, Class, Race, and the Politics of Patriotic Citizenship in Georgia, 1890–1925." *Negotiating Boundaries of Southern Womanhood: Dealing with the Powers That Be*. Eds. Coryell, Appleton, Sims, Treadway. Columbia: U of Missouri P, 2000. 174–98.

Patterson, Betty Benton. *Mammy Lou's Cook Book*. New York: R. M. McBride & Company, 1931.

Porter, M. E. *Mrs. Porter's New Southern Cookery Book*. 1871. New York: Arno, 1973.

Richards, Ellen. *Euthenics, the Science of Controllable Environment: A Plea for Better Living Conditions as a First Step Toward Higher Human Efficiency*. Boston: Whitcomb & Barrows, 1910.

Roberts, Robert. *The House Servant's Directory, or A Monitor for Private Families.* New York: Charles S. Francis, 1827.

Russell, Malinda. *A Domestic Cook Book*. 1866. Ann Arbor: William L. Clements Library, 2007.

Rutledge, Sarah. *The Carolina Housewife*. 1847. Columbia: U of South Carolina P, 1979.

Sharpless, Rebecca. *Cooking in Other Women's Kitchens: Domestic Workers in the South, 1865–1960*. Chapel Hill: U of North Carolina P, 2010.

Silber, Nina. *The Romance of Reunion: Northerners and the South, 1865–1900*. Chapel Hill: U of North Carolina P, 1993.

Smith-Rosenberg, Carroll. *Disorderly Conduct: Visions of Gender in Victorian America*. New York: Alfred A. Knopf, 1985.

Turner, Bertha L., ed. *The Federation Cook Book*. 1910. Bedford, MA: Applewood Books, 2007.

Tyree, Marion Fontaine Cabell. *Housekeeping in Old Virginia*. New York, 1877.

Wallace-Sanders, Kimberly. *Mammy: A Century of Race, Gender, and Southern Memory*. Ann Arbor: U of Michigan P, 2008.

Witt, Doris. *Black Hunger: Soul Food and America*. Minneapolis: U of Minnesota P, 2004.

———. "From Fiction to Foodways: Working at the Intersections of African American Literary and Culinary Studies." *African American Foodways: Explorations of History and Culture*. Ed. Anne L. Bower. Urbana and Chicago: U of Illinois P, 2007. 101–25.

Zafar, Rafia. "Recipes for Respect: Black Hospitality Entrepreneurs before World War I." *African American Foodways: Explorations of History and Culture*. Ed. Anne L. Bower. Urbana and Chicago: U of Illinois P, 2007. 139–52.

Chapter Five

THE COOKBOOK STORY
Transitional Narratives in Southern Foodways

ELIZABETH S. D. ENGELHARDT

"'Twas a long mont' 'fo' I seen Miss Honey ergin. One day she trip offen de train an' come ter me. She stood quiet while I han' up ter a gent'mun at de winder two pieces uv chicken, two pieces uv pie, an' two cups uv dripping coffee . . . 'Leah,' she says, 'I jes' got a few minits. How's business?'"
—**"Aunt Sanna Terry,"** Landon R. Dashiell (359)

In the midst of World War I, Landonia Randolph Dashiell, under the pen name Landon R. Dashiell, published a short story that later would be picked up by William Dean Howells for inclusion in his *Great Modern American Stories* volume of 1921. Dashiell's "Aunt Sanna Terry" portrays a series of interactions between an African American woman who makes a living selling food at her local rail platform and a young white woman who frequently travels there. What sets the short story apart, however, is its precise directions for brewing coffee, serving chicken, and preparing hygienic meals. Those directions work whether one is marketing to rail passengers in the South or cooking in one's own kitchen after an afternoon of short story reading.

Dashiell successfully created a document from which a specific recipe could be learned. She also embedded what she believed were best practices in service, hygienic preparation, and sophisticated presentation of foods. Yet Dashiell did not choose to employ the format and strategy of the era's cookbooks or advice manuals. Within the pages of "Aunt Sanna Terry," one does not find lists of ingredients or measurements set off from the surrounding story, there are no section headings to announce the next recipe or course in the meal, and the directions for preparation are never distilled into bulletpoint format. Instead, Dashiell created a southern black narrator who has a chance encounter with a presumed cooking school graduate. Over the course of "Aunt Sanna Terry," readers become invested in the resulting transformation of her business as well as her extended family's prospects. Given the background of Jim Crow against which the story takes place and in which Dashiell lived, we should tread carefully in describing the relationship between black and white female characters here. As a starting point, however, we can say Dashiell embraced a woman's club ethos of "lifting as we climb" in her story of women encountering changing transportation and technology and finding ways to talk to each other about it (White 23).

Dashiell's story is different from most pieces that describe food for travelers. While trips south on the railroads are dramatized by authors such as Rebecca Harding Davis and Frederick Law Olmstead, such authors do not discuss how to cook the food they encounter. On the other hand, Dashiell was not the only author to write such an alternative cooking guidebook. Hers, however, is inflected by its southern setting and its author's resultant sensibilities. This essay recovers a little-known moment in southern food writing in order to explore the text's particular interventions in Jim Crow's racial, gender, and technological economies. It examines why some authors at the turn of the century avoided the cookbook format and instead created narrative texts as cookbooks, with plots to follow, characters with which to identify, and settings through which to engage the attention of readers. Developing alongside the codification of recipe formats and modern cookbook conventions, the cookbook-as-novel and cookbook-as-short-story are more than artifacts of failed experiments. Rather, they make rhetorical space to negotiate changing definitions of gender, race, region, technology, and class. Understanding them as parallel strategies in conversation with, but separate from, other southern cookbooks allows a richer conversation about the stakes of food, time, and place.

For School and Community Improvement: Clubwoman and Author

Landonia Randolph Sparrow Dashiell was herself very much a figure of her time and place. The 1914–1915 edition of *Woman's Who's Who of America* ticks off her qualifications as a leading white citizen of Virginia (Leonard 229). Born in 1855, she was educated at a Richmond, Virginia, private school. Her marriage to William Sparrow Dashiell in 1883 brought together its own who's who of prominent family lines, some of which boasted lineal connections with the British royalty and the Plymouth colony (Browning 168; Leonard 229). Not only did Dashiell produce two sons in the later nineteenth century, but she also took on leadership positions in the clubwomen's world of turn-of-the-century Virginia. On the local level, she belonged to a group called the "Woman's Club and Country Club" in Richmond. Dashiell operated in statewide organizations as well, joining and participating in the leadership of groups such as the National Municipal League, the Colonial Dames of Virginia, and the Association for Preservation of Virginia Antiquities, the first statewide organization for historic preservation in the United States. With many of her fellow white clubwomen, hers was a racialized history, as she also belonged to the Confederate Museum and the United Daughters of Confederacy, groups devoted to creating and documenting a southern story of whiteness and privilege along with memorializing war experiences for fathers and brothers (Leonard 229; Janney 133–66).

The brunt of her activism, however, focused on educational issues. Her fiction emerges from this particular set of concerns. Dashiell belonged to the Richmond Educational Association and the Cooperative Education Association of Virginia. She spoke at the national "Conference for Education in the South" at least once (Dashiell, "Report," 41–44), and her obituary suggests she attended regularly, leading the Virginia contingent (Mitchell 52). She was an especially strong voice for "community improvement" in rural communities, of which education formed a centerpiece, and the *Woman's Who's Who* describes her as an "author of circulars and pamphlets on community improvement" (Leonard 229). Some of that work engaged African American or Native American Virginians, especially those connected to Hampton Institute, the prominent school serving black and Native students from across the United States. Such work was no brief commitment for Dashiell. She was active in improving "schools, roads, public health, and the growth of community life" from as early as 1900 through to her death in 1925 (Mitchell 52).

Her obituary, published in the *Southern Workman*, the journal headquartered at Hampton, sums up Dashiell as a "friend" of the school and its graduates. More than that, the obituary explains, "She saw clearly that the two races in the South must advance together in a spirit of mutual helpfulness." It pointedly calls her an "ardent supporter of all education in Virginia" (Mitchell 52–53). Given the range of her activism—and reflected in the plot of "Aunt Sanna Terry"—education meant more than classroom lessons to Dashiell. Exchanges on the side of railroad tracks, over shared meals, and concerning businesses headed up by women across Virginia all could be chances for "friends" to listen, learn, and teach each other important lessons for improving individual and civic life.

The Curious History and Plot of "Aunt Sanna Terry"

While Dashiell was a significant figure in community work, she left light traces on the literary landscape. An unpublished journal of her poetry resides in the archives of the Virginia Historical Society (Dashiell, "Album"). "Aunt Sanna Terry" appears to be the only foray she made into the world of fiction, and it certainly is her only story to draw attention from literary circles. Her longstanding affiliations with Hampton Institute may explain the story's publication in the *Southern Workman*. The story was not buried deep in the issue; instead, it and its author headlined the front cover of the journal's 1918 edition. Perhaps the prominent placement caught the eye of noted editor and tastemaker William Dean Howells. Whatever the trajectory, Dashiell's story did indeed catch Howells's attention—though he expressed surprise to find it in the Hampton publication and to find it so good.

In his introduction to *Great Modern American Stories*, Howells claims that "there is nothing better here [in the volume] than the episode of *Aunt Sanna Terry*, which a beneficent chance vouchsafed to one of us in the very unexpected pages of *The Southern Workman* where the humor of Miss Dashiell had lavished it on that organ of Hampton Institute." Putting aside Howells's real or feigned surprise that there could be humor or literary merit in Hampton's publication, we find him comparing Dashiell to Joel Chandler Harris, Mark Twain, and George Washington Cable, saying (somewhat convolutedly), "[T]here is to my thinking, no superior to ['Aunt Sanna Terry'] in the whole range of colored character, as the mastery of the South which knows it best has portrayed it in *Uncle Remus*, and Mark Twain and Mr. Cable's very varied and exquisitely rendered shades and differences of the race unsurpassedly known to him" (Howells x). Evoking the stories of Twain, Cable, and Harris introduces precisely the tension between broad stereotype, regional dialect and humor, and subtle, sophisticated character play that concerns us as we tease out the rhetoric of this early twentieth-century cookbook story. While the story's "colored character" occupied Howells's attention, cooking and the food business occupied the attention of that character, Dashiell's fictional "Aunt Sanna Terry."

The story, written in the era's broadest of dialect, is narrated by Mrs. Leah Heber Jenkins, dubbed "Aunt Sanna Terry"—that is, sanitary—by the younger, white cooking school graduate, whom Jenkins calls Miss Honey. The story is told in past tense, as Jenkins reflects upon the changes to her business, income, and family after a chance encounter with Honey on the railroad platform. Selling food to rail passengers is nothing new to Jenkins—she has been in the business of "fried chicken an' coffee, pies an' milk" for more than twenty years (352).[1] With at least ten trains passing through each day, the business supports Jenkins and her now-adult son with a house and food for both. Jenkins pays regular installments on her house and lot on the edge of the unnamed town where she raises her chickens (352).

However, at the story's beginning, Jenkins faces two distinct challenges. First, her son is in jail for drinking (Dashiell inserts a subtheme of temperance through the son's trials; he is not bad, but he just cannot stay away from alcohol). Second, the growing railroad industry coupled with changing food technology has created new competition for women like Jenkins. As a result, Jenkins admits, she is now struggling to pay her house note. Consolidation of industry means that the railroad now owns the platform and the hotel next to it, and they have advanced young black men to the titles of waiters and authorized them to sell food directly from the hotel to passengers. Women like Jenkins have been pushed to the other side of the tracks, in a more awkward, less professional setting. They must prepare and pack up their food at home, make the long walk across town carrying food, umbrellas, and cooking equipment, and set up their business anew each day (352–53). What Miss Honey has realized—and what Jenkins must learn—over the course of the story is that customer expectations have embraced the new technologies of hygiene, sanitation, and food preparation, adding extra difficulties to the women serving food from the dusty and dog-infested "wrong" side of the tracks.

At their first encounter, Honey compliments Jenkins's cooking skills, especially with the chicken and pies. But she tries to convince Jenkins to "wear here at de depot a white cap, a large white ap'on an' white cotton gloves an' a lovely white han'kerchief folded ercross dis way" (354). Honey promises Jenkins that her sales will double if she will just don the uniform of sanitary food preparation. More than that, she sends Jenkins the uniform at no cost. A point of distinction to which we will return in a moment: Jenkins is already mostly practicing clean food service, which the story details. She wraps her foods in paper before selling them, she separates her different products, and she wages a war against the animals and insects. But Honey insists that customers are hard pressed to know Jenkins follows such standards of cleanliness without the uniform's visible markers. Jenkins at first resists the gloves, and describes in detail the reactions of both the other women and the male waiters—both of which prod her into making the suggested changes in full (355–56).

By the time Honey returns a week later, Jenkins's sales have, in fact, increased as promised. She has even taken on an employee, hiring someone to help her make the extra chicken and pies she can now sell in a given day. Honey has one more alteration to make. The main recipe of the story is conveyed through Honey's introduction of a coffee percolator and her detailed directions to Jenkins about how to use it. They discuss the thorough daily cleansing and set up of the equipment, the heat needed, the amounts of coffee, the precise pints and beginning temperature of the water, and the ideal time for percolation. They debate the merits of cream-versus-milk and granulated-versus-lump sugar for coffee's best flavor. Finally, Honey emphasizes a name change to distinguish the previously offered "boiled coffee" from this, "drip coffee" (357–58).

The final scene of the story takes place a month later, when Honey returns once again. This time, Jenkins reports not only on her successful coffee sales, but also on how the expansion of the business means that her house note will be completely paid off by the following week. Her son is out of jail, and the county has "gone probation"—in other words, has voted in Prohibition—so coffee is all he has to drink while holding down a new job. Times have changed for Honey as well, since on this trip she brings her new husband along, and the story ends with Jenkins offering to come cook for them and the husband accepting on the merits of the fried chicken he has just tasted (359–60).

Historical Kin: The Waiter Carriers of Virginia

Leah Heber Jenkins is, in fact, the fictional sister of the historical "waiter carriers" of Virginia. In her exploration of women, fried chicken, and power in the United States, *Building Houses Out of Chicken Legs*, Psyche Williams-Forson analyzes interviews with descendants of African American women who lived and worked in Gordonsville, Virginia. Indeed, Williams-Forson's title comes from the daughter of a waiter carrier who says her mother "paid for this place"—by which she means their home—"out of chicken legs" (32). Jenkins would very much understand. Today, a historical marker vaguely describes the waiter carriers' contribution to the community, to the comfort of rail passengers, and, importantly, to the history of restaurants, black entrepreneurship, and the ultimate dismantling of Jim Crow racial codes in the South (36). Williams-Forson documents how the marker's historical memories have been flattened to emphasize the feel-good small business and empowered femininity of the waiter carriers' contribution. As a result, the tensions, often deeply racist ones, of code enforcement—ironically, in terms of our discussion, on the grounds of hygiene and sanitation—versus home-based businesses, of national rail companies versus local platform practices, and of white community memory-makers versus African American histories have been difficult to unearth and understand. Dashiell's story, while not historical fact, is nonetheless a reflection of a particular historical time and place, through which we can glimpse not only an author's dramatic interests but also an era's racial, class, and food battles.

Virginia was not the only state in which female black entrepreneurs sold "fried chicken, biscuits and breads, hard-boiled eggs, fruit pies, and 'their famous hot coffee which was sold in old fashioned pots'" to rail passengers and at street markets (Williams-Forson 32). Williams-Forson here quotes John T. Edge, who found similar stories of women at rail depots in Mississippi. Photographs and sketches from the late nineteenth and early twentieth centuries place such women across the Chesapeake Bay, and, in particular, in Dashiell's hometown of Richmond (Williams-Forson 234n60).

While in the story a white woman teaches an African American woman best cooking practices, in early century Virginia and across the South that lesson was more likely to take place between African American women (Sharpless 21–22). For instance, in the same volume of the *Southern Workman* in which "Aunt Sanna Terry" appears, we can also find an excerpt from the United States' Department of Agriculture *Weekly News Letter* about "Negro home demonstration agents" who "not only help the Negroes in their homes, but also give instruction to women who are regular cooks . . . in the work given to cooks greater emphasis is put on food preparation and food and fuel conservation" ("Race" 427). Especially with the outbreak of World War I, funding for black home extension work was more plentiful, resulting in a fleet of such women spreading about the states with their messages of hygiene and care (Gilmore 197–99). Virginia had earlier pioneered such "master teachers" through the foundation of a white Quaker woman, Anna Jeanes, that trained African American women to be "Jeanes teachers," tasked with training students to, in turn, instruct widening circles of friends, classmates, and neighbors. The later founding of the Department of Agriculture's home service explicitly studied and borrowed the methods of Virginia's Jeanes teachers (Reck 137–38). Extension programs also hired some African American women into more stable government positions where they interacted with similarly professional white women. While the classes each group taught were rarely integrated, the training of agents often was. Thus, the technical conversation Dashiell portrayed, while constrained by the racial segregation of the story's setting, was nonetheless possible in the era's progressive extension and women's club outreach.

What the historical sources are hard pressed to tell us, though, are the ways black and white women imagined talking to each other. While fictional, "Aunt Sanna Terry" is one white woman's version of how the conversation might go. More than that, its author is a white woman who we know had some of those encounters in her volunteer activities. It is important not to overstate the progressivism here—the story is not written by someone who personally experienced the oppression of Jim Crow Virginia, nor does it portray an African American woman teaching a white woman, for instance. At no time does it challenge the social systems that give Leah privilege and Jenkins space by the side of the tracks. Its "comic" effects, so embraced by Howells, never stray from white conventions of black speech and manner. Yet many authors in Dashiell's position were comfortable presenting accomplished southern black women's cooking as purely intuitive, untaught, and "natural" (Levenstein 14). Dashiell conformed to her era's dialect expectations, but she presented Jenkins's food as expertly prepared and her exchange with Leah as that between professionals talking about efficiency, profit, and best practices.

Aunt Sanna Terry's Food Issues: How Coffee Might Save the South

Today, coffee may not seem like something one need turn to a cookbook or cooking expert to learn. Yet in the nineteenth century, coffee was an important topic in cooking schools, home economics programs, and educational cookbooks. While we often think of the South as one of the few outposts of tea drinkers in the United States—a history that lingers today in the quantities of iced tea consumed—evidence also suggests great devotion to hot coffee. For instance, we know from early cookbooks that southerners invented and employed numerous and ingenious coffee substitutes in times of scarcity (Edge 40). Similarly, an 1899 editorial from the rival Postum company, which appeared in newspapers from Bangor, Maine, to Portland, Oregon, appealed directly to southern consumers of coffee (Tullar 3). Historian Mark Pendergrast argues that, for the nation as a whole, "By the end of the nineteenth century, the United States would consume nearly half of the world's coffee" (42). Nonetheless, the poor quality of boardinghouse coffee, the frequency of burnt coffee beans in private homes, and the health effects of dirty coffee pots and equipment all were fervently discussed in magazines, travel journals, and newspapers. Befitting its cultural context, Dashiell's "Aunt Sanna Terry" hinged not on the introduction of a new foodways, but, rather, it turned on the improvement of existing practices.

The other reason so much ink was spilled at the turn of the century over coffee preparation can be glimpsed in the number of temperance advocates who generated that ink. To them, coffee was a struggle over high stakes citizenship, national health, and individual morality. For instance, the editors of *Good Housekeeping* magazine brought together six of the best-known cooking teachers and columnists, Maria Parloa, Catherine Owen, Marion Harland, Juliet Corson, "Mrs. Helen Campbell," and "Mrs. D. A. Lincoln," to collaborate on *Six Cups of Coffee: Prepared for the Public Palate by the Best Authorities on Coffee Making* in 1887. Writing in the introduction, Hester M. Poole claimed that poorly prepared coffee was "injurious and depressing" to individuals and society as a whole (Parloa et al. 3). Later in the volume, she expanded on her statement, saying, "That coffee is a medicine in cases of extreme alcoholism is well known, but it is hardly understood to what extent this exhilarating and potent beverage might be used in place of liquor" (48). Juliet Corson upped the stakes further, suggesting that coffee's "free use is unfavorable to indulgence in intoxicants of any character" (20). And, in fact, many of the cooking schools saw their lessons as at the forefront of the temperance movement.

Since so much coffee was already consumed in the United States and alcohol rates still soared, the health reformers had a problem. They could not argue any coffee would help, so they instead claimed only properly prepared coffee worked. By extension, then, bad coffee was dangerous, a social problem that must be addressed. If people could be made to drink better—in this case, properly brewed and healthful coffee—then they would be less likely to succumb to alcohol and the attendant abuse and violence that so often accompanied it. Dashiell's odd subplot of the alcoholic son, while ostensibly resolved by the town's Prohibition edict, surely was received by many readers also as a success story of well-prepared coffee such as Jenkins's new percolator produces (359). Judging from *Good Housekeeping*'s desire to draw together some of their best writers into a single volume on the topic, the editorial staff must have been convinced of a robust market of people interested in coffee lessons. As did Dashiell, the authors had a serious message for their readers beyond their pages-long directions for the most delicious cup of hot coffee.

That percolator is a crucial piece of the food story underlying "Aunt Sanna Terry" and *Six Cups of Coffee* alike. Invented in the middle of the nineteenth century, the percolator saw its heyday in the first decades of the twentieth. Once electric power lines reached their home, many households chose to make the percolator one of their first electric appliances purchased (Pendergrast 110). Accustomed to the taste and in support of their private consumer choice, travelers looked for similarly brewed coffee on their trips. Honey has clearly brought Jenkins a percolator more like the stovetop or campfire ones we still see occasionally today—because it does not rely on electricity, she can brew fresh coffee all day long over a small wood or coal fire that she builds. In between batches, she can scrub the pot clean and discard the old grounds. As a side effect of her increased sales, Jenkins is able to offer richer cream rather than milk and keep using the more economical granulated sugar rather than lumps (358). The story suggests that her percolator may be new to Jenkins, but it is recognizable to her customers, who lean out of the train as soon as they smell the drip coffee at her side, expecting fresher, more sanitary, and more hygienic food to follow (359). The trappings of Jenkins's new uniform, her continued devotion to proper food safety, and now her newer brewing methods that come with their own marketing campaigns promising sanitation confirm potential customers' expectations. Jenkins embodies Honey's nickname for her; Sanna Terry becomes a symbol of sanitary travel food.

Sanitation, however, cut in negative as well as positive directions for actual African American Virginians in the early twentieth century. Dashiell's story ends on a hopeful premise that simply wearing the signs and practicing the newest breakthroughs in sanitary food preparation will be enough to uplift the lives of people like Jenkins and communities like the larger one in which she lives. Interestingly, the daughter of the Gordonsville waiter carrier also discusses hygiene. She recalls the town's white "health regulators" who would frequently give citations to the African American women for not being sanitary enough with their practices. Given the racialized rhetoric around cleanliness that propped up Jim Crow's separation of black and white in dining facilities, water fountains, and more—which rarely limited whites' abilities to hire black women to cook for them privately—not unlike the very end of "Aunt Sanna Terry." Some health regulators surely came to the deeply racist conclusion that African Americans simply never could be sanitary in their efforts (Hale 128). In such a hostile environment, it would be very difficult even to continue, much less thrive in the business.

Unlike the white author Dashiell, for whom hygiene is only a positive for which to strive, the African American women in Gordonsville also identified citations as sometimes not being about their food safety practices at all. Instead, they "believed that most of these interventions were in an effort to gain information about their recipes" (Williams-Forson 34). As scholars such as Rebecca Sharpless and Jacqueline Jones have explored, one of the few sources of power—albeit highly constrained—reliably available to African American women in the United States South was located in the kitchen, in their own recipes, and in their role in creating what was fast becoming a fabled cuisine, southern cooking (Sharpless 167–69; Jones 128–34). While Williams-Forson cannot offer proof of unnamed white male inspectors' motivation to co-opt recipes and—it is implied—repurpose them for white businesses, it should not surprise us that the mechanisms of southern society might be deployed in support of white privilege and enforcement and in order to disempower African American women in one of their few terrains.

Additionally, businesses like Jenkins's were fleeting in the 1920s. Williams-Forson outlines changes in the railroad industry that proved the end of waiter carriers in Gordonsville: first, business was siphoned off by the advent of dining cars on the rails; second, rail companies introduced closed vestibules between cars, which made it hard to reach customers; finally, air-conditioning in passenger cars led to windows being sealed, shutting off the last access point between the women and hungry customers (34). And, of course, soon after World War I, the reign of the automobile reached full ascendance. The epilogue to the Gordonsville waiter carriers is a long struggle, shared by African American entrepreneurs and workers, to break into the restaurant business, navigate the new interstate road system, and ultimately break down the system of segregation and violence that kept them out of many successful food business ventures.

Jenkins demonstrates one small bit of resistance in the story: she does not replace her boiled coffee with the drip version. Instead, she offers both products, arguing that some of her customers are loyal to the older process (359). The fictional detail could reflect Dashiell's experience working in actual communities and with African American as well as white Virginians. Consumer practices, especially around food, rarely follow single truths or straight lines—taste preferences may very much mean that a market remains for boiled coffee despite the arguments mounted for the superiority of the drip coffee. Jenkins may also be preserving a lower-cost option for travelers without as much access to cash—whatever their race. The detail functions in the story to establish Jenkins's independent character and to allow a possibility of resistance or subversion between Jenkins and Honey or even between the author and her readers. With this racialized historical context more clearly in view, then, we can turn to questions of genre and cooking.

The Cookbook Story: Transitional Narrative Strategies

Dashiell did not invent the genre of cookbooks in the form of novels or stories. While some early nineteenth-century advice manuals take the form of narratives between an older, experienced author and a younger interrogator, the cookbook novel phenomenon really blossomed in the last three decades of the 1800s. I count among them stories that have narrators and plots, characters in which readers become invested, and fully realized settings that influence the people and foods, but which also give detailed directions in the dialogue or narrator's voice of how to prepare specific recipes. Such pieces start popping up in the magazines, serialized newspaper columns, and publishing catalogs of the late century. While today they can be hard to find as a group (in part because they are differently categorized across archives— sometimes in cookbook lists, other times in collections of early American fiction, and still other times as sketches or columns), readers at the time were aware of the model, comparing works to ones by other authors, and driving at least some kind of market for the publications. As scholars, perhaps we should be on the lookout for food writing in unexpected places.

One of the authors of *Six Cups of Coffee*, Catherine Owen, was perhaps the most well-known author in the genre. In works such as *Ten Dollars Enough* (1887), *Molly Bishop's Family* (1888), and *The Gentle Breadwinners* (1888), she returned repeatedly to the model of plotting, character building, kitchen design, and food preparation techniques paired with specific recipes to be mastered. The first two novels feature a cooking school graduate managing her first home and then supporting a young family, and they are deeply involved in the choice and training of kitchen and nursery assistants (Cohen 107–22). But both *Ten Dollars Enough* and *Molly Bishop's Family* each contain more than fifty fully discussed and described recipes over their chapters. *Gentle Breadwinners* bears more surface similarity to "Aunt Sanna Terry" as it is the story of a young woman thrust out on her own who slowly builds a cake- and candy-making business that eventually supports both herself and her sister in relative comfort. Also as in "Aunt Sanna Terry," a strong clubwomen's ethic prevails. The titular gentle breadwinner sells most of her products through the Woman's Exchange, a cooperative club meant to connect wealthy patrons with deserving enterprising businesswomen. All of Owen's novels are set in the Northeast, and they reflect that region's German and Irish immigrant culture, as well as the middle-class relocation to early suburbs. While Jenkins's encounter with Honey is much more accidental, Honey would fit in well on the board of directors of the Woman's Exchange.

Similarly, in *Cooking and Castle Building* (1880), the home economics pioneer Emma Pike Ewing united a world-weary mother and daughter with a friend who is an accomplished cook while they spend the summer at a reputedly haunted house in rural Massachusetts. Readers turn the pages to see if the friend's efforts to reinvent the cookbook and teach the daughter to embrace cooking as an empowering identity will transform both mother and daughter and banish the ghosts of older decades. Lesser-known but similar works include Jehiel Keeler Hoyt's *Romance of the Table* (1872), which is particularly concerned with poor bread baking. The anonymously published *Six Hundred Dollars a Year* (1867) is predicated on a household tax enacted by Congress and the wild economic swings of the post–Civil War economy. To its recipes, it adds in household accounting for furniture and heating bills, arguing that they are all parts of running a house that women should know.

Many in the genre are juvenile books, written for children to teach them to cook. Examples include Elizabeth S. Kirkland's *Six Little Cooks: Or, Aunt Jane's Cooking Class* (1877), which includes cake recipes using alcohol, and its quickly released follow-up, *Dora's Housekeeping* (1877), which does not in deference to temperance advocates. The *Mary Frances Cook Book* (1912) and its variations were similar, with the addition of lovely full-color illustrations of the talking kitchen implements that help Mary Frances learn. The scholar Jan Longone discusses at least one ethnic cookbook, in which the Dutch main characters address American children to tell them about and give directions for Dutch cuisine (Longone 107). Some of these have explicit religious messages, such as Caroline E. Kelly Davis's *Sunny Path* (ca. 1887) and *Prudy Keeping House* (1870) by Sophie May. As Longone points out, some of the juvenile works result in what we might call useful cooking skills—breakfasts, lunches, and dinners fully realized. Others focus solely on gendered sweets and dainty confections reflective of middle- and upper-class white assumptions of girls' decorative function in a home (Longone 107). Such stories are, needless to say, far away from Dashiell's adult character running a business and supporting whole families off her entrepreneurship.

Nonetheless, all of these stories share certain conventions and practices (and this is why I am calling them a genre). Not only do they talk through how to prepare a recipe, they also often discuss how to shop for the raw ingredients, where to economize, and when to buy quality. They dwell on the necessary preparation ahead of time or on when the cook will be able to take breaks and accomplish other work while waiting for the recipe to come together. They anticipate problems—mistakes the cook may make or difficult-to-predict variables that show up once the process has begun. Many provide course corrections to faltering cooks. Finally, directions for reheating, storing, and making second or third meals out of the recipes are included.

Food scholars' research helps explain why authors like Dashiell chose to narrate recipes and create characters to cook them. The format of recipes is a socially constructed convention, which, in the United States, developed along with home economics, reliable scientific instrumentation, and concomitant instruction in their uses (Levenstein 72–85). Kitchen technology was in flux well into the twentieth century, with some cooks having electric stoves, others using gas ones, others still cooking over wood or coal, and far-flung readers even cooking over open flames. Measuring cups and spoons, while coming into greater use, still varied in accuracy, and cooks were not accustomed to using them precisely (Shapiro 100–105). Deeply layered debates about gender normativity, inseparable from race and class hierarchies, played out over such cooking innovations (Inness 1–16). Ingredients themselves varied greatly—no one had dictated the size of eggs, amount of leavening in different "baking powders," percent of gluten in flour, or fat in meats butchered at home and from markets. Because of these variables, and because many readers were used to learning how to cook from mothers, grandmothers, or friends of whom they could ask questions and have lengthy exchanges, readers of cookbook novels and short stories were comfortable with more narrative, conversational lessons than the short lists that became standard cookbook convention.

Dashiell's Southern Strategy: The Public Lessons of Aunt Sanna Terry

Thus, we should not conclude that Dashiell invented the genre of cookbooks as novels or short stories. In fact, she is a relatively late entry into the field. However, Dashiell's is one of the few southern stories in the genre—set in a southern city, written by a southern author, featuring southern recipes and foodways, and marked by the era's signs and signals of southern speech and politics. More than that, it is one of the few that dwells on public food, on nondomestic space, and on increased profit for the producer rather than savings for the consumer. As such, it is worth a second glance for what it can tell us specifically about southern literature and food.

The cookbook in the form of a short story or novel was not a gimmick or an odd eddy in the history of cooking. Rather, in an era in which the best practices of cooking had yet to be internalized, for which technology was still changing at breakneck pace, and during which consumer demand was rising—the format was particularly useful. "Aunt Sanna Terry" is a literary cookbook of foodways, not recipes. It develops a shared language of food, across class, across place, and through time. The surface discussion of hygiene, taste, and efficient cooking technologies is on a deeper level an exploration of racial hierarchy, market-based capitalism, and gendered activism.

Honey and Leah Jenkins can talk and laugh and the inexperienced white woman can make suggestions that improve the business profitability of the older, independent black woman precisely because they are not employer and employee, precisely because "Aunt Sanna Terry" takes place in the liminal space of the wrong side of the tracks. Their gender solidarity can result in a comfortable uplift even with the unsettling racialized dialect, ignorance, and sterotypes circling around them. Dashiell seemed to recognize as much with her carefully scripted ending of the story. Lest Jenkins become too independent or too empowered, her acceptance of the much more typical role of cook (and likely nurse and mammy) in the newly formed middle-class white household between Honey and her husband in the end reinstalls her in an easily understood and confined social position for Dashiell's white Virginia and for Howells's national audience.

Just for a moment, however, through the method of a narrative cookbook, a coalition for community improvement in and of rural Virginia can be glimpsed. As scholars trying to understand the meanings, power, and potential of food in literature, we would be well served to listen to what is being said both by character and by genre. The cookbook novel may indeed still hold narrative strategies that illuminate the stakes of food, culture, and region in the early twentieth century.

Note

1. Page references throughout refer to the version of "Aunt Sanna Terry" in the Howells collection.

Works Cited

Browning, Charles Henry. *Americans of Royal Descent: Collection of Genealogies Showing the Lineal Descent from Kings of Some American Families*. 7th ed. Baltimore: Baltimore Genealogical Publishing, 1969.

Cohen, Kim. "'True and Faithful in Everything': Recipes for Servant and Class Reform in Catherine Owen's Cookbook Novels." *Culinary Aesthetics and Practices in Nineteenth-Century American Literature*. Ed. Monika Elbert and Marie Drews. New York: Palgrave Macmillan, 2009. 107–22.

Dashiell, Landon R. "Aunt Sanna Terry." *The Great Modern American Stories: An Anthology*. Ed. William Dean Howells. New York: Boni and Liveright, 1920. 352–60.

———. "Aunt Sanna Terry." *Southern Workman* 47:9 (September 1918): 449–55.

———. "Report upon the Richmond Education Association." *Proceedings of the Ninth Conference for Education in the South, Lexington, KY. May 2–4, 1906*. Published by the Executive Committee of the Conference, S. C. Mitchell, Chairman. Chattanooga: Time Printing, 1906. 41–44.

Dashiell, Landonia Randolph Minor. "Album." Mss 5:5 D2604: 1. Virginia Historical Society, Richmond, Virginia.

Davis, Caroline E. Kelly. *Sunny Path*. Nashville: Publishing House of the Methodist Episcopal Church, South, J. D. Barbee, Agent, ca. 1887.

Davis, Rebecca Harding. *Silhouettes of American Life*. New York: Scribner's, 1892.

Edge, John T., ed. *Foodways. The New Encyclopedia of Southern Culture*, Vol. 7. Chapel Hill: U of North Carolina P, 2007.

Fryer, Jane Eyre. *The Mary Frances Cook Book: Or, Adventures Among the Kitchen People*. Philadelphia: John C. Winston, 1912.

Gilmore, Glenda Elizabeth. *Gender and Jim Crow: Women and the Politics of White Supremacy in North Carolina, 1896–1920*. Chapel Hill: U of North Carolina P, 1996.

Hale, Grace Elizabeth. *Making Whiteness: The Culture of Segregation in the South, 1890–1940*. New York: Vintage, 1999.

Howells, William Dean. "A Reminiscent Introduction." *The Great Modern American Stories: An Anthology*. Ed. William Dean Howells. New York: Boni and Liveright, 1920. vii–xiv.

Hoyt, Jehiel Keeler. *Romance of the Table*. New Brunswick, NJ: Times Publishing, 1872.

Inness, Sherrie. *Dinner Roles: American Women and Culinary Culture*. Ames: U of Iowa P, 2001.

Janney, Caroline. *Burying the Dead But Not the Past: Ladies' Memorial Associations and the Lost Cause*. Chapel Hill: U of North Carolina P, 2012.

Jones, Jacqueline. *Labor of Love, Labor of Sorrow: Black Women, Work, and the Family, from Slavery to the Present*. New York: Vintage, 1986.

Kirkland, Elizabeth S. *Dora's Housekeeping*. Chicago: Jansen, McClurg, 1877.

———. *Six Little Cooks: Or, Aunt Jane's Cooking Class*. Chicago: Jansen, McClurg, 1877.

Leonard, John William, ed. *Woman's Who's Who of America: A Biographical Dictionary of Contemporary Women of the United States and Canada, 1914–1915*. 1914. Detroit: Gale Research, 1976.

Levenstein, Harvey. *Revolution at the Table: The Transformation of the American Diet*. Berkeley: U of California P, 2003.

Longone, Jan. "'As Worthless as Savorless Salt'?: Teaching Children to Cook, Clean, and (Often) Conform." *Gastronomica: The Journal of Food and Culture* 3.2 (Spring 2003): 104–10.

May, Sophie, pseud. Rebecca Sophia Clarke. *Prudy Keeping House*. Boston: Lee and Shepard, 1870.

Mitchell, S. C. "Landonia R. Dashiell." *Southern Workman* 55.2 (February 1926): 52–53.

Olmsted, Frederick Law. *The Cotton Kingdom: A Traveller's Observations on Cotton and Slavery in the American Slave States*. New York: Mason Brothers, 1861.

Owen, Catherine, pseud. Helen Alice Matthews Nitsch. *Gentle Breadwinners: The Story of One of Them*. Boston: Houghton, Mifflin, 1888.

———. *Molly Bishop's Family*. Boston: Houghton, Mifflin, 1888.

———. *Ten Dollars Enough: Keeping House Well on Ten Dollars a Week; How It Has Been Done; How It May Be Done Again*. Boston: Houghton, Mifflin, 1887.

Parloa, Maria, et al. *Six Cups of Coffee: Prepared for the Public Palate by the Best Authorities on Coffee Making*. With the Story of Coffee by Hester M. Poole. Good Housekeeping Press, Clark W. Bryan & Co., Springfield, Mass., 1887.

Pendergrast, Mark. *Uncommon Grounds: The History of Coffee and How It Transformed Our World*. Rev. ed. New York: Basic, 2010.

Poling-Kempes, Lesley. *The Harvey Girls: Women Who Opened the West*. New York: Marlowe, 1991.

"Race Relations: Press Comment." *Southern Workman* 47.9 (September 1918): 427.

Reck, Franklin M. *The 4-H Story: A History of 4-H Club Work*. Ames: Iowa State College P, 1951.

Shapiro, Laura. *Perfection Salad: Women and Cooking at the Turn of the Century*. New York: Farrar, Straus, Giroux, 1986.

Sharpless, Rebecca. *Cooking in Other Women's Kitchens: Domestic Workers in the South, 1865–1960*. Chapel Hill: U of North Carolina P, 2010.

Six Hundred Dollars a Year: A Wife's Efforts at Low Living Under High Prices. Boston: Tichnor and Fields, 1867.

Tullar, Myra. "Southerners and Coffee: A Cooking School Teacher from the South." *Daily Whig and Courier* [Bangor, Maine] 17 July 1899: 3.

White, Deborah Gray. *Too Heavy a Load: Black Women in Defense of Themselves, 1894–1994.* New York: W. W. Norton, 1999.

Williams-Forson, Psyche. *Building Houses Out of Chicken Legs: Black Women, Food, and Power.* Chapel Hill: U of North Carolina P, 2006.

Chapter Six

THE DOUBLE BIND OF SOUTHERN FOOD IN WILLA CATHER'S *SAPPHIRA AND THE SLAVE GIRL*

ANN ROMINES

I n Willa Cather's last novel, *Sapphira and the Slave Girl* (1940), food and food service are a major subject and subtext throughout. The book literally begins at the breakfast table where "Henry Colbert, the miller, always breakfasted with his wife," and it ends in the kitchen (7). It is set in 1856, on a small northern Virginia plantation where the major source of income is a mill, much like the plantation of Cather's maternal great-grandparents, Jacob and Ruhamah Seibert, who are prototypes for Sapphira and Henry Colbert, the slaveholding owners of the place. As Henry and his wife sit at breakfast, discussing the central matter of this book—the disposal of the "slave girl," Nancy—we also learn about the dining chairs, how the meal is served by an elderly male slave at the command of Sapphira's bell and her silent, peremptory gestures, about the menu of bacon and coffee, and about the table service of "good china" and silver. With rigorous and unsentimental details, such as those of the breakfast service, Cather confronts, more directly than she ever had before, the Virginia slaveholding culture in which her family was long implicated, and she shows us how slavery (and class) were intricately negotiated, often through food.

At the novel's end, in the epilogue set twenty-five years later, about 1881, we find ourselves still in the same region of Virginia, with the same family—Cather's own. For the first time in her career, Cather represents herself as a character—a five-year-old girl—and the point of view becomes explicitly hers. Southern food is very much on this narrator's mind; the last scene is set in the kitchen of her Virginia childhood, which is recalled with vivid and affectionate specificity.

... to me it [the kitchen] was the pleasantest room in the house,—the most interesting.... Besides the eight-hole range, there was a great fireplace with a crane....

We had three kitchen tables: one for kneading bread, another for making cakes and pastry, and a third with a zinc top, for dismembering fowls and rabbits and stuffing turkeys. The tall cupboards stored sugar and spices and groceries; our farm wagons brought supplies out from Winchester in large quantities. Behind the doors of a very special corner cupboard stood all the jars of brandied fruit, and glass jars of ginger and orange peel soaking in whisky. Canned vegetables, and the preserved fruits not put down in alcohol, were kept in a very cold cellar: a stream ran through it, actually! (279–80)

This passage is a literal portrait of the kitchen at Willow Shade, Cather's Virginia home for her first nine years. In nostalgic detail, she recalls a generous space that welcomes both whites and blacks. Her white grandmother, daughter of the slaveholder Sapphira, sits and visits with two African American women friends who are former slaves of Sapphira's. This roomy kitchen accommodates multiple workers, and with three worktables, it is equipped for sophisticated food preparation. It retains its original cooking fireplace as well as a large, "modern" cast-iron stove, and it provides storage space for ample and varied provisions, both homegrown, on the prosperous family sheep farm, and purchased in a nearby, well-provisioned small city. Cather, who was born during Reconstruction in 1873, lovingly recalls the camaraderie of that kitchen, where she enjoyed the delectable bounty of the Virginia countryside as it was preserved, prepared, and served forth by skilled cooks. The ambiance is very different from that of Sapphira's breakfast table of the book's first pages, with the well-ordered charade of silent slave food service as master and mistress quarrel over the sale of a slave. The epilogue celebrates the return of Nancy for a visit with her mother, "Aunt Till," twenty-five years after her Underground Railroad escape to Montreal, where she has become a successful professional housekeeper. For five-year-old Willa, this visit was a "thrilling" event and a lifelong memory.

When Cather began writing *Sapphira*, she had already published a substantial body of fiction set in Nebraska, New York, Pittsburgh, Quebec, and New Mexico. These were all places where she had lived or made long, repeated visits, but she had never written a novel set in Virginia, where she spent her first nine years and where her ancestors had lived since 1730.[1] Her companion, Edith Lewis, speculated that Cather had been reluctant "to break through to those old memories that seemed to belong to another life." When her elderly parents died, her father suddenly in 1927 and her mother after a long, agonizing illness in 1931, Cather mourned them deeply and, as their eldest daughter, found herself the oldest member of the oldest generation of her family—a strange new experience, she said, and one that may have put her in the position of family storyteller, as her grandmothers and parents had been. Lewis believed that the death of Cather's parents and of other elders who had Virginia ties, such as the beloved family servant, Marjorie Anderson, was the catalyst for her last novel: "the long train of associations and memories their death set in motion led her to write *Sapphira*" (181–82).

The novel, probably begun in 1936, her sixty-third year, was written during what Cather called the worst years of her life. The deaths of family members and close friends continued, her health declined and impeded her writing progress, and the acceleration of World War II in Europe distressed her deeply. Writing about nineteenth-century Virginia, where she had been a privileged firstborn child in a relatively prosperous household and where all the people who were dearest to her were either safely alive or as yet unborn, provided a much-needed respite. She wrote to a writer/editor friend, Viola Roseboro, that "writing the book. . . . eased the hurt of bitter sorrow, because when the present was painful, it was a help to me to turn back to those very early memories" (28 Dec. 1940). She also told Roseboro that "not very much of" *Sapphira* "is actually fiction. It is so largely made up of old family stories and neighborhood stories that I scarcely know where my own contribution to it begins" (9 Nov. 1940).

Cather acknowledged the pleasant surfaces of the Virginia life she remembered[2]—as we can see in her description of the Willow Shade kitchen—and created an atmosphere of plenitude and peace where a former abused slave girl has become an honored guest. But in the body of this novel, she also looks critically at the nineteenth-century history of her native state, especially as experienced by her maternal ancestors, almost all of whom were slaveowners. Here, her medium is largely domestic and often spelled out in the language of food. She confided to Roseboro, a fellow southerner and trusted critic, that "there is something else which eludes and eludes—I mean the Terrible, domesticated and a part of easy every day life. That's what I was thinking about" (9 Nov. 1940). This "Terrible" lies beneath Sapphira's disputes with her slave cook and her daughter Rachel's labors in a cramped basement kitchen in Washington, to prepare luxurious meals for her congressman husband and his all-male companions above. Even in the largely benign epilogue, young Willa does not question that although Nancy is received at Willow Shade as a long-awaited guest, she and her mother are not allowed to eat in the dining room with the white family. They are served "the same dinner as the family," yes, but at a later second table. For the five-year-old child, such race-based distinctions and exclusions are already taken for granted as a "domesticated ... part of easy every day life."

As she wrote her twelfth novel, Cather was already fluent in the language of food. For example, she had used it to sketch the struggles of midwestern immigrants to resist the strictures of Americanization and to retain some features of their native European cultures while making a home in a new world, as in the kolache and other Bohemian "fancy breads" in *O Pioneers!* and *My Antonia*, as well as the French onion soup that brings "a thousand years" of French culture and history to New Mexico in *Death Comes for the Archbishop* (41). Yet one of these priests in that book also acquires a taste for the local food as well, and he grows "to like *chili colorado* and mutton fat" (217). As in these examples, food provides important thematic threads in most of Cather's fiction.[3]

Cather's letters, interviews, and journalism also demonstrate her lifelong interest in food and cooking. Recalling her childhood homesickness for the South after the family's move to Nebraska, she told an interviewer that she decided that "I would not eat much until I got back to Virginia and could get some fresh mutton," such as she had eaten on the family sheep farm (Bohlke 10). Once she had adjusted to the Nebraska menu, she celebrated the cooks there as well. In a 1921 interview she said, "There is real art in cooking a roast just right. . . . The farmer's wife who 'cooks for her family' can experience the real creative joy . . . which marks the great artist" (Bohlke 47). The principal cook in Cather's family was her grandmother Rachel Seibert Boak, who supervised the family kitchen both in Virginia and in Nebraska, until her death in 1893, when Willa was in college. "Grandma Boak" is also a constant kitchen presence in *Sapphira*, for she was the literal model for an important character, Rachel Blake—Sapphira's daughter and Willa's grandmother.

Cather's interests in food continued to expand, including her pleasure in shopping in New York greenmarkets, in ordering provisions for her summer house on Grand Manan Island, New Brunswick, and in her thrilling introduction to the French food she encountered on her first trip to Europe. French cuisine became a lifelong pleasure, and she employed an excellent French cook for much of her adult life in New York City. However, the southern food of her early childhood, which her family had continued to enjoy in Nebraska, remained a constant in her life. When she returned for summer visits with her parents, she spent long hours in the kitchen, learning to make piecrust and preparing puddings and other sweets from "old Virginia recipes" (Lewis 12). In the 1930s, as she was writing *Sapphira*, a favorite brother, Douglass, joined Cather and her companion Edith Lewis in their Park Avenue apartment to celebrate Thanksgiving. Despite her own considerable prosperity in those years and all the available culinary resources of New York City, Cather chose to prepare the turkey herself. For only she knew how to prepare it as Grandma Boak had done—in Virginia style.

When Cather turned to her last novel—which was also her first fully southern novel—the vocabulary of southern food, specifically northern Virginia food, was at her disposal, as it had been all her life. She made subtle and wide-ranging use of that language, which spells out distinctions of class, servitude, nurturing, charity, care, and deprivation, to create the most politically confrontational—and controversial—fiction of her career. In this essay, I point to some of the ways in which she employed that vocabulary, ultimately creating a double bind of political confrontation and nostalgia that still surrounds the subject of southern food today.

◆ ◆ ◆

Sapphira Colbert, the novel's title character, has been an active and effective plantation mistress, typically overseeing gardening, cooking, preserving, and other domestic tasks. She dictates the work of the kitchen, although she seldom goes there and does not lower herself to the work of cooking (Fox-Genovese 109–12). Now, in 1856, Sapphira is disabled and increasingly immobilized by heart disease, and she is engaged in a power struggle with her excellent slave cook, Lizzie. Historian Eugene D. Genovese calls this frequent plantation combat "culinary despotism" (quoted in Harris 16) and, as we see, Sapphira and Lizzie contend to be culinary despots. When her oldest, African-born slave, Jezebel, dies, Sapphira plans to observe proprieties with relatively lavish funeral observances. She summons Lizzie to give her orders, and chastises her for the menu she produced for a previous slave funeral: "I won't have any skimping for the watchers, as there was when Manuel died.... you put disgrace on me and it was talked about all up and down the creek. Cold batter-cakes and ponhos for the watchers; whoever heard of such stinginess!" (101). Lizzie protests and promises food that will honor Jezebel properly: "Yes mam! I sho'ly will put my bes' foot for'ard fo' ole Aunt Jezebel an' all de yeahs she carry. But dat triflin' li'l Manuel wa'nt no 'count nohow, an' his pappy not much bettah—" (101–2). Although the two women are apparently in agreement on the menu for Jezebel's funeral, their motivations are very different. Sapphira is concerned with maintaining her own prestige in the eyes of her white neighbors, avoiding "disgrace" to her reputation as a liberal slave mistress. Lizzie's primary concern is the slaves who are being buried and her own evaluation of them. She saw Manuel as a "triflin'" boy from a "no 'count" family, while "Aunt Jezebel," with her honorific title in the slave community, is revered for her ninety years of tough, intrepid endurance.

Although Sapphira recognizes and values Lizzie's excellent cooking skills, she does not trust her to plan the funeral menu. Instead, she dictates: "Now remember, there will be two nights to cook for. You are to boil a ham and fry up plenty of middling meat. Mrs. Blake [Sapphira's daughter] will tell you how many loaves of light bread to bake, and there must be plenty of corn bread, and sugar-cakes and ginger-cakes. Master is going to invite all Mr. Lockheart's niggers to come over and sit up, and likely some of Jezebel's grandchildren will come out from Winchester" (101–2). Although the mourners for whom Lizzie will be cooking will be slaves, Sapphira's menu acknowledges the importance of this occasion by including foods normally reserved for whites of some affluence: ham, "light bread" made with wheat flour and yeast, and the white sugar that is an ingredient of sugar-cakes. Nevertheless, Sapphira makes it clear that this is not a menu for her white peers by including inexpensive foods that are part of a standard slave diet, "middling meat"[4] and cornbread. Although wheat could be grown in northern Virginia, cornbread was the standard bread of the South, and in this book, cornbread is only mentioned as a food eaten by slaves. The "batter-cakes" that Sapphira mentions as stingy fare for Manuel's funeral are one of the simplest forms of cornbread, baked on a griddle. And the "panhos" that Lizzie served to Manuel's watchers was also very much an economy food, made with scraps of pork not good enough for sausage.[5] This hierarchy of southern foodstuffs was clearly a vocabulary that Sapphira and her slaves and her neighbors understood well, and Cather wants to make sure that her readers will pick up on the nuances of this language as well. *Sapphira* includes only two authorial footnotes: one defines "panhos" and the other defines "light bread." Obviously Sapphira's menu, as executed by Lizzie, conveys the message that the mistress intended: both white and black mourners are pleased, and agree that "Miss Sapphy sho'ly give Jezebel a beautiful laying away" (104).

To insure these "beautiful" results, Sapphira plays her trump card in her ongoing contest with Lizzie: she threatens to sell the cook's adolescent daughter. "'Remember this; if you don't do me credit at Jezebel's wake, I will send Bluebell back to Loudoun County for good.' . . . Sending Bluebell over to Loudoun County meant selling her there, and Lizzie knew it" (102). Lizzie, like many cooks, kept her daughter near her—to "help" her in the kitchen—and protected her from arduous work and made sure she was well fed, as they both are. Lizzie is routinely called "fat Lizzie," and when she is summoned from the kitchen, she always seems to be swallowing a "last mouthful" of something. Both Lizzie and her daughter wear "very full" skirts with numerous pockets, for secreting choice foods not intended for slave consumption. However much she may threaten Bluebell's sale, Sapphira will never sell Lizzie's daughter, even though she and her husband agree that Bluebell is, as he says, "the laziest, trashiest wench on the place" (64). Sapphira admits that "if it wasn't for Lizzie's feelings," she would sell her "tomorrow. I'd give her away! But we've got the only good cook west of Winchester, and so we have to have Bluebell. Lizzie would always be in the sulks, and when a cook is out of temper she can spoil every dish" (54). Sapphira and Lizzie hold each other in thrall, and their precarious relations are typical. According to Fox-Genovese, "notoriously, cooks challenged their mistresses' greatest diplomacy in supervision," and highly skilled plantation cooks, like Lizzie, "occupied positions of considerable prestige—and knew it" (159–61).[6]

The novel's other major occasion for "company" entertaining at Sapphira's Mill House table is a special dinner served to welcome an arriving guest, Henry's nephew, Martin Colbert. Sapphira has invited him with the intention that he will "ruin" the slave girl Nancy by raping her. Although there are only three persons at table, this is an important occasion with animated conversation and bottles of the "best" Madeira. We see the scene from the viewpoint of a slave child:

> [T]welve-year-old Katie, barefoot, in a stiffly starched red calico dress, walked round and round the table waving a long flybrush made of a peacock's tail. Even in town houses the flybrush was part of the table service....
>
> Katie, excited as she was by the talk, had even keener joys in anticipation. Her eyes gloated over the good things Mr. Washington [the elderly table servant] carried in to the table. She knew she would get a taste of them, though Bluebell always had the best of what went back to the kitchen. Lizzie had promised to make ice cream enough for everybody. Tap had brought squares and chunks of ice in a wheelbarrow up from the icehouse.... Since six o'clock old Jeff had been seated behind the laundry cabin, turning the big freezer. In winter, whenever there was a snowfall, Lizzie made "snow-cream" for the Mistress, beating the fresh, clean snow into a bowl of thick cream, well flavoured with sugar and brandy. But she made ice cream only on special occasions. (158–59, 163–64)

This passage underlines Lizzie's control of the kitchen. She determines who eats what, and even a slave child like Katie, near the bottom of the plantation hierarchy, knows that she will taste every delicacy served at the table—although Lizzie's favored daughter will get the best. Ice cream is a special treat, expensive and labor-intensive, and Cather spells out the work involved. It is Lizzie who "promises" that the slaves, as well as privileged whites, will eat ice cream. Ice cream is a relatively new food in America in 1856. It was invented as a European "royal dessert," served only to aristocracy, and we see vestiges of that in the "snow cream" that Lizzie prepares only for her mistress, although we may suspect that Bluebell gets a taste. But by mid-nineteenth century new technology was available in the form of a home ice cream freezer invented by an American woman in 1846, and ice cream was becoming "something of a social institution in America." The 1853 cookbook[7] that the Cather household used at Willow Shade includes recipes for both ice cream and snow cream. Lizzie's decision to make ice cream for both white owners and their slaves underlines her power in her kitchen realm, and it illustrates the ongoing "democratization of ice cream," extending even to slaves (Weaver lxiii; Quinzio 314–15).

Through her cooking skills, Lizzie has created a power base where she makes and executes key decisions. She decides, for example, which slaves will eat at the kitchen table and who (like Tansy Dave) is too dirty and must eat outside. Her mistress must attend to "Lizzie's feelings," to insure that she will produce fine food. And, perhaps most important, Lizzie is able to pamper her beloved daughter, despite the fact that Bluebell is "worthless" to Sapphira, and to protect her from the worst abuses of slavery. As David Wyatt points out, one of the horrors of slavery, for slave women, was that it denied them "the freedom to love their children" (281). Lizzie, who is inseparable from her daughter, has been able to preserve that freedom. By contrast, Sapphira's slave housekeeper Till, her mistress's most trusted slave, cannot protect her adolescent daughter Nancy against Sapphira's malicious abuse. When Till tries to advise Nancy on how to regain the mistress's favor, she recommends food service: "Now honey, if I was you, I'd make a nice egg-nog.... I'd take it to her on the small silvah salvah, with a white napkin and some cold biscuit.... I'd smile, an' look happy to serve her, an' she'll smile back." This strategy doesn't work, of course. Sapphira's animosity is too intense, and, as Nancy knows, the kitchen is controlled by Lizzie, who dislikes her: "Lizzie, she don't like to have me meddlin' round the kitchen to do anything" (46). Later in the book, when Sapphira dies, her husband, Henry, immediately frees all her slaves, and he goes to great trouble to find them paying jobs, including "a good place" in the kitchen of the best Winchester hotel for Lizzie and Bluebell. But they prefer to remain at the Mill House, "hangin' round the kitchen. In the end he [Henry] had to drive 'em into town himself an' put 'em down at the hotel" (281). As a slave cook, Lizzie had created a kitchen realm where she wielded considerable power, power that she was reluctant to give up for the uncertainties of life as free persons of color for herself and Bluebell.

In addition to her power struggle with Lizzie, Sapphira engages in another food-related power contest with her oldest slave, Jezebel, now a bedridden invalid near death. When she pays a watchful and (supposedly) benevolent bedside visit to the old woman, Sapphira reads a psalm from her prayer book and directs Jezebel to "be resigned." Jezebel appears to acquiesce, an obedient slave: "'Yes'm, I'se resigned,' the old woman whispered" (89). But when her mistress goes on to give orders to Jezebel about her eating, the slave is no longer acquiescent. She has been refusing to eat, thus hastening her death and exercising one of the few opportunities for self-determination available to her. Sapphira orders, "You *must eat* to keep up your strength." At Jezebel's refusal, she persists: "Can't you think of anything that would taste good to you? . . . *tell me* [emphases mine]." Jezebel resists: "The old woman gave a sly chuckle; one paper eyelid winked, and her eyes gave out a flash of grim humour. 'No'm, I cain't think of nothin' I could relish, lessen maybe it was a li'l pickaninny's hand" (91). Jezebel spent her first eighteen years in a cannibal tribe in Africa,[8] near the Gold Coast, where the flesh of children was indeed sometimes eaten to celebrate the harvest. Although Sapphira claims that she "knows" her aged slave "through and through," Jezebel's comment indicates that she has appetites, and food preferences, that her mistress *cannot* know, embedded in her African memories. The "sly" "grim humour" of this reply is anything but acquiescent, and it shocks her timid, American-born great-granddaughter Nancy, who is standing by. As a dying slave, old Jezebel asserts her African otherness and self-possession by suggesting an appetite for violating one of the most powerful American food taboos, against eating human flesh.

The slave girl Nancy lacks her great-grandmother's sly assertiveness. She is suffering from the jealous abuse of her mistress Sapphira, who suspects (wrongly) that the girl is sleeping with Henry and that her husband and Nancy have an affectionate personal relationship. Exhausted by the relentless sexual pursuit of the visiting Martin Colbert, which Sapphira encourages, Nancy contemplates suicide, and her desperation is so apparent that her one confidant, Sapphira's daughter Rachel, eventually decides to facilitate the girl's escape by Underground Railroad. Nevertheless, the Mill Farm is the only home Nancy has ever known, and she feels an intense and romantic love for the place and the blooming Virginia countryside, not unlike young Willa Cather's love for her Virginia home. To Nancy, there is no "lovelier spot in the world than this right here. . . . She loved everybody in those vine-covered [slave] cabins, everybody. This morning she would be glad to see even fat Lizzie and Bluebell" (195–96). The pleasure of picking and eating homegrown food is a part of that "lovely" southern world, and it is intertwined with her pleasure in her own developing, still virginal, sexuality. After a terrified, sleepless night on a pallet outside her mistress's bedroom door, where Sapphira has ordered her to sleep so that she will be far from Sapphira's husband and easily available for Martin's advances, Nancy is nevertheless "lighthearted" in the fresh morning, as she "run[s] away to the old cherry trees behind the smokehouse," which is tended by her Pappy Jeff. In this safe, lovely spot, which is defined by familiar and delicious foods, Nancy goes cherry-picking, seeking a momentary escape from enslavement. "She loved to pick cherries, and she loved being up in a tree. Someway no troubles followed a body up there; nothing but the foolish, dreamy, nigger side of her nature climbed the tree with her. She knew she had left half her work undone, but here nobody would find her out to scold her" (176–77). Unlike Bluebell, Nancy is normally a conscientious and careful worker. She has been well schooled in a work ethic by her mother and Sapphira, and she thinks of her truant cherry-picking self in disparaging terms: "foolish," "nigger." Yet that self is also deliciously "dreamy"; in the tree, she can let her exploratory imagination wander with a freedom a "slave girl" usually doesn't have, and enjoy the sensual pleasure of eating cherries for herself: "She ate the ripest ones." The cherries themselves seem closely associated with nubile Nancy, with their traditional associations with sexuality and virginity, and the association is more specific because these cherries are "*black*hearts" (emphasis mine) and "sweet," not sour. While Nancy is in the cherry tree, Martin pursues her there and says persuasively, "Come now, you're going to give me something, Nancy." The dreamy, exploratory Nancy of the cherry tree "somehow didn't feel scared of him as he stood down there. . . . He didn't look wicked. Maybe he only meant to tease her." Cautiously, she begins to flirt with Martin; "she laughed a soft darky laugh and dropped a bunch of cherries down to him" (177–78). Her pleasure turns to terror as he begins to assault her, and she screams for help to Pappy Jeff, nearby in the fragrant smokehouse. In this scene, food—the large, sweet, heart-shaped blackheart cherries—triggers Nancy's exploration of her sexuality and the possibilities of freedom, as in picking cherries—and possibly lovers?—for herself. But when Martin seizes her, we see again the "Terrible" that can wait for a vulnerable girl under the sweet-tasting surfaces of home. The cherry-picking scene raises troubling questions. In a "home place" that offers rich natural nourishment, like the cherries, how can a slave girl negotiate her appetites for sex and for food, her self-esteem, and her freedom?

◆ ◆ ◆

On Henry and Sapphira Colbert's plantation/farm, the business is food. Henry is a miller and, as he says, "The first miller who has ever made a living in these parts" (10). Several of Willa Cather's ancestors were Virginia millers in the nineteenth century, including Jacob Seibert, prototype for Henry, whose family ran the mill on Back Creek, where this novel takes place, for about forty years, from the mid-1830s to 1873. The upper Shenandoah Valley of Virginia, where Cather's family lived, was largely a region of small farmers, with a few larger plantations and farms, like the Colberts'. In this northerly region, wheat was "an ideal crop for the small farmer . . . profitable on any scale" (Hofstra 126). Grain was a product with high value that was easy to transport, and its value was increased by the skill of a "competent miller" (Gordon and Malone 75), like Henry. A typical mill served a community with a radius of five to eight miles, in Henry's case, the village of Back Creek Valley and the surrounding farms (Kerns 15). Like other country mills, this mill ground corn, wheat, buckwheat, and other grains to order between millstones, and it was powered by a water wheel with a dam built across a substantial stream, Back Creek. By mid-nineteenth century, this area was specializing in grain crops, and Frederick County was Virginia's largest producer of wheat and flour (Hofstra, *Separate Place* 25, 30). During the Civil War, the much-contested Shenandoah Valley was commonly called "the breadbasket of the Confederacy." Thus, for both poor and prosperous local farmers, Henry Colbert's mill was at the center of the local economy—and food chain. The mill has increasingly become the center of Henry's life. He sleeps there, and not with his wife, most nights, and when called to the house, he is often covered with a thick coating of flour-dust.

With the help of his male slave workers, Henry runs a model mill, and his only problem is getting his poorer farmer-customers to pay their bills. Unlike his wife, who comes from a wealthy slaveowning family and believes in the plantation model, based on slave labor, Henry, whose father was also a miller, comes from a family of Flemish immigrants that has never owned slaves, and he has deep doubts about the morality of slavery. While Sapphira and her slave cook are always combatants, at some level, Henry and Sampson, his chief slave assistant at the mill, are cooperating collaborators. The mill seems an almost utopian place, where technology (the mill wheel) works with nature (Back Creek) to grind grain into a usable, profitable foodstuff, and where white owner and slaves work together equitably. Henry, for example, spends most of his time in the shared workspace of the mill, while Sapphira—although she gives orders to Lizzie—is never seen in the kitchen.

In fact, Henry thinks so highly of Sampson that he formulates a plan to buy him from Sapphira and manumit him, finding him a good job in a free state, at "the Quaker mills in Philadelphia." But Sampson, who is highly capable, intelligent, and self-possessed, breaks down when Henry proposes this plan to him. "This was his home. Here he knew everybody. He didn't want to go out among strangers." He could never keep his wife and children "in a city as well off as they were here. . . . Anyhow, he'd a'most sooner leave the chillun than leave the mill, when they'd got everything fixed up so nice and could bolt finer white flour than you could buy in town" (111). Sampson's view of the mill is clearly utopian, and he takes pride in its finest product, "fine white flour." "In the small hours of the night," Sampson actually bakes the bread for his family (196). Presumably this is time-consuming light bread, not the usual slave food, quickly baked cornbread, and Sampson's access to wheat flour is a privilege of his position at the mill. When Sampson is freed with the other Colbert slaves, after Sapphira's death in 1857, Henry does find him a "wonderful good place" in a Pennsylvania roller mill, where he and his children prosper. But on a postwar return visit to Till, he craves her light bread, made with the local milled flour, a taste for which he is deeply nostalgic. Till says, "He told me how in the big mill where he works the grindin' is all done by steam, and the machines runs so fast an' gits so hot, an' burns all the taste out-a the flour. 'They is no real bread but what's made out-a water-ground flour,' he says to me" (282). Food historians confirm that roller mills, like the one where Sampson works, aimed to create "a bright white flour that had a long shelf life," and so they added technology that removed the bran and wheat germ, which could quickly become rancid, but helped give bread made from water-ground flour its complex taste and "dense, chewy crust. . . . commercial bread became softer, sweeter, moister, and whiter" (Smith 64). Thus, the taste of the antebellum Shenandoah Valley bread that Sampson fondly remembered was lost.

There is a hierarchy of bread in this novel, and its terms are well known to all. "Light bread" is at the top, and unleavened cornbread at the bottom. This vocabulary clearly establishes distinctions of race and class. Rachel Blake, Henry and Sapphira's widowed, thirty-seven-year-old daughter, who works as a local, often unpaid, nurse, understands this hierarchy especially well. When she calls on Mandy Ringer, a poor white friend with an injured foot who lives on a poor farm at the edge of the Appalachians, she carries in her basket not only simple remedies, but also foods that she knows will be unaccustomed treats for the Ringers: "a fruit jar full of fresh-ground coffee, half a baking of sugar cakes, and a loaf of 'light' bread. The poor folks on the Ridge esteemed coffee and wheat bread great delicacies" (119). Mrs. Ringer is modeled on Willa Cather's favorite childhood nurse and storyteller, Mary Ann Anderson, and she is a spirited, enduring character whose good qualities are illustrated by her respect for food and food service. When Rachel arrives and unpacks her basket of special foods, Mrs. Ringer brings out her best "blue [Staffordshire] chiney" and a fresh white cloth to honor the food and the company. The family's major resource is one cow, which Mrs. Ringer cares for herself, and milk is carefully preserved in a spring-cooled cellar, even though the spring is far from the house and the disabled Ringer son must walk there to provide proper cream for the women's coffee. "Born interested," Mrs. Ringer finds both interest and pleasure in providing the basic diet of her family, which largely comes from her vegetable garden and her cow. "When she woke in the morning, she got into her calico dress in a flash and ran out to see what her garden had done overnight. Then she took a bucket and went to milk Sukey in the shed" (120).

Despite Mrs. Ringer's low place in the local food chain and class hierarchy, Rachel respects her and finds her "better company than many people who . . . came of better blood, and had farms and raised sheep and pigs for market" (120). Rachel understands and negotiates the local language of food on every level. For Jezebel's funeral, for example, it is she who conveys her aristocratic mother's food orders to Lizzie and the other slave kitchen workers. Although she grew up in the slaveholding Colbert household, Rachel herself quietly opposes slavery and has never owned slaves. When she returned to Back Creek Valley after the death of her congressman husband left her without financial resources, Rachel became what her mother has never been, her own housekeeper and hands-on cook. The foods she takes to Mrs. Ringer, and everything she feeds her children, are prepared by her. As Nghana Tamu Lewis argues, Rachel is in many ways the moral center of this book,[9] and some of her moral authority comes from her cooking and the way that she is willing to use her skills to express charity, caring, and concern for others. She also knows how to prioritize. One morning Nancy arrives in Rachel's kitchen, hoping that her confidant will accompany her on a laurel-picking expedition ordered by Sapphira, to help her fend off the advances of the predatory Martin, who is in pursuit. Rachel is just ready to put her day's baking of light bread in the oven, and delay might spoil the risen bread. She tells Nancy, "The baking can wait. I'll just check the damper and go along with you" (167). Clearly she recognizes that the vulnerable slave girl's protection is more important than risking a few loaves of bread.

Near the novel's end, Rachel's two little girls contract diphtheria in a local epidemic. Rachel cares for them according to the instructions of the ignorant country doctor, who orders that the children must have no food or drink. But the local minister, David Fairhead, is helping Rachel to nurse, and she cooks for him, preparing a nourishing chicken broth and leaving it on the kitchen table. When Fairhead steps outside for a breath of air, he looks in the window and sees one of the sick girls, Mary, come down the stairs "barefoot, in her nightgown, as if she were walking in her sleep. She reached the table, sank down on a wooden chair, and lifted the bowl of broth in her two hands. . . . She drank slowly. . . . Fairhead knew he ought to go in and take the soup from her. But he was unable to move. There was something solemn in what he saw . . . like a Communion service" (255). A little later, Fairhead finds Mary upstairs in her bed, sleeping peacefully. The next day, Sapphira's excellent doctor arrives to treat the girls, and Fairhead confesses to him the silent scene he saw in the kitchen. The doctor confirms that the soup has saved Mary's life. "The child was hungry. Your warm broth satisfied that craving" (259–60). Mary will recover, while her sister Betty, who had no soup, will die. This scene is based on a Cather family legend, in which one of Grandma Rachel Boak's daughters did indeed survive a life-threatening illness after eating a forbidden bowl of soup. In the story as Cather tells it, the surviving child, Mary, is based on Willa's mother, Mary Virginia Boak Cather. In a sense, Cather owes her own existence to that bowl of soup, prepared by her grandmother and consumed by her mother. Here, a simple food takes on almost holy significance, "like a Communion service."

After Rachel's loving marriage at sixteen to a handsome, pleasure-loving congressman, Michael Blake, she lived in Washington for thirteen years, and there she encountered an alternative to the food hierarchy of her mother's plantation household. The Blakes had no slaves, so Rachel did their cooking herself, in their "narrow rented house," and her husband did the marketing at a "big market" near Capitol Hill. Perhaps drawing on her own pleasure in shopping at New York greenmarkets,[10] Cather describes the bounty of nineteenth-century Washington markets:

> In those days the Washington markets were second to none in the world for fish and game: wild ducks, partridges, pheasants, wild turkeys . . . the woods were full of wildfowl. The uncontaminated bays and rivers swarmed with fish: Potomac shad, Baltimore oysters, shrimps, scallops, lobsters, and terrapin. In the spring the Dutch truck gardeners brought in the first salads and asparagus and strawberries. (139–40)

This is the most extended, luxurious and sensuous description of food in the body of this novel, and it is worth noting that its subject is not Sapphira's slave-served plantation table but an urban market, accessible to all.

Rachel delights in pleasing her husband by preparing delicious meals based on his market purchases. "Rachel became expert in cookery. . . . she put herself under the instruction" of an expert cook, Sarah, a former slave from New Orleans, who "now made her living by cooking for dinner parties" (139). With Sarah's assistance in cooking and serving, Rachel prepares elaborate meals for her husband and his male friends. She works in the cramped basement kitchen, while the men feast in the dining room above, and they invite her up to join them for dessert, after the work of cooking and serving is done. By making herself the pupil of a former slave, she has become an accomplished and sophisticated cook and has defied the plantation traditions of her childhood home. But in her desire to please her beloved husband and to satisfy his appetites, she comes close to enslaving herself; there was always "something of the devotee in Rachel" (141). Michael and their son die of yellow fever on a visit to New Orleans, and Rachel discovers that he has let his insurance policy lapse, and there is no money left for her and the two surviving daughters. She collapses, locks herself in her room, and Sarah, her only woman friend and ally in Washington, cares for the children. After Henry Colbert rescues his daughter and granddaughters and returns them to Back Creek, Rachel tries to forget the alternative world of Washington. When asked about her life there, she replies, "I hardly remember. All that is gone. I'd take it kindly of you not to bring it back to me" (146). Back in her birthplace, she is a somewhat austere and solitary figure despite her moral authority. The foods she prepares in her kitchen are not the opulent dishes she cooked in Washington, but simple staples such as light bread, chicken broth, and roasted coffee, which nevertheless require careful preparation. The 1856 kitchen at Sapphira's Mill House was detached, about thirty feet from the house. This was common plantation practice because detached kitchens reduced risks of fire and separated slaveowners from "the heat, noise, odors, and general commotion associated with the preparation of meals." They also enforced racial segregation: "the detached kitchen was an important emblem of hardening social boundaries" (Vlach 43). However, the kitchen where the novel's epilogue is set, at Willow Shade, is not detached, but an integral part of the dwelling house. Willa's paternal grandfather, William Cather, built this house, which still stands, in 1851, and the kitchen architecture is a political statement of his antislavery principles.[11] In the idyllic postbellum southern kitchen of the epilogue, white and black workers gather around the fireplace in evenings, cracking nuts and telling stories, and former slaves Till and Nancy sit side by side with the daughter and great-granddaughter of their former owner, doing needlework and telling stories.

Willa's aging grandmother, Rachel Blake/Boak, presides over this capacious, welcoming kitchen, and it is perhaps the most gratifying space she has ever inhabited. Here she is no longer solitary or taciturn, but a voluble storyteller. Now able to express her emotions more fully, she welcomes the returning Nancy with open affection: "Tears were shining in the deep creases on either side of Mrs. Blake's nose. 'Well, Nancy, child, you've made us right proud of you,' she said" (276). A few years earlier, in 1931, Willa Cather had built one of her best stories, "Old Mrs. Harris," around another portrait of her Grandmother Boak, as title character. In that story, Grandma Harris has been transported out of the South, with her family, to a cramped house with a too-small kitchen in a little western town, a house closely resembling Willa Cather's childhood home in Nebraska. Back in their spacious southern home, she had presided over the kitchen according to local custom: "every young married woman [like her daughter, modeled on Willa's mother] had an older woman in the house . . . who managed the household economies and directed the help. . . . [These] old women spent most of their lives in the kitchen. . . . but there they ordered life to their own taste, entertained friends, dispensed charity" (644–45). Mrs. Harris deeply misses that southern kitchen, and when Cather created an expanded portrait of her Grandmother Boak in *Sapphira*, she finally portrayed her at her best, in a post-Emancipation southern family kitchen.

While Nancy is visiting her mother, she and Till come to the Willow Shade kitchen often. Whether they come as visitors or workers is not entirely clear. Nancy brings with her "a fresh apron, and insisted on helping Mrs. Blake and Moses's Sally [a servant and probably a former family slave] with whatever housework was under way" (279). The apron, of course, is the emblem of the domestic worker and indicates that Nancy may still see herself as a servant, although not a slave, in this family's dwelling. But "Till and Nancy usually came for [noon] dinner, and after the dishes were washed they sat down with Mrs. Blake in the wooden rocking-chairs" and "took out their sewing or knitting." It would have been customary for guests to share dinner but not necessarily the dishwashing after, and women visitors often brought their own needlework to do as they chatted with friends. "While the pound cake or the marble cake [traditional southern recipes] was baking in a slow oven, they talked about old times," and Willa "was allowed to sit with them and sew patchwork" (280). In this kitchen, both cooking and storytelling are under way, and Till and Nancy take part in both. Till, who was trained as a slave girl by an excellent British housekeeper, is eager to demonstrate her cooking skill: "I'll just turn the bread fur you, Mrs. Blake. I seem to smell it's about ready" (281). And Nancy, now an equally accomplished professional housekeeper, is eager to roast and brew coffee: "I'll grind a little and make us all a cup, by your leave" (179). Now she is making coffee for all the women to enjoy, not preparing special treats for the mistress only. But she does ask Rachel's permission: "by your leave." Is this simply a courteous guest speaking or a servant?

The Willow Shade kitchen, presided over by Rachel, is clearly a more hospitable and inclusive environment than Sapphira's plantation ever offered. But it is also an ambivalent space where, through their cooking and visiting, these white and black women are still negotiating their troubled plantation history. This ambivalence is expressed by the two former slaves who return to Back Creek for postbellum visits. When Sampson visits Till, he asks for foods he ate as a slave: "greens an' a little fat pork, an' plenty of light bread," made from the water-ground flour from the mill where he once worked. He hungers for the flavors of the preindustrial southern past, even though he was a slave in that past. And Nancy, now living in tea-drinking Montreal, "begged to be allowed to roast the coffee. 'The smell of it is sweeter than roses to me, Mrs. Blake,' she said laughing. 'Up there the coffee is always poor'" (279). Despite the satisfactions of her free Canadian life, to which she will soon gladly return, she longs for the "sweet" smell of coffee roasting in the kitchen oven. Nancy's and Sampson's ambivalence echoes some of Willa Cather's own mixed feelings about her southern heritage, which emerge in this novel.

Sapphira demonstrates how southern food is deeply implicated in histories of race and class abuse and, at the same time, retains a delicious appeal that is alluring to both blacks and whites. The southern kitchen of the novel's epilogue, where young Willa is nourished both by southern cooking and by the stories that the cooks tell—stories which became the stuff of this novel[12]— is still a deeply compelling place. In *Sapphira and the Slave Girl*, Willa Cather powerfully conveys the double bind of southern food's appeal, which remains with us today.

Notes

1. For a fuller account of the Virginia history of Cather's family, see Romines, "Historical Essay," 299–316.

2. In a letter to her former editor, Ferris Greenslett, Cather emphasized that she had intended to give a balaced view of the "strange" domestic institution of slavery, rendering both its pleasant surfaces and what lay beneath them—although her own family had not given much thought to what lay underneath (WC to FG, 13 Dec. 1940).

3. Two recent sources explore the language of food in Cather's fiction and life: *At Willa Cather's Tables: The Willa Cather Cookbook* and a special issue of *The Willa Cather Newsletter and Review* (fall 2010), "Food and Drink and the Art of Willa Cather."

4. Middling meat, or "fatback," was pork side meat, preserved by salting or smoking, and not considered so choice as ham or tenderloin. "Such meat made up the bulk of the slaves' meat ration on most plantations" (Hilliard 46–47).

5. "Panhos" (a Pennsylvania German word) is still a common term—and foodstuff—in the Shenandoah Valley, where German settlers, including some of Willa Cather's ancestors, were numerous. It refers to scrapple, a mush made of pork scraps and cornmeal and/or buckwheat, which is formed into loaves, sliced, and fried (Weaver 342–43).

6. As Elizabeth Fox-Genovese notes, slave cooks were in "a privileged position for poisoning" or contaminating their owners' food, a fact "which did much to exacerbate the disquiet of the slaveholding class" (159–61).

7. The most-used cookbook in the Cather family collection (now at the Willa Cather Foundation Archives in Red Cloud, NE) was an 1853 edition of Elizabeth Ellicott Lea's *Domestic Cookery,* published in Baltimore in 1851. Lea, a Quaker (as were several Cather relatives), lived on a Maryland farm, and her recipes featured the simple, economical cookery of the rural upper South (Weaver).

8. See Romines, "Old Jezebel's Story," on Jezebel's African history.

9. Lewis writes, "*Sapphira*'s narrative logic . . . converges on Rachel's thoughts and actions—the source of racial liberation" (145).

10. Elizabeth Sergeant describes Cather's pleasure in these markets: "It was fun to market with her, for she enjoyed turning countrywoman, and frowning over a housekeeper's list; selecting items of her prediction, like fresh plump chickens and mellow fruits, and ripe French Camembert" (126).

11. This house also contains an upstairs hiding place, concealed under a closet floor, that may have been used by slaves escaping via the Underground Railroad.

12. In several letters, Cather emphasizes that her major sources for *Sapphira* were her grandmother Rachel Boak and "Aunt Till" (Matilda Jefferson), and the stories she heard from them as a child in Virginia.

Works Cited

Bohlke, Brent, ed. *Willa Cather in Person: Interviews, Speeches, and Letters.* Lincoln: U of Nebraska P, 1986.

Cather, Willa. *Death Comes for the Archbishop.* Willa Cather Scholarly Edition. Historical Essay and Explanatory Notes by John J. Murphy. Textual Editing by Charles W. Mignon with Frederick M. Link and Kari A. Ronning. Lincoln: U of Nebraska P, 1999.

———. Letter to Ferris Greenslett. 13 Dec. 1940. MS. Houghton Library, Harvard University.

———. Letters to Viola Roseboro. 9 Nov. and 28 Dec., 1940. MS. Alderman Library, University of Virginia.

———. *Sapphira and the Slave Girl.* Willa Cather Scholarly Edition. Historical Essay and Explanatory Notes by Ann Romines. Textual Essay and Editing by Charles W. Mignon with Kari A. Ronning. Lincoln: U of Nebraska P, 2009.

Fox-Genovese, Elizabeth. *Within the Plantation Household: Black and White Women of the Old South.* Chapel Hill: U of North Carolina P, 1988.

Gordon, Robert B., and Patrick M. Malone. *The Texture of Industry: An Archaeological View of the Industrialization of North America.* New York: Oxford UP, 1994.

Harris, Jessica B. "African American Foodways." *Foodways.* Vol. 7 of *The New Encyclopedia of Southern Culture.* Ed. John T. Edge. Chapel Hill: U of North Carolina P, 2007. 15–18.

Hilliard, Sam Bowers. *Hog Meat and Hoecake: Food Supply in the Old South, 1840–1860.* Carbondale: Southern Illinois UP, 1972.

Hofstra, Warren R. *A Separate Place: The Formation of Clarke County, Virginia*. 1986. Madison, Wis.: Madison House, 1999.

———. "These Fine Prospects: Frederick County, Virginia, 1738–1840." Diss., U of Virginia, 1985.

Kerns, Wilmer L. *Historical Records of Old Frederick and Hampshire Counties, Virginia*. Bowie, Md.: Heritage Books, 1991.

Lewis, Edith. *Willa Cather Living: A Personal Record*. 1953. Lincoln: U of Nebraska P, 2000.

Lewis, Nghana Tamu. *Entitled to the Pedestal: Place, Race, and Progress in White Southern Women's Writing, 1920–1945*. Iowa City: U of Iowa P, 2007.

Quinzio, Jeri. "Ice Cream and Ices." *The Oxford Companion to American Food and Drink*. Ed. Andrew F. Smith. Oxford: Oxford UP, 2007. 314–15.

Romines, Ann, ed. *At Willa Cather's Tables: The Cather Foundation Cookbook*. Red Cloud, Neb: Willa Cather Foundation, 2010.

———, ed. *Food and Drink and the Art of Willa Cather*. Spec. issue of *The Willa Cather Newsletter and Review* 54:2 (2010): 29–92.

———. "Historical Essay." *Sapphira and the Slave Girl*. Willa Cather Scholarly Edition. 297–404.

———. "Losing and Finding 'Race': Old Jezebel's African Story." *Willa Cather: A Writer's Worlds*. Ed. John J. Murphy, Francoise Palleau-Pepin, and Robert Thacker. Lincoln: U of Nebraska P, 2010.

Sergeant, Elizabeth Shepley. *Willa Cather: A Memoir*. 1953. Athens: Ohio UP, 1992.

Smith, Andrew F. "Bread." *The Oxford Companion to American Food and Drink*. Ed. Andrew F. Smith. Oxford: Oxford UP, 2007. 63–66.

Vlach, John Michael. *Back of the Big House: The Architecture of Plantation Slavery*. Chapel Hill: U of North Carolina P, 1993.

Weaver, William Woys, ed. *A Quaker Woman's Cookbook: The Domestic Cookery of Elizabeth Ellicott Lea*. Philadelphia: U of Pennsylvania P, 1982.

Wyatt, David. *Secret Histories: Reading Twentieth-Century American Literature*. Baltimore: Johns Hopkins UP, 2010.

Chapter Seven

EATING POETRY IN NEW ORLEANS

RUTH SALVAGGIO

There is no happiness like mine.
I have been eating poetry.
—**Mark Strand**

A potato may not seem an especially poetic vegetable, but it claims special poetic status among the songs of the early Americas. We come upon this potato in an old Creole slave song that dates back to the time when Indians and Africans gathered in a place called Congo Square, just on the edge of the newly forming city of New Orleans. The song follows the sound of the *bamboula*—an African dance that takes its beat from a confluence of tango rhythms that pulsed throughout the historic Atlantic world. Its lyrics are composed of a single repeated phrase: *Quand patate le cuite na va mangé li!* Simply translated, the words say: *When the potato is cooked, you must eat it.* But the meanings of the words turn out to be not so simple. A perfectly cooked potato calls attention not only to the right moment to eat, but also to act. One historian cites the song to introduce her study of African slave uprisings in the 1790s in Louisiana, and another critic links its lyrics to similar encoded messages about slavery and freedom, offering this interpretation: "When freedom comes we shall devour it."[1] But the most revealing hint of the song's meaning comes from an African cook who moved with her owners from Saint Domingue to New Orleans at the turn of the nineteenth century. Her name was Sally, and she seems to have deeply affected the white Creole children under her care, among them the famous musician Louis Gottschalk who set this song about a potato to his equally famous pianoforte. He obviously got the song from Sally, who tended the coals while his grandmother told terrifying stories about the slave uprising in Saint Domingue that would culminate in the Haitian revolution. Sally, it seems, was always having encounters with ghosts and zombies in their New Orleans household, where she stirred the fires of the coals and "baked her sweet potatoes, to the recital of this terrible negro insurrection" (Sublette 253). Baked, sung, danced to, and eaten, the sweet potato becomes the first recorded transformation in New Orleans of food into poetry.

Potatoes, as we will see, become poetically transformed into all sorts of messages and stories and historic encounters in the city—from the humble fried potato po-boy sandwich to the puffed *pommes de terre soufflés* dipped in béarnaise sauce at Galatoire's Restaurant. A catalogue of potatoes in New Orleans might well be launched like a catalogue of ships in an epic poem, setting up the story of the city's history. Long before Africans gathered in Congo Square to dance and sing to the *bamboula*, the Houma Indians held their corn festivals in this area—or more precisely, their "pre-corn" festivals, since numerous varieties of corn and grain and root vegetables were harvested by the many Indian tribes in these surrounds (Kniffen 205). If Africans gave the potato its distinctive song and dance in Congo Square, the potato itself is a vegetable indigenous to the Americas. The specific sweet potato of Sally's song was a root vegetable that grew wild in the region and that was consumed by Indian tribes throughout the lower Mississippi valley—the Houma, Choctaw, Tangipahoa, Chitimacha, Opelousa, Caddo, and others—who traded their food there long before Europeans arrived. Indians and their entrenched knowledge of local food production are responsible for nothing less than saving the early French colony from starvation, and Africans, who arrived mainly from Senegambia by way of the French slave trade, brought with them their own sophisticated agricultural and marketing expertise (Johnson 5, 9–11).[2] A hardy group of Rhinelanders also arrived when the new colony was forming, and brought a variety of vegetables to the farms they established north of New Orleans, a region still known today as the German coast (Tucker and Roahen 142).[3] By the 1720s, all these unique people—the accomplished Indians, the expert Africans, the farming Rhinelanders, and the nearly starving French—found themselves tossed together in a place that was gifted with rich river soil, a climate ripe for growing vegetables, loads of fish and seafood, and markets where food always circulated with song.

Congo Square itself—long associated with African song and dance—actually began as a public market, where lyric festivities typically followed the commercial exchange of food items.[4] Food literally fed these musical gatherings that would commence when all the trade of the day was done. Among the many foods distinctive to and exchanged among Indians and Africans—grains, beans, fish and shellfish, vegetables and herbs such as okra and sassafras famously informing the base for all gumbos—only the potato emerges with a song all its own. But food hawkers, especially women, would call out their food items, such that cakes and vegetables were set to certain chants and rhythms before they were ever eaten. As a child growing up in New Orleans, I recall walking through the French Market where every vegetable was chanted for sale, most often delivered in polyrhythmic invocations and cataloging: "I got watermelon, I got some okra, I got the baby cucumber, I got sweet potato." Sweet potatoes grew wild in the gulf region long before they were domesticated into crops, and they grew on vines in songs, like the version of the folksong we learned where a monkey played his fiddle on the sweet potato vine. Archaeologists tell us that Indian dancers often imitated the movements of raccoons, rabbits, and turtles, and it seems likely that they also called forth vegetation at their harvest festivals—just as surely as certain fish dances called forth the fish to the dancer and just as young Indian women danced to the rhythm of winnowing corn into their baskets (Kniffen 282). It could be that an African song about a potato has some antecedent in an Indian song, now lost to us, centered on such a prodigious root vegetable—a single one said to have grown as large as twenty pounds (Kniffen 191). Imagine the vine that must have sustained its songs.

The connections between potatoes and songs, vegetables and lyrics, and the lyrical impulse of poetry which has its own roots in song and dance, thus become perfectly situated in Congo Square—the heartbeat of lyric impulse in early North America. And Congo Square, where the potato gets perfectly cooked, becomes the perfect place to indulge what Mark Strand describes when he writes: "There is no happiness like mine. / I have been eating poetry." Poetry, of course, is made of language, not food—or not quite of food. Yet anyone who indulges the fragrant spice beds and orchards of *Song of Songs*, one of the most beautiful and sensual poems ever sung, or who reads Milton's lush description of the seductive garden in *Paradise Lost*, or who sips the sweet honey and nectar of Sappho's lyrics or tastes the bitter history of Rita Dove's "Parsley" knows that the poetics of language is steeped in the sensual world of food. Given the cultivation of poetry and fruit and vegetables in fertile river valley cultures across the globe, it is hardly surprising that poetic language indulges in food for its most sensuous and nourishing metaphors. Food presents itself to the poet's hand and mouth and to the dancer's body. When Bienville first encountered the Houma Indians, they greeted him in a ceremonial fashion by rubbing their bellies together, and later, he observed their dancing, where drums and *chychycoucy*, gourds with seeds in them, marked the beat of the music (Sublette 37). Among the many foods documented in the market of Congo Square—from steaming coffee and cakes and pralines to a Creole beer made of ginger root, fermented apples, and mellow pine—we come upon the sweet potato which also makes its way into a song. And we come upon a variety of *calas*, the rice cakes that originated in Africa (*kala*), that also appeared as sweet potato cakes in poetic markets in and around the city. A scholar of African Creole musical traditions once described a special version of *calas* served at Creole dances as *Pains patatte*, a sliced sweet potato pudding (Evans 110, 113).[5]

Eating poetry in New Orleans always hinges on this primal connection of food and song, a lyricism inherent in wild sweet potatoes or *chychycoucy* or *calas*. And this lyricism, in turn, relies on the substance of food to form its poetic expressions. *Poiesis*, from the Greek term meaning *to make*, to shape and give form, describes a process that we typically associate with the mixing and shaping of words and things in poetry, an alchemy all its own (Stewart 12). But *poiesis* can also apply to the alchemical shaping of food, or any other distinctive formative practice—just as an architect writes of a poetics of space, or a poet describes a poetics of spatial relations.[6] A poetics of food would reveal not only how certain prepared meals are *formed* and *made* of select and wildly abundant ingredients, but also how some of these alchemical formations produce remarkable cuisines and how cuisines establish themselves and are also further transformed over time in the hands of people who converge across the globe even under tragic circumstances and who find themselves trading vegetables at an oddly festive market situated near the mouth of a great river. Eating poetry in New Orleans is to open one's mouth to the wild sweet potato of a song, to swallow its messages, to taste its transformations over cultures and geographies and time.

The transformations of the grassy grain of wheat alone testify to the city's vast culinary poetics. As anyone who has ever tried to make gumbo knows, *first you make a roux*. You *make* it, and you make it by combining flour and oil. A roux, like a poem, is a creative act of melding, a mixture of tasty, aromatic ingredients. Practically speaking, a roux is the slow mixture of flour and oil over a medium heat, so that the flour gradually turns a dark shade of brown—not too dark or it will burn but dark enough for its deep, tasty flavor. Poetically speaking, a roux gives form to grain and oil, shaping them into something like a thick chocolate paste. In both indigenous North America and in Africa, pounded grains and nuts and fruit and root vegetables were commonly mixed together and baked, fried, boiled, or steamed. The making of roux is at least as old as these distinctive early New Orleans cultures, as old as ritual mixtures of bread and wine, and as much of a miracle as proliferating loaves of bread that keep generating as if from generosity itself. Or how else to explain the miracle of Margaret Haughery, "The Breadwoman of New Orleans," a poor Irish immigrant who was orphaned at the age of nine yet whose success as a humble baker fed thousands of the city's homeless and needy and funded the building of several orphanages. The flour that makes the roux is the same miracle flour that makes the bread for orphans and the homeless, the same flour that makes French bread and that makes the muffaletta and the po-boy sandwiches, and the same flour used by Annie Laura Squalls who for twenty-five years was the head baker at the Ponchartrain Hotel. Working in the famous Caribbean Room of this hotel that did not allow black people among its clients, this distinguished black chef created an entire cuisine of her own signature breads, pastries, and desserts. She would constantly change and transform her recipes and ingredients, explaining how she made her bread pudding with "regular bread, not French," to which she added diced apples, fresh coconut, and crushed pineapple. "Vanilla sauce goes nicely with it," she concluded. Her ideas for *making* an icing progress quickly from the blending of cream and eggs to the poetics of yet another version of the potato: "If you are making an icing, a pinch of cream of tartar helps to harden it; it also helps to thicken egg white for a meringue. When I make sweet potato turnovers, I add whiskey to the filling" (Burton and Lombard 17–21).

The Caribbean Room of this once-segregated grand hotel—long-ago closed and now reopened in its latest reincarnation as luxury apartments for the elderly—emerges as the choice place for the transformation of "regular bread" into Squalls's fruit-infused bread pudding, for her transformation of flour into cherry cobbler, sweet rolls, and orange cake, and for her sheer and abundant transformation of a racially exclusive hotel into a culinary legacy punctuated by a touch of whiskey in a poetic potato turnover. While the bread of Margaret Haughery and the cakes of Annie Laura Squalls may not be able to eradicate famine in Ireland, hunger in New Orleans, or the unbearable burdens of slavery that extend from the early Caribbean islands to the Caribbean Room of the Ponchartrain Hotel, the culinary poetics of these two women alone gives rise to a miracle, a recompense for sorrow and suffering. As if issuing from both the sacred and the profane dimensions of history, miracle food appears in New Orleans as a kind of reconciliation with the past, perhaps also the means of reconciliation between and among people who might otherwise never enjoy, or even be allowed to enjoy, meaningful relations with each other. This poetic transformation of food has a long history in New Orleans and sustains well into our own age. Just stop by Café Reconcile for lunch in Central City, one of the most economically impoverished but artistically rich areas of the city, where young people are given a chance to learn to cook signature New Orleans cuisine and in the process get a chance for a decent life despite all the hardships they were dealt. Sit down there and enjoy a dish of shrimp Creole and bread pudding for a taste of culinary history. You will find yourself helplessly immersed in poetic reconciliation.

Reconciliation may not at first seem the best term to describe anything in a city whose history has always been laced with tragedy. From the slave trade to the plight of Irish immigrants worked to death building a canal, from fires and yellow fever epidemics on through Katrina, the city has been built and rebuilt on the backs of people who would have every reason to become life-long enemies of those who made their own lives miserable. Yet reconciliation describes exactly what people in this city manage to do, through thick and thin, and most often through the eating of shared food. After Katrina, food stands and food trucks dotted the flooded neighborhoods, offering not simply packaged sandwiches and plastic bottles of water, but also small tasty dishes of crawfish and pasta, red beans and rice, and yes, shrimp Creole and bread pudding. Food emerged as a miracle on a flooded wasteland. But then food has always been a kind of miracle in this city, approaching something like the ritual mixing and melding of ingredients that mark sacramental transforma-tion. A sacrament—like a poem, like so many ritual practices—involves the distinctive mixture of words and material things, *verba* and *res*.

One need not visit a St. Joseph's Day altar and its abundance of prepared foods to understand that food is holy in this city and gets served from altars. No wonder a flooded city welcomed food stalls as if they were altars of salva-tion, dispensing miracle food that might soon be followed with songs. Ever since large numbers of Sicilians arrived in New Orleans in the nineteenth century, St. Joseph's Day altars have flourished in the city, offering bread and fish, olives and olive salad, seeded cakes and coconut cakes and fig cakes, stuffed artichokes and green bean and artichoke casseroles, fried eggplant and meatless pastas, and bowls of dried fava beans to honor the saint who once saved Sicilians from famine. In a miracle that turns on a fava bean, St. Joseph apparently warded off famine by ensuring that these beans would grow. And they did grow, just like all the best foods and restaurants cropped up again after a great modern flood. St. Joseph must have been presiding at two special neighborhood restaurants after the flood—Il Tony's on the lake-front and Vincent's uptown—both Creole Italian restaurants and among the first to open their doors after Katrina to welcome those returning to the dark and devastated city. Eating poetry in New Orleans takes you back to familiar foods that survived the near destruction of the city—as if one is meeting back up again with an old friend. *Reconcile*—from the Latin *reconciliare*, meaning to come back and to meet.

The poetics of food in New Orleans always seems to involve a mixture or meeting that comes back to reconcile with the past, to meet back up with old dishes and lost neighbors. If this kind of mixture possesses sacramental status in the city, then it may have its source in what is known as the culinary Holy Trinity that presides in New Orleans—onion, celery, and green pepper sautéed in oil, with garlic and parsley serving as always respectable substitutes or additions. Forming a base, like roux, in which all other alchemical transformations unfold, this Holy Trinity pays perfect reverence to the spirits in a city where Catholics lapse into food for their most venerable adorations, and where food facilitates a meeting with the past. The ancestry of the stuffed artichoke—packed with seasoned breadcrumbs and drizzled with sacramental olive oil, a single slice of lemon delicately placed on its top—forms a miracle all its own, and takes us back across geographies, cultures, and time. The actual artichoke thrives in the heat and ashy soil of Sicily, but it was not Sicilians who brought the artichoke to New Orleans. Nor was it Sicilians who gave us the distinctive preparation of the stuffed artichoke. People claim that artichokes have grown in New Orleans for centuries, and at least one food writer claims that an artichoke plantation once existed in today's Warehouse District, appropriately the home now of several top-notch restaurants serving visitors who convene at the convention center along the river, and where thousands of Katrina evacuees took refuge for a week before anyone even noticed they were there without food or water. The early German farmers from the Rhinelands who helped save the French colony from starvation also grew artichokes, and it is likely that later French and Italians who came to the city also brought artichokes and artichoke recipes with them (Roahen 63–64).[7] But the making of the stuffed artichoke remains a mystery, and we must reconcile with the past to begin to understand this mystery. The artichoke is described in some cookbooks as a Creole, rather than an Italian or Sicilian, dish, and is said to be served as an appetizer or complement to a meal. Given the largess of the term Creole to describe both food and people in the city, it is likely that the artichoke was stuffed by the same amalgam of people in New Orleans who love to stuff all vegetables, especially artichokes, squash, eggplant, and the prized Creole tomato—not to mention muffaletta and po-boy sandwiches. At Brennan's Restaurant, you can order shrimp Sardou, fried shrimp served on the bed of an artichoke heart. According to Catholic Church doctrine, there must be proof that a person has performed three miracles in order to be granted the status of saint. The artichoke has undergone far more poetic metamorphoses than the mere three requisite for sainthood, and rightly assumes its anointed place on St. Joseph's Day altars as St. Artichoke, stuffed with sacramental bread(crumbs) and oil.

Eating poetry in New Orleans may offer special indulgences as well. If it does not afford time off in purgatory, then it certainly indulges in the culinary cultures of a vast array of people and food from across the globe. To indulge this food is to meld into a sumptuous past, not simply some proverbial "melting pot" where everything ends up tasting the same, but instead a concoction that only the word "gumbo" can describe. The sassafras pounded into a powder by Indians becomes file, a thickener for gumbo, made from a roux which has its grainy sources all over the globe and which gets its principal vegetable ingredient, okra, from Africa. Gumbo may get its name from Africa, where okra was pronounced in the Central Bantu dialect of West Africa as *"ki ngombo,"* or it may get its name from the Choctaw word *"kombo,"* for sassafras. From the start, gumbo mixes indigenous and African New Orleans in a thick cultural stew that is recalled today by the Mardi Gras Indians—who, by the way, dance in the streets on both Mardi Gras Day and on Super Sunday, the Sunday closest to St. Joseph's Day when food-infused altars throughout the city pay tribute to the saint. Indians, Africans, and Sicilians meet back up with St. Joseph in this oddly Latinate city, where you can indulge a sumptuous bowl of gumbo at Brennan's and Commander's Palace, signature restaurants of the Brennan family whose founder was born in the Irish Channel, the son of a poor Irish metal worker whose labor ultimately gave rise to one of the finest French restaurants in the city.

The convergence of Indians, Africans, Sicilians, Irish, and French through the metamorphosis of food and its ritual preparations only begins to hint at the complex alchemy of food and cultures in this feast day of a city. A quick survey of at least the major groups who have brought their food and food traditions to the city must include not only the Indians and Africans who mixed sassafras and okra for the city's most famous dish, but also the Germans and French and Sicilians who ate it, the Spanish whose sautéed blending of onions, garlic, and peppers played no small role in solidifying the Holy Trinity of foods in the city, the Islenos of the Canary Islands who brought their expertise with fish and wild game, the Acadians from Novia Scotia who utterly transformed seafood culture and preparation in the bayou country surrounding New Orleans, the émigrés from St. Domingue and the Haitian revolution who passed through Cuba on their way and brought their own distinctive African, French, and Spanish Creole food traditions from the West Indies, the Irish who must have remembered the haunting hologram of the white potato and its blight that sent them crossing the ocean to the city's Irish Channel where Owen Brennan was born and where Margaret Haughery baked her miracle bread, the Hondurans who brought bananas to New Orleans which would be unloaded from the boats by Sicilian dock workers and then transformed into Brennan's culinary creation of bananas Foster, the Vietnamese whose pistolettes of sliced meats, carrots, chiles, and cilantro form the Vietnamese po-boy, and the Mexicans who continue to labor to rebuild the city after Katrina and whose taco trucks have already left their sustaining and spicy imprint on a city craving tasty food. A recent and wonderful cookbook, entitled *You Are Where You Eat: Stories and Recipes from the Neighborhoods of New Orleans*, and compiled by Swedish journalist Elsa Hahne, features recipes from people who cook at home, and it reads like the records of a world summit on contemporary global cuisine. Among its at-home chefs and dishes are Bellazar Wilcox's "Mexican Meringue Frosting," Kalpana Saxena's "Crawfish Balls with Cilantro Chutney," Marietta Esther Schleh Herr's "Sour Cream and Onion Pie (Zwiebelkuchen)," Ronald William Lewis's "Tupelo Street Barbecue," Bertin Bernard Esteves's "Satsumas with Sangria Syrup," Asare Dankwah's "Fufu," Chin Thi Nguyen's "Mung Bean Sweet Rice Dipping Sauce," Alina Sierra Sedlander's "Black Beans and Rice (moros y Christianos)," Estella Francesca Cirincione Mantia's "Sesame Cookies for St. Joseph," Beulah Kenney Labostrie's "Filé Gumbo," and Eric Paul "Esquizito" Perez's "Sweet Potato Smoothie."

All this and we have yet to approach the great confluences that have produced red beans and rice. Taking its place with gumbo as one of the two most famous dishes of New Orleans, red beans and rice harbors a very special poetics all its own. Unlike gumbo, it forms a dish that rarely makes its way onto the menus of New Orleans's finest restaurants. Look for red beans instead at neighborhood restaurants, smaller seafood eateries, festivals where it is dished out to you from huge communal pots, and of course, look for it at home. Both gumbo and red beans and rice are foods native to the household, but of the two, red beans remains the humble stalwart of the homey kitchen. And as we all know, the people who most often prepare any food in the kitchen are women, the *femme* of what is known as *bonne femme* cuisine. Food writers use the term *bonne femme* to refer to food produced in the household and by the "good housewife," the woman who presumably becomes "good" by behaving and performing her duties as a cook. Long and diverse traditions of good women—extending from slaves to domestic servants to well-behaved and not-so-well-behaved wives, and from nuns and courtesans and lesbians to saints and voodoo queens—have prepared food in the city, and rightly deserve to reclaim the term *bonne femme* for their distinctive poetic culinary creations. Yet *bonne femme* cuisine takes a decidedly second place to traditions of *haute cuisine*, literally the "high" cuisine marked by its fine sauces and delicate preparation, and associated with such restaurants as Antoine's, Arnaud's, Brennan's, Commander's Palace, Galatoire's, Broussard's. In the nineteenth century, many such restaurants were connected to the finest hotels—the St. Charles, St. Louis, and Tremoulet—where the high business transactions of the day commenced, and where women and black people were simply not allowed.[8]

Red beans and rice is the revenge for their exclusion. Prepared by good women, and more than a few good humble men of the kitchen, red beans and rice refuses to be seated at the table of *haute cuisine* establishments. It represents a mixture of the oldest foods on the earth, and yet it will not mix with *haute* and haughty food traditions. It is the food of women who labor in the kitchen, distinctive among them, black women. As tradition has it, red beans and rice was typically prepared every Monday, the day for doing laundry and other household tasks, when it was easy to leave the slow-cooking dish on the stove, simmering to perfection. Since the women of the household, and women slaves and servants in particular, actually performed this labor of laundry and cooking, red beans and rice sets a cuisine to the calendar of women's labor. St. Joseph who saved the Sicilians from famine has his fava beans and his one feast day each year, but the women of New Orleans have every single Monday to remind the world that they are and remain the poets who mix and meld the world's most ancient foods.

To eat red beans and rice is to indulge the distinctly feminine poetic metamorphosis of ancient foods and household labor. If red beans and rice takes its seat at the *bonne femme* kitchen table, it also insistently turns our attention to the women who have always prepared food in this city where food is formed like a poem. We are reminded that women have always cooked the most delicately spiced dishes even as they rarely number among a long legacy of great chefs, just as women have always produced poetry yet have rarely been acknowledged in *haute poetics*. In New Orleans, these two feminine artistic practices—one that feeds the shaping of poems and the other that nourishes the shaping of food—have long been linked. In her book *Women and New Orleans: A History*, Mary Gehman describes how Indian and African women were especially crucial in the production, trading, and cooking of food in early New Orleans (Gehman 1–3). And in her recent book *Congo Square*, Freddi Williams Evans describes the city's originary market culture as one that "resided largely in the hands of market women," reflecting a "continuation of African market culture." Market women, she tells us, were also calling women, women who sold their goods "calling out their wares with melodic chants." From the call of Sally and the emancipatory potato song to the call of women who sing the praises of their cakes, the "calling women" of New Orleans harbor a long poetic legacy. Their markets and their voices permeated the city—from Congo Square itself to streets and alleys and levees, at houses and businesses and public places. Some of them carried their markets in huge baskets balanced on their heads, and others covered their tables and stalls with pecan pies and cakes, coconuts, pralines, and croquettes (Evans 109).

The praline alone harbors its own feminine heritage. Creole scholar and poet Sybil Kein tells us that it was supposedly invented by the female cook for one Marshall Dupleses-Preslin (1598–1675), whose name obscures hers. But her creation survives anything about him. Kein goes on to explain how the markets of both Africa and early New Orleans were filled with the voices of women "calling out praises of the cakes they had baked for sale [and] candies they made out of sugar cane, which they peeled and boiled to extract the syrupy liquid" (Kein 250–51).⁹ Pralines, it seems, had their origins in both the creative hands and poetic voices of African women—a fine *bonne femme* tradition deserving of *haute* distinction. Food would be passed from hand to hand just as food traditions and recipes would be passed down by women through the generations. Writer and critic Joyce Zonana passes on several recipes that extend back to those of her mother and other Sephardic Jews in Egypt, recipes that then find their place in the kitchen of Zonana's small house in the Gentilly Terrace section of New Orleans. Today, Mona's grocery store in Midcity, where Zonana would shop, supports the ancient connection of Jews, Africans, and Europeans through their shared Mediterranean cuisines.

Matters of ancestry and history are of no small consequence when talking about red beans and rice. Rice, the seeming secondary component of this dish, assumes primary status as an African food with longstanding connections to song. Historians have documented that rice accompanied the first slaves taken to Louisiana during the French slave trade, and that Africans had long cultivated rice, along with other varieties of corn and vegetables, in the fertile Senegal River valley. The laborers in these fields were accompanied by *griots* who sang to the beat of drums, limning the rhythmic movements of bodies tending the soil (Hall 34–37).¹⁰ Not surprisingly, rice proliferated in the early French colony thanks to the expertise and labors of Africans, and found its way as a staple food in the city's cuisine. If the poetics of red beans and rice accounts for the feminine metamorphosis of ancient food and household labor, the poetics of rice alone has its own story: its cultivation was accompanied by song, and some of its most singular preparations were sustained by women's song-like callings. The *calas*, or rice fritters, that could also be made from wheat or even sliced sweet potato pudding, were among the many tasty items traded in the markets of early New Orleans and sold by the "cala women" who called out praises and chants for their delicacies. "Louisiana rice," or *Le Riz de la Louisiane*, gets its own chapter in the historic collection of recipes found in *The Picayune Creole Cookbook*, which tells its own story of the *calas* and its women callers—"Belle Cala! Tout Chaud!" (184). Rice also harbors its own special mixed cultural heritage in New Orleans, where Spain joins with Africa and indigenous America to shape the particular ways in which red beans and rice gets served. The method of cooking rice in water so that it produces separate grains differs from the general European practices of cooking rice in vegetable or animal oils, and generates a pearly assortment of simple carbohydrates which will then be doused with the creamy sauce of slowly simmered red beans.

The red bean and its many culinary cousins have their origin in Central America, where dark kidney beans were the first beans of the Americas to be sent to Europe in the sixteenth century (Leathem 136–38).[11] Understanding kidney beans as indigenous to Mesoamerica explains not only the obvious plentiful presence of beans in dishes throughout Mexico and the southwestern United States, but the more mysterious presence of the red bean in dishes throughout the Americas. This presence explains to me, for instance, why my sister-in-law from Honduras prepares a delicious version of red beans which she calls red bean soup that includes, among other ingredients, eggs. Traveling from Honduras to Havana, the red bean gets darker, though Haiti is often cited as the source for the New Orleans red bean. Beans and rice were often cooked together or separately—but not cooked separately and served one atop the other as they are in New Orleans. Pinto beans in Mexico, black beans in Cuba, red beans in Haiti and New Orleans all seem to possess the same mother bean. Whatever the travels and travails of the Central American red bean, I feel quite certain that a woman, who likely also did the laundry, is the one who created and passed down the dish we now know as red beans and rice, this most magnificent testimony to the poetics of *bonne femme* cuisine.

If *bonne femme* food welcomes people to the table without reservation, it also serves as the social, communal cuisine—the food of the kitchen table, of the gathered group and extended family, the cuisine of the neighborhood. As such, it is the food most intimately and socially linked to language. Cooking and calling women make way for talking people. The poetics of *bonne femme* accounts for this special blending of food and conversation. Louis Armstrong, who signed all his correspondence with the phrase "Red Beans and Ricely Yours," once famously described the aura of music in New Orleans. It was an aura that always included food: "In the evening, people colored and white, used to give parties on the lawns in front of their houses—set up with lemonade and sandwiches and fried chicken and gumbo and the band sit down in front of the door on the porch and play. And people dance. . . . Yeah, music all around you. The pie man and the waffle man . . . [and] banana man, he'd be hollering 'Yellow ripe bananas, lady, 15 cents a bunch! Yellow ripe bananas!' Oh, yeah, always had music all around me of some kind" (Armstrong 25–26).

Calling women make way for men who call out to ladies, and cacophonous music swirled all around and everybody talked over food. The phrase *gumbo ya ya* refers precisely to the overflow of talk when everyone is gathered at the table, as if both the aroma and taste of food carries the sound of voices, and vice versa. The po-boy sandwiches and little waxed boxes of olive salad that we sometimes ordered out when I was a child—the only food I can ever recall that was not prepared at home—were delivered from Sauro's by young boys on bicycles. I never actually knew where Sauro's was located, and so it seemed to me that its food kept circulating on bicycles with its smells wafting throughout the streets of our 9th Ward neighborhood, waiting for all of us to eat and talk. The talk that commences over food can often revolve around hefty matters, the kind of conversation that can change your mind, and the world. Leah Chase, longtime cook and master maternal chef at Dookie Chase's restaurant in Tremé, describes how "a good meal can really make you think different." She goes on to describe how civil rights workers ate and planned at her establishment. "They came, and they ate. Always had gumbo. *Always had gumbo.* They ate, and then they would say what they were going to do, and then they would go out and do it. Some would go to jail. Some would do this. Then when they got out, they would come back here and eat again." Pondering world problems, she adds: "If you talked over things. Come to dinner. Sit down to a good meal. And then we'll talk. Sit down. We'll talk" (Chase 16).

Talk itself, calling out to each other over food, joins with the lyric call of poetry through which we sustain our most basic connections. Red beans and rice calls us together, maybe to talk about a world of problems. Maybe food talks to us, calling us to each other and also back in time—back into tragic and transformed histories, back into the fusion of African and European and Indian cultures of grains and vegetables, back into the melodic melding of rice and song, back to the good women who have always cooked good food, and always back to my mother's kitchen where Camilla red beans simmered slowly with the pickled pork she sent me to buy at Wagner's Supermarket on nearby Desire Street. When I prepare them today, I skip the pickled pork. But the desire remains.

◆ ◆ ◆

Bonne femme cuisine sustains the desire to talk as the traditionally female art of conversation infusing the very food itself, as if meals were imbued with meanings and messages. No wonder *haute cuisine* restaurants in the nineteenth century excluded women and black people. Yet these cuisines and their delicacies can hardly be sidelined, and it may well be the case, as Richard

Collin claims, that what makes New Orleans "one of the great eating cities of the world" is that both *bonne femme* and *haute cuisine* preside there,[12] where they sometimes form and inform each other (Collin 17–18). Gumbo has made its way into the fine food establishments just as *poisson meunière amandine* and *shrimp rémoulade* are served in neighborhood cafes. And bread pudding in all its infinite variety appears virtually everywhere. The potato, that poetic image from an old slave song, offers itself as perfect example of this poetic fusion of *bonne femme* and *haute cuisine* as they have shaped each other over time and circumstances. Fried potatoes and roast beef gravy formed the original po-boy sandwich, made at Martin's sandwich shop during a streetcar strike in the 1920s, to feed the striking workers, forever linking the potato of emancipation with the potato of unions and fair wages ("French Bread" 46–53).[13] (I recall a sandwich shop just a few blocks from my high school on St. Claude Avenue that skipped the potatoes, and served us simply gravy po-boys dressed with mayonnaise, sliced tomato, and shredded lettuce: a fine indulgence for nineteen cents.) But the same potato of the striking workers' potato and gravy po-boys had already undergone transformation at *haute cuisine* establishments, emerging as *pommes de terre soufflés in béarnaise sauce.* Story has it that the chef of King Louis-Philippe in France accidentally invented this dish for the king who loved fried potatoes. Once, the story goes, after the chef prepared for the king his favorite sliced fried potatoes, Louis-Philippe was delayed for dinner. By the time he arrived, the chef had no fresh potatoes to fry, so he simply refried the ones originally prepared such that his double-fried potatoes emerged as "an accidental masterpiece: the stuffed potatoes puffed into balloon-like French fries" (244–45).[14] Antoine Alciatore, who founded Antoine's restaurant in 1840, re-created the recipe and produced *pomme de terre soufflés*, which is not only served at Antoine's and at restaurants throughout the city, but passed on in cookbooks for generations.

From the wild sweet potato to the *pomme de terre*, literally translated from the French as "apple of the earth," there is a vegetable presence in New Orleans that vies only with seafood—and decidedly *not* meat—for prime distinction in the city's cuisine: potatoes and red beans, artichokes and eggplant, olives, okra, Creole tomatoes, and the Holy Trinity of onion, celery, and peppers mixed with the ancient grains of corn and rice. Even a seafood boil—where huge mounds of boiled crawfish, crabs, and shrimp are piled onto newspaper-covered tables and where people talk ceaselessly and eat all day and night—must be accompanied by the corn and potatoes and garlic thrown into the brew. And even the *boeuf gras* of Mardi Gras, signaling the height and the end of carnival (the word carnival from *carne*, or meat—carnival presaging the meatless days of Lent) makes way for a cuisine that historically tends to use smaller bits of meat for spicing rather than larger hunks for gorging. The city's finest foods—in *bonne femme, haute*, or their combined traditions, and though often infused with bits of ham or slices of sausage or the proverbial pickled pork of red beans—rise from vegetables mixed and melded in herbed oil, fried and simmered and stuffed, always the stuff of poetic metamorphosis. Seventeenth-century British poet Andrew Marvell once described his love for a woman as a "vegetable love that grows / vaster than empires." Although New Orleans owes next to nothing to England for its poetry and (thank goodness) for its food, the city's miracle of food does bear remarkable resemblance to a vegetable love that grows vaster than empires. In a loving act of vegetable alchemy, cooks in New Orleans have transformed the ravages of empire—conquest and slavery—into one of the world's most distinctive and famous cuisines. The sugar of horrific plantation economies miraculously reappears as a praline, or as the multicolored and multiflavored syrups poured onto the city's signature summer treat, the sno-ball, its flavors relished with such passion that a recent lawsuit was filed to contest the ownership of several of these select transformations of sugar (Simerman A1, A5). The rice of these same plantation encampments emerges as jambayala (the city's version of Spain's paella) and as the *calas* of all the calling women who chanted and so transformed their foods into poems. Bananas from a poor Central American country become bananas Foster. A single fava bean carries forth its legacy of halting famine, and the red bean alone brings women into their own as poets and *femme* chefs. The love of vegetables becomes a vegetable love that permeates the city, and then keeps getting stuffed back into the vegetables—stuffed eggplant, stuffed artichoke, stuffed cabbage leaves (especially on St. Patrick's Day after the parade), the stuffed shells of crabs, oysters (Rockefeller, Bienville, Thermidor), and crawfish (for crawfish bisque). For Joyce Zonana, grape leaves stuffed with chickpeas, tomatoes, and rice in her Gentilly kitchen sustain the memory of a faraway Jewish home in Egypt. For me, memories of New Orleans will forever be stuffed into the magically translucent skin of the city's signature vegetable, the mirliton.

The stuffed mirliton, which is formed through a special *poiesis* which melds and molds its honeydew sweetness with the sacramental oil and bread(crumbs) of the Holy Trinity, fills the present moment with tastes and aromas from the past. The object of nostalgia and longing that always calls one back to the kitchen, the mirliton forms nothing less than the very stuff of memory in New Orleans, and presides as poet laureate in a city where poetry is eaten. It connects us, through taste and smell, with what is gone—no small task for a city that nearly lost everything in a great flood. It creeps along the vine in the backyard of everyone's childhood, growing vaster than empires.

It is itself the child of empires and has outlasted every single one of them. It originated in Mexico, was transported by the Spanish to Jamaica and Cuba, and then by Saint Domingue refugees to New Orleans, perhaps also brought by Acadians to the city since they, too, had once taken refuge in Jamaica and Cuba. Perhaps, too, the mirliton arrived when the first bananas did from Honduras. Known in Mexico as the chayote, it harbors at least thirty-two other names which all sound somewhat like chayote, so that the New Orleans name of mirliton remains a mystery to this day. In French, *mirliton* refers to a kazoo-type flute, so we can only wonder if the fusion of food and song, food and music, food and poetry in New Orleans is epitomized in this seeming musical instrument of a vegetable (147–52).[15]

The mirliton vine, like the vine of the wild sweet potato of an old Creole song, extends its vast domain over backyards and sheds in the city, so impressive in its sheer determination to spread that it implants itself in mind and memory. It keeps creeping up from behind. Its abundant fruit—a green squash that looks like a big pear but with a single large seed at the center, an indulgence all its own—is harvested in both fall and spring, coinciding with the catch of white shrimp in fall and brown shrimp in spring, which are in turn sautéed into the Holy Trinity and mixed with breadcrumbs and the honeydew pulp of the mirliton itself, and then stuffed back into its translucent skin. Baked to perfection, its taste and message are all about how the past keeps creeping us on us, how it never fully departs. The mirliton forms the vigorous vine that holds tight to the past while it keeps reaching toward tomorrow.

Memory, we are told, is far more deeply coded in the body than the mind. A scent can bring back overwhelming remembrances, and taste can stun you with a surprise vision of something long forgotten. But it is the actual process of *making* the stuffed mirliton, its peculiar *poiesis*, that brings me back to the kitchen of a small house where my mother and I once stuffed twenty halves of mirlitons, all from the extending vine that grew across the backyard fence and shed before a flood washed them all away. Far away now, I can still smell mirlitons baking in the oven, as if they were an image being cooked to perfection in a poem. My vegetable love.

On that day, we were preparing the mirlitons for Thanksgiving dinner— and thank goodness that now, after my own vine drowned, mirliton vines have returned and are quietly creeping throughout neighborhood yards in the city. I like to remember New Orleans as forever filled with these miracle vegetables, each one a poem infused in sacramental oil and breadcrumbs. Anointed and granted sainthood in this city filled with saints of all varieties, St. Mirliton ensures the ritual salvation that food grants in New Orleans—where potatoes carry messages and magically blow up like balloons, where red beans and rice reveals the poetry of good women, where gumbo sustains civil rights, and where mirlitons feed a memory that grows forever on a backyard vine.

Notes

1. Among the citations and translations of this Creole song, see George Washington Cable, "The Dance in Place Congo," 524, 529, which follows his fulsome description of the *bamboula*. The song, he claims, all comes to "one nonsense line meaning only, 'When that 'tater's cooked don't you eat it up!'" But the provocative negative can signal precisely an invitation to "eat it," as most other translations indicate. Gwenlodyn Midlo Hall relies on the translation of Alcée Fortier, "When the potato is cooked, it must be eaten," in her study *Africans in Colonial Louisiana*, 316; and Martha Ward relies on several primary sources for the fuller song and translation she prints: "When the potato will be cooked, we shall eat it, we shall eat it, / Even if it is in the soup, even if it is in the ashes, / Even if it is in the syrup, we shall eat it, we shall eat it," *Voodoo Queen: The Spirited Lives of Marie Laveau*, 91.

2. Jerah Johnson, *Congo Square in New Orleans*, 5, 9–11. Johnson also cites Benjamin Latrobe's famous description of Congo Square published in the early nineteenth century, where Latrobe's decidedly nervous account of the market people along the river included an abundance of food for exchange—"'wild ducks, oysters, poultry of all kinds . . . bananas, piles of oranges, sugar cane, sweet and Irish potatoes,'" 1–2.

3. See Susan Tucker and Sara Roahen, "Mirliton and Shrimp," in *New Orleans Cuisine: Fourteen Signature Dishes and Their Histories*, 142.

4. See Johnson, *Congo Square in New Orleans*, 5–13; and Freddi Williams Evans, *Congo Square: African Roots in New Orleans*, 109–13.

5. Evans documents these appearances of the sweet potato, 110 and 113. For a discussion of *calas* as they appeared in one of the earliest of New Orleans cookbooks, *The Creole Cookery Book*, see Karen Trahan and Sharon Stallworth Nossiter, "Red Beans and Rice," in *New Orleans Cuisine*, 134–35.

6. For example, Gaston Bachelard, *The Poetics of Space*, and Edouard Glissant, *Poetics of Relation*.

7. See Tucker and Roahen, "Shrimp and Mirliton," in *New Orleans Cuisine*, 143–44; and see Sarah Roahen's discussion of the artichoke in her book *Gumbo Tales: Finding My Place at the New Orleans Table*, 63–64.

8. See the discussion of such matters in Susan Tucker, et al., "Setting the Table in New Orleans," in *New Orleans Cuisine*, 14–17.

9. See Kein's essay "Louisiana Creole Food Culture" in her edited book *Creole*, where she cites several sources on the foods and chants of women in Africa and throughout the Caribbean world, 250–51. For a study of the dominant and pervasive influence of Africa in food throughout the American South, see Jessica Harris's classic *Beyond Gumbo: Creole Fusion Food from the Atlantic Rim*.

10. See Hall, 34–37, and Leathem and Nossiter, "Red Beans and Rice," in *New Orleans Cuisine*, 133–35.

11. See this discussion of "Red Beans and Rice" in *New Orleans Cuisine*, 136–38.

12. Richard Collin, *The Revised New Orleans Underground Gourmet*, 17–18. Also see "Setting the Table in New Orleans," in *New Orleans Cuisine*, 16–17, n. 11.

13. See the account and other legends of the po-boy sandwich in "French Bread," *New Orleans Cuisine*, 46–53.

14. The story is related in "Mirliton and Shrimp," in *New Orleans Cuisine*, 144–45.

15. See the full and fine discussion of the mirliton in "Mirliton and Shrimp," in *New Orleans Cuisine*, especially pp. 147–52.

Works Cited

Armstrong, Louis. "Growing Up in New Orleans." *New Orleans Stories: Great Writers on the City*. Ed. John Miller. San Francisco: Chronicle Books, 1992. 25–26.

Bachelard, Gaston. *The Poetics of Space*. Boston: Beacon Press, 1969.

Burton, Nathaniel, and Rudy Lombard. *Creole Feast: 15 Master Chefs of New Orleans Reveal their Secrets*. New York: Random House, 1978.

Cable, George Washington. "The Dance in Place Congo." *Century Magazine* (February 1886): 524–29.

Chase, Leah. "Come to Dinner." *Louisiana Cultural Vistas* (Summer 2011): 16.

Collin, Richard. *The Revised New Orleans Underground Gourmet*. New York: Simon and Schuster, 1973.

Evans, Freddi Williams. *Congo Square: African Roots in New Orleans*. Lafayette, LA: U of Louisiana at Lafayette P, 2011.

Gehman, Mary. *Women and New Orleans: A History*. New Orleans: Margaret Media, 1988.

Glissant, Edouard. *Poetics of Relation*. Ann Arbor: U of Michigan P, 1997.

Hahne, Elsa, ed. *You Are Where You Eat: Stories and Recipes from the Neighborhoods of New Orleans*. Jackson: UP of Mississippi, 2008.

Hall, Gwenlodyn Midlo. *Africans in Colonial Louisiana*. Baton Rouge: Louisiana State University P, 1992.

Harris, Jessica. *Beyond Gumbo: Creole Fusion Food from the Atlantic Rim*. New York: Simon and Schuster, 2003.

Johnson, Jerah. *Congo Square in New Orleans*. New Orleans: Louisiana Landmarks Society, 1995.

Kniffen, Fred B., Hiram F. Gregory, and George A. Stokes. *The Historic Indian Tribes of Louisiana: From 1542 to the Present*. Baton Rouge: Louisiana State University P, 1987.

The Picayune Creole Cookbook: The Original Second and Best Edition of the Greatest Classic of Louisiana French Cooking. 1901. New York: Dover Publications, 1971.

Roahen, Sarah. *Gumbo Tales: Finding My Place at the New Orleans Table*. New York: W. W. Norton, 2008.

Simerman, John. "Suit lobs curve into snowball fight." New Orleans *Times-Picayune*, July 5, 2011, A1, A5.

Stewart, Susan. *Poetry and the Fate of the Senses.* Chicago: U of Chicago P, 2002.

Strand, Mark. "Eating Poetry." *New Selected Poems.* New York: Alfred A. Knopf, 2007. 36.

Sublette, Ned. *The World That Made New Orleans: From Spanish Silver to Congo Square.* Chicago: Lawrence Hill Books, 2008.

Tucker, Susan, ed. *New Orleans Cuisine: Fourteen Signature Dishes and Their Histories.* Jackson: UP of Mississippi, 2009.

Ward, Martha. *Voodoo Queen: The Spirited Lives of Marie Laveau.* Jackson: UP of Mississippi, 2004.

Zonana, Joyce. *Dream Homes: From Cairo to Katrina, An Exile's Journey.* New York: The Feminist Press, 2008.

Chapter Eight

A MATTER OF TASTE

Reading Food and Class in Appalachian Literature

ERICA ABRAMS LOCKLEAR

In 1888, Charles Dudley Warner, an editor and writer, colleague of Mark Twain, and patron of Sarah Orne Jewett, traveled through parts of Appalachia. He later published a narrative about his experience in which he commented that "it should be said that before the country can attract and retain travelers, its inhabitants must learn something about the preparation of food" (77). Lee Smith's upper-class Richard Burlage from *Oral History* (1983), a novel set in the early part of the century, seems to share Warner's opinion because he writes, "The food [in the mountains] is abominable" (112). Progressive-era missionaries Katherine Petit and May Stone, meanwhile, were invested in changing what mountain people ate because they believed that biscuits were more hygienic than cornbread (Engelhardt, *Greens* 51–52). Appalachians who came into contact with missionaries such as Petit and Stone or who read travel accounts like Warner's or other literature set in the mountains were quite literally taught to feel ashamed of their regional fare. Leather britches, creasy (or creecy) greens, and poke sallet were depicted in local color literature and missionary reports about the region as the barbaric food of the uncivilized. In John Fox Junior's *The Little Shepard of Kingdom Come*, for example, a character named Chad boards with a mountain family, and the narrator describes the "coarse food" as "strangely disagreeable" (153). Negative descriptions of Appalachian food permeate the literature about the region, separating both Appalachians and the food that they consume from the rest of the nation. When the Appalachian region became conceptually distinct near the beginning of the twentieth century, the food that mountain people ate became affiliated with a particular mountain identity, one closely aligned with class hierarchies and systems of oppression. In the introduction to *Cornbread Nation 3: Foods of the Mountain South*, editor Ronni Lundy

writes that by "looking through the lens of real Southern mountain food ...
we discovered lurking under the dinner table an unexpected subject inextricably connected to the food above ... we discovered that the visitor under the
table looked suspiciously like class and the prejudices that accompany it" (2).
Food became another means by which Appalachians were socially marginalized, until writers from the mountains began responding.

As the genre of Appalachian literature grew throughout the middle of the
twentieth century to include works of literature written by Appalachian people—not just works written about them—depictions of food began to change,
often celebrating the distinctiveness of mountain food and metaphorically
inviting readers to take part in the feast. Yet as this essay explores, the connections between class and food still plague many Appalachian residents, only
now the scrutinized foods are not ramps or creasy greens but soda and other
processed, cheap foods. Media-perpetuated representations linking mountain people with the overconsumption of Mountain Dew, for example, send
a potent message about the class of people who consume such fare, one that
serves the same purpose as a century earlier: to categorize mountain residents
as low class. As with earlier depictions of Appalachians that linked an undesir-
able position on the social hierarchy with what were once considered "lowly"
foods—foods that are now notably chic, like ramps—contemporary representations take the same approach but through a different category of foods.
In the same way that twentieth-century Appalachian writers responded to
disparaging portrayals from local color fiction, so too are contemporary writers usefully complicating these simplistic generalizations about the kind of
people who consume these maligned foods.

Appalachian foods occupy a particular category, and, likewise, the Mountain South has long been considered part of, yet distinctly different from, the
rest of the South. Literary critic Rodger Cunningham calls Appalachia the
South's Other, "a region marked by a double otherness" (42). As many scholars
have noted, this idea took root in the latter part of the nineteenth century, as
evidenced by articles like Will Wallace Harney's 1873 "A Strange Land and
a Peculiar People," published in *Lippincott's Magazine*, and William Goodell
Frost's now famous "Our Contemporary Ancestors," published in *The Atlantic Monthly* in 1899. Twentieth- and twenty-first-century scholars including
Cratis Williams, Henry Shapiro, and Allen Batteau have written extensively
about the notion of Appalachia as an anomalous region, examining how this
phenomenon originated in the American consciousness, and many Appalachian studies scholars have published and continue to publish books and
articles that help debunk myths about Appalachia that were created during
the last century.[1] Yet as anyone who saw the 2009 *20/20* special narrated by

Diane Sawyer, "A Hidden America: Children of the Mountains," knows, the perception that Appalachia is a region apart is alive and well. Several ideas about mountain people and the region—many of them gross overgeneralizations—contribute to this view: assumed regional loyalty, distinctive speech patterns, supposed racial, ethnic, and socioeconomic homogeneity, and most important for the purposes of this essay, food.

Food associated with Appalachia undoubtedly contributes to the double othering that Cunningham notes. Leather britches, creasy greens, poke sallet, and other unique foods comprise a regionally specific microcuisine far different from the gumbo-laden tables of southern Louisiana or the shrimp and grits breakfasts favored in Charleston. Foodways scholars have taken note of this difference, as evidenced by the publication of such books as *Cornbread Nation 3: Foods of the Mountain South*. In fact, Appalachian foods are now experiencing exposure to national consumers thanks to the inclusion of ramps and other mountain ingredients into recipes by chefs Emeril Lagasse and Bobby Flay. In 2008 the Biltmore Estate hosted the "Field to Table Festival: A Taste of Appalachia," where chefs and connoisseurs gathered to praise mountain dishes including pickled watermelon and apple stack cake. Likewise, foodies perusing the "Cooking and Eating" section of the May 28–29, 2011, issue of *The Wall Street Journal* were no doubt interested to find a half-page article, complete with mouth-watering photographs, extolling the virtues of an asparagus and ramp skillet soufflé (Reusing). But as the work of multiple Appalachian authors reveals, these recent developments mark a notable shift in perceptions of mountain food.

The current spotlight on Appalachian foodways seems unexpected because for so long, mainstream America viewed Appalachians—and the food that they ate—as socially deviant and in need of reform. Travel literature written about the region dating back to the nineteenth century reveals the trend of denigrating Appalachian food. In 1888, Charles Dudley Warner published *On Horseback: Tour in Virginia, North Carolina, and Tennessee with Notes of Travel in Mexico and California*, a book that chronicles his journey with his friend, the Professor. At the time Warner was a well-known editor and essayist, and he and his wife, Sarah, were affluent enough to build a house "on a plot adjacent to the properties of [Mark] Twain and [Harriet Beecher] Stowe" (Leach 331). Literary critic Eugene Leach even describes Warner as the "squire of Nook Farm" and contends that "the good life at Nook Farm made Warner a man of letters" (329, 332). Warner's lofty class status matters in the context of this argument. As he demonstrates throughout his travel narrative, he viewed himself as superior in both culinary knowledge and general status when compared with the mountain cuisine he consumed and the people who prepared it. His account functions as a microcosmic view of how mainstream America in the late 1800s positioned itself in relation to "backwards" Appalachian dishes and those who ate them, a trend that continued well into the twentieth century and that lingers today.

In his narrative, Warner initially appears relatively open-minded about the food he will encounter on his trip. Early in their journey, after departing from Abingdon, Virginia, the pair dines at Ramsey's boardinghouse, because it "had been recommended to [them] as a royal palace of entertainment, the best in all the region" (13). Warner and the Professor first pass Ramsey's without recognizing it, and they comment that "everybody about the place was barefooted, except the mistress" (14). But the "comely daughter of eighteen, who served [their] dinner in the kitchen" seems to ameliorate any misgivings that they have about eating food prepared by people who are not wearing shoes (15). Warner writes a glowing description of their fare, one that provides a stark juxtaposition to the food that they encounter later in their trip, when mountain people provide them with meals out of their homes, not a boardinghouse: "On the table were hot biscuit, ham, pork, and green beans, apple-sauce, blackberry preserves, cucumbers, coffee, plenty of milk, honey, and apple and blackberry pie" (15). He even goes on to reflect that "the dinner was abundant, and though it seemed to us incongruous at the time, we were not twelve hours older when we looked back upon it with longing" (15). Though Warner is clearly skeptical of this establishment when he and the Professor first arrive, the bounteous table that the hostess provides makes up for any judgments about mountain people. But his positive impression soon begins to change.

After leaving Ramsey's, the duo crosses into Tennessee, and they are told that they should visit the Eggers farm, where Mr. and Mrs. Eggers will likely take them in for the night. The Eggerses agree to provide lodging and food for the pair, but Mrs. Eggers only serves dinner after 9 p.m., after the family's chores are completed. Warner seems displeased by this fact, insinuating that this mountain family should alter their regular work schedule to accommodate his preferred dining time. Warner's description of his meal is not altogether negative, but the food he describes is a departure from the dishes offered at Ramsey's. They are served:

corn-pone (Indian meal stirred up with water and heated through), hot biscuit slack-baked and livid, fried salt-pork swimming in grease, apple-butter, pickled beets, onions and cucumbers raw, coffee, so-called buttermilk, and sweet milk when specially asked for (the correct taste, however, is for buttermilk), and pie. This was not the pie of commerce, but the pie of the country—two thick slabs of dough, with a squeezing of apple in between. (22–23)

Warner lists some items (apple-butter, pickled beets, and coffee) without further comment, but most of the dishes he mentions appear with a qualifier or further description; phrases like "fried salt-pork swimming in grease" and "so-called buttermilk" suggest that he is not nearly as pleased with this meal as the one he enjoyed at Ramsey's. He also seems especially attuned to the fact that he is dining in a setting more rural than the previous boarding-house, and for Warner, this difference carries with it distinct class divisions. His remark that the pie he consumed was "of the country" underscores one of this essay's main assertions: the food with which people are associated is intimately connected to social class. While much of his narrative falls in line with other travel writing from the early part of the twentieth century, Warner admits at times that local color narratives had overromanticized their portrayals of mountain people, commenting that "the modest and pretty young lady with frank and open blue eyes [whom they met], who wore gloves and used the common English speech, had never figured in the diction of the region," prompting him to conclude that "cherished illusions vanish often on near approach" (24).

Despite his vanishing illusion of wild mountain women, Warner becomes increasingly unhappy with the food he and his companion are offered as they continue their travels. Even though he comments upon the beauty of the scenery that they encounter, he wryly remarks that "there is no landscape in the world that is agreeable after two days of rusty bacon and slack biscuit" (31). In the mountains of North Carolina, he is supremely disappointed to find that moonshine does not flow freely in the hills, as he had anticipated it would. "We had found no bread since we left Virginia," he laments, "we had seen corn-meal and water, slack-baked; we had seen potatoes fried in grease, and bacon encrusted with salt (all thirst-provokers), but nothing to drink stronger than buttermilk" (38). By the time they arrive in Burnsville, North Carolina, his estimation of mountain food has reached a new low. He warns ominously, "[I]t should be said that before the country can attract and retain travelers, its inhabitants must learn something about the preparation of food" (77). Warner privileges nonmountain food preparation, even writing, "if, for instance, the landlord's wife at Burnsville had traveled with her husband, her table would probably have been more on a level with his knowledge of the world" (77). Taking an obviously condescending tone, he fails to acknowledge that his travels to the mountains and consumption of Appalachian food broaden his culinary repertoire. He further reveals his bias when he comments upon arriving in the city of Asheville, North Carolina, that he and the Professor "had reached ice-water, barbers, waiters, civilization" (110).

By this point in the narrative, Warner clearly distinguishes between rural and urban Appalachia. It appears that the further he and his companion travel into rural areas, the less content they are with the food that is served to them, and the more judgmental he becomes of the people who offer it to him. Earlier in the narrative, he admits that he is "on a tour in search of the picturesque," and it seems that when he finds "the picturesque," he is neither pleased with it nor with the food that accompanies it (43). As such, he makes several comments about "rusty bacon" and "slack biscuits," suggesting that the preparers of such food rank far lower on the social hierarchy than those who could afford luxuries like ice water in Asheville.

Maria Louise Pool's 1896 novel, *In Buncombe County,* provides even more damning portrayals of mountain people based on the food that they consume. Loosely based on her own traveling experience to western North Carolina, the novel chronicles the adventures of the narrator and her companion, Amabel. The narrator takes a voyeuristically judgmental stance, at one point making derogatory comments about a mountain woman who offers to feed and shelter her and Amabel. After remarking on the woman's "dingy neck," she explains that her hostess is "not old," but instead "reveal[s] what a woman looks like who works at the plow, who eats hog and drinks whiskey, who sucks at a wad of snuff, who is as licentious as the worst women in cities," deciding that "it was easy to guess at many of her sins" (51–52). In this instance, the narrator uses a type of faulty judgmental reasoning to draw connections between labor deemed unfit for women, food and drink choice, tobacco consumption, and immoral behavior. Even so, the narrator admits that "it was also easy to see that she had the virtue of hospitality" because "plainly she enjoyed mixing the corn pone and frying the bacon" (52). In commenting upon the woman's potential, the narrator employs a common strategy used by missionaries ministering to "mountain whites" around the turn of the century: the recognition of one admirable quality suggested that more such qualities might emerge with proper encouragement.[2] But in the turn-of-the-century words of William Goodell Frost, "the aim should be to make [mountain people] intelligent without making them sophisticated" (319). Part of that sophistication involved making changes to Appalachian food, because as folklorist Lucy Long explains, "[M]ountain food itself tended to be seen as primitive and simple, reflecting a lack of culinary discernment that was indicative of either the perceived backwardness and depravity of mountain residents or their forced protection from the influences of time and progress" (4–5). Part of Frost's agenda involved introducing the influences of time and progress that Long discusses, but he notably wanted to do so without shifting the way the rest of America viewed the class status of mountaineers.

Hindman Settlement School founders Katherine Petit and May Stone envisioned similar goals in their campaign to change the food that mountain people ate and how they prepared it. Elizabeth Engelhardt points out that during the Progressive Era, one of the immediate concerns of Appalachian settlement school founders involved efforts to convert cornbread-loving mountain folk to biscuit-eating citizens, believing that biscuits were more "hygienic" than cornbread. As Engelhardt explains, "[T]o some observers, one meant high culture, modern hygiene, and Progressive womanhood. Biscuit making demonstrated class consciousness, the ability to acquire specialized ingredients, racially-coded leisure time for certain women, consumer-marketed equipment, and nationally standardized consumption. Cornbread, on the other hand, symbolized ignorance, disease, and poverty" (Engelhardt, *Greens* 52). Engelhardt goes on to write that "the biscuit, in other words, marked middle- and upper-class status in 1900" (Engelhardt, *Greens* 61). She contends that the Hindman Settlement School founders could have focused on any number of mountain foods to change, but by singling out cornbread as an object worthy of food outreach, they were making a political statement as well. Engelhardt asserts that "portraying cornbread-eating Appalachians nostalgically as 'our contemporary ancestors,' to use the term of the day, made them worthy (and needy) American subjects for funding—and, thus, let the Progressive women set forth with their lectures and lessons in cooking" (Engelhardt, "Beating the Biscuits" 35). Petit and Stone's crusade against cornbread and for labor-, time-, and resource-intensive beaten biscuits represents just one facet of a larger social dynamic at work during the Progressive Era that extended from then onward: mountain food was generally viewed as intrinsically aberrant by those sent to minister to and presumably "civilize" mountain people. Foods not typically found in urban areas, like leather britches, were deemed unacceptable and unfit for consumption. These judgments have had a lasting impact on mountain people and on the way that they viewed, and to some extent still view, their own culinary traditions.

Such devaluing of mountain dishes provides ample material for Appalachian authors, and while these instances abound in Appalachian literature, the scope of this essay only affords a brief examination of a few of them. In Lee Smith's 1983 novel, *Oral History*, for example, Richmond-born Richard Burlage travels to the mountains of Virginia on "a pilgrimage to a simpler era" (93). During his train ride into the region he encounters "a cumbersome old country woman" with a large goiter on her neck who offers him "chicken, pound cake, deviled eggs, [and] dried peaches" (98, 103). Despite this woman's presumed iodine deficiency, she still offers Burlage food that she could likely use herself (assuming it contains iodized salt, which it might not), and he eats the items offered to him but not without clearly judging the woman as socially inferior.

Like Warner and the Professor, Burlage boards with a mountain family (the Justices) for a time. He proclaims that "the food there is abominable: boiled beef, rough as brogans; thick flat peas; sticky yams with an acrid, burned taste; green beans cooked to death in a kind of greasy gruel; and the ubiquitous cornbread which appears at every meal" (112). He goes on to conclude, "No wonder that these people, often handsome and hardy in youth, sicken and die so soon! Their diet is not only inedible but appalling from a nutritional standpoint (sanitary precautions being, of course, unknown)" (112). Though fictional, Burlage would no doubt agree with Warner and Pool about what they deem substandard in mountain diets. Burlage's opinion of the food he receives from the Justice family is important, because Smith's rendering of such negative judgments associating mountain foods with the region's inhabitants points to the pervasiveness of this perception.

Despite mainstream messages proclaiming the inferiority of mountain foods, many Appalachians remained, and still remain, proud of mountain dishes. The selections in *Cornbread Nation 3*, for example, not only teach readers about papaws, greasy cut-short beans, ramps, leather britches, possum, fried pies (apple, of course), molasses, and so much more, but they also leave readers longing for foods that they may not be able to access for lack of raw material, preparation know-how, or both. While contributor Janisse Ray, for instance, admits that not everyone enjoys molasses, for "those of us raised on it, who never had Aunt Jemima, who didn't know anything else, we sop[ped] it up with hot biscuits and pour[ed] it over griddle cakes and wet our cornbread with it. We boil[ed] it up and pour[ed] it over popcorn" (145). This kind of loving description suggests that not knowing "anything else" was in fact a privilege, one that allowed mountain residents the gift of experiencing molasses, something not all readers will have done. Notably, this collection was only published in 2005; such a recent publication date suggests that this trend of venerating mountain foods is a new one, a hypothesis further validated by additional examination of Appalachian authors' portrayals of food. If early literature about Appalachia supported Progressive Era mandates to civilize savage hillbillies by way of culinary redemption, then literature written in the mid-twentieth century and onward about Appalachia—but by Appalachians, not local color writers in search of the picturesque—reveals that authors are taking stock of such negative judgments regarding Appalachian food, and they are fighting back. In the 1954 novel *The Dollmaker*, for example, Harriette Arnow makes clear to readers that the protagonist, Gertie Nevels, has the resources to prepare a scrumptious meal in the hills of Kentucky but not in the tenement housing of Detroit, where fresh produce is difficult to obtain, let alone grow. In scene after scene of multiple works, mountain writers describe distinctly Appalachian food with finesse and grace, leaving readers salivating, not pitying the poor mountaineers left to their cornbread.

These proud assertions of culinary pride also often reveal the kind of internalized shame over mountain food that Petit and Stone encouraged. The connection between mountain food and social class that Lundy notes in her introduction to *Cornbread Nation 3* appears repeatedly in Appalachian literature, but these instances of Appalachian characters feeling shame over mountain cuisine are routinely countered with descriptions of bounteous tables overflowing with mouthwatering mountain meals. Read in this way, these instances of fictionalized agency appear to presage the contemporary interest in traditional mountain foods. If authors are including characters proud of creasy greens, ramps, and poke sallet, then the popularization of these traditional foods on both local and national levels suggests that such fiction is becoming reality.

But this trend is a relatively new one, and many twentieth and twenty-first century fictional portrayals of mountain people and their cuisine depict the kind of devaluing that educators like Petit and Stone supported. Jim Wayne Miller's partially autobiographical novel, *Newfound* (1989), provides one particularly revealing example of such internalized shaming over food. Narrated by a young boy named Robert, the novel chronicles his coming-of-age story, one that involves a school consolidation to a facility named West Madison and exposure to children from different socioeconomic backgrounds. When Robert first describes the school building, readers anticipate that great change awaits him:

> West Madison was very modern, bright and colorful. There were skylights in the rooms and halls; smooth tiled floors, which janitors swept with green sawdust; pink, yellow, and green rooms; desks arranged in a semicircle around the teacher's; green writing boards with yellow chalk. But [Robert] longed for Newfound School, with its old desks bolted to the oil-soaked floor, and the huge oak tree in the yard, scarred with everyone's initials. [He] yearned for the good hours when the teacher taught the other side of the room and [he] read and heard the faraway chugging of the engine and the singing of the saw as it cut through timber at the sawmill down by the creek. (97–98)

In this passage, Miller compares and contrasts Robert's reactions to the two schools, preparing readers to make their own judgments about which learning environment and set of cultural standards is preferable.

A few paragraphs later, we learn about Robert's teacher, Miss Hudspeth, a former missionary who had served in Central America and has come to similarly minister to Appalachia's children. Robert narrates that "she disapproved of our sack lunches," instead recommending a "hot nourishing meal" for "only pennies a day" (98). Apparently oblivious to the socioeconomic status of her pupils, she routinely tells the children to "be sure to tell [their] fathers and mothers" about the option of school-bought lunches (98). Such condescending advice results in substantial internal strife for Robert, as when he recalls, "I never grew accustomed to feeling shame. Each time, it flared up hotter than before, and raced from the center out, popping and cracking like a brush fire, leaving everything black and smoldering inside" (98). Here Miller uses words like "popping," "cracking," "black," and "smoldering" to describe Robert's reaction to Miss Hudspeth's teachings, words that evoke images of failed attempts at cooking. Miss Hudspeth's efforts to reshape Robert's view of the food options available to him backfire like a failed recipe, resulting only in a charred, inedible product that must be discarded.

In an even more revealing scene that chronicles the effects of Miss Hudspeth's notions about "proper" food, Robert remembers watching a film with the rest of his class called "The Wheel of Good Health." A promotional film about proper nutrition, the film admonishes children to partake daily of the "basic seven daily requirements for good nutrition" (99). To further emphasize the importance of such advice, Miss Hudspeth calls on several students and asks them what they ate for breakfast. As Robert recalls, several of the children "recited . . . bacon, eggs, toast, milk, cereal—all the lovely, approved things," but when she calls on Robert's brother, Eugene, he answers in a high voice, "Biscuits . . . and sawmill gravy . . . and molasses, *new* molasses!" (99). In a display revealing that Robert has learned the proper denigration for his own food, he emits "a half-mad, hysterical laugh [that] rose to the high ceiling of the gym and bounced back" before he realizes that the sound came from him. Upon this realization, he recalls that he "cringed down, all crumbling ashes inside, and looked to see whether anyone on either side of [him] knew Eugene was [his] brother" (99). Once again Miller's description evokes the product of an inexperienced or none-too-talented baker with phrases like "crumbling ashes," an image that aptly echoes the way Miss Hudspeth makes Robert feel about the food he and his brother consume on a daily basis: unworthy.

Although Miller's narrator feels embarrassed about the food that his brother brings to school, he immediately feels guilty for his initial reaction. At other times in the novel Robert describes mountain food with such reverence that readers understand that even if he sometimes feels ashamed of it, Appalachian cuisine comprises an important part of his cultural identity. Earlier in the novel Robert describes "tender new potatoes . . . okra and cucumbers, onions, peppers, and tomatoes from the garden," as well as sweet corn, rhubarb pie, blackberries, and a "truckload of peaches" (56). In only a few short paragraphs, Miller establishes that Robert's family does not suffer from a lack of nutritional food, and when Robert remembers picking chinquapins on the hill after school and gathering black walnuts, Miller makes clear that Robert cherishes this time spent with family. Later in the novel Robert explains that after his mother, brother, and he move in with his mother's parents, they "didn't buy as many groceries out of the store" since "[t]hey raised almost all their food" (81). These foods include "potatoes stored in a big cone-shaped mound, beneath straw . . . dried apples, ham and sausage from the smokehouse, and vegetables fresh from the garden or canned" (81–82). The kind of sustainable life that Robert describes here sounds remarkably similar to the current trend of growing one's own food, participating in CSAs (Community Supported Agriculture), and buying locally at farmers' markets and tailgate markets, a trend that well-known American author Barbara Kingsolver advocates in her best seller, *Animal, Vegetable, Miracle.*

If Robert's positive descriptions of mountain fare outweigh the shame that he feels under the scrutiny of Miss Hudspeth, then Miller also appears to overcome these kinds of negative associations with mountain food. In an essay called "From Oats to Grits, Mutton to Pork: North British Foodways in Southern Appalachia," Miller is quick to assert that

> Food is not medicine, a class marker, or a badge of discrimination (though food may be all these things to some people). I certainly no longer feel apologetic about or ashamed of any food, as Robert does in *Newfound* when his little brother recites what he ate for breakfast. I do not assume, as Robert did, that the humble fare carried from home to school was automatically inferior to "storebought" foods or food served in the school cafeteria. (71)

Notably, Miller uses the words "no longer," indicating that he did, in fact, once feel shame over the food that he brought to school. Similarly, his careful attention in remarking that "food is not . . . a class marker" suggests that he once believed that they were connected, indicating that for some people, they still are.

In her novels, Denise Giardina resists the same kind of internalized shame that Robert experiences. In *Storming Heaven* (1987), a novel that fictionalizes the Battle of Blair Mountain, Giardina repeatedly describes mountain food not to highlight the shame that consumers feel over it, but rather to elicit admiration and longing from readers. Early in the novel, one of the main characters, Carrie Bishop, takes her future husband, Albion Freeman, to a molasses making. The portrayal of the dishes served at this important social event hardly presents people in need of food. Carrie recalls that "the women set out the food on tables inside the cabin: fried chicken and salty ham, mashed potatoes swimming in butter, green beans cooked with hunks of fatback, hot pickled corn, biscuits, yellow cornbread, boiled cabbage, sweet potatoes, green poke sallet in bacon grease, fresh kale, squirrel meat with dumplings, venison steaks, groundhog, red-eye gravy, milk gravy, stack cakes, apple pies" (44–45). Carrie remembers that "when we were done eating, it was difficult to stand up" (45). The description here echoes Charles Dudley Warner's remembrance of the meal he and the Professor consumed at the Eggers family farm, but Carrie's chronicling is clearly positive, while Warner's is not. Scenes like these likely place the reader in a state of wanting, bordering on needing, to dine on the same sumptuous fare. Portrayals like this trigger feelings of curiosity about dishes such as groundhog or squirrel, while also negating beliefs that all mountain people are lacking in food (though some were and still are).

Even so, Giardina is only able to place the reader in such a vulnerable, possibly hungry, position when outside forces akin to Katherine Petit, May Stone, and Miss Hudspeth are not present. In an earlier scene in the novel narrated by Rondal Lloyd, he describes how his teacher, Miss Radcliffe, would invite her pupils to her room at the boardinghouse for tea and cookies, where she would "talk about the importance of an education, about how [the students] had the obligation to raise [themselves] above [their parents] and save [their mountain people] from ignorance" (15). Rondal remembers how different his teacher's living space was compared to his at home, noting that she led her pupils into her room "with the air of a genie revealing a treasure" (14). He goes on to explain that "she served the cookies on bone-white china, and [they] had hot tea served in delicate cups with handles so small that even a child could not get a proper grip without being burned" (15). In calling attention to the literal fact that the food Miss Radcliffe serves her pupils is somewhat dangerous, Giardina suggests that what she is teaching them during these lessons on etiquette and dining may have similarly dangerous consequences for the way they feel about their mountain heritage, including its culinary traditions.

When the tea session ends, Rondal is finally able to escape, and his description of his home—and his mother's cooking—stands in stark contrast to Miss Radcliffe's oriental rug, cookies, and tea: "When I went inside, I smelled grease. Mommy was scraping the bacon leavings in the iron skillet for gravy. I scuffed my bare feet across the gritty wood floor, sprinkled with coal dust despite Mommy's daily scrubbings. Yellowing newspapers plastered the wall to keep out the cold" (15). After revealing to his younger brothers that he has saved some of the cookies for them as a surprise after supper, Rondal remembers, "I sighed, lay back on the bed, and was glad to be home" (15). Although Rondal's home circumstances are not as plush as Miss Radcliffe's, he still prefers them, signaling to readers a stubborn resistance to any belief that would privilege her living situation—and the foods available there—over his own. And yet Rondal recognizes the value of the cookies that Miss Radcliffe offers, thoughtfully saving them for his siblings. Read metaphorically, this gesture signals to readers that mountain people are not so resistant that they shun new foods, but rather, that they want those new foods to rest on equal footing with their own.

Similarly, Gertie Nevels in Harriette Simpson Arnow's *The Dollmaker* longs for the rich meals she was able to prepare in Kentucky but not in Detroit. While in Kentucky the family eats well, even though they are poor. In one description of the meal Gertie provides for her family, Arnow urges readers to imagine sitting down to such a meal:

> Gertie, sitting at the foot of the table with a lard bucket of sweet milk on one side of her, buttermilk on the other, a great platter of hot smoking cornbread in front, and other bowls and platters within easy reach, was kept busy filling glasses with milk, buttering bread, and dishing out the hominy fried in lard and seasoned with sweet milk and black pepper. It was good with the shuck beans, baked sweet potatoes, cucumber pickles, and green tomato ketchup. Gertie served it up with pride, for everything, even the meal in the bread, was a product of her farming. (85–86)

After the family moves to Detroit so that Gertie's husband may work in the factories, however, she must purchase all of her ingredients. The narrator explains that "the buying of potatoes was a part of the never ending strangeness. Back home, no matter what the season, she had always raised enough to carry her from one potato-digging time to the next" (207). Arnow also repeatedly emphasizes the substandard quality of food that Gertie purchases in the city, and along with some other authors considered in this essay, she overturns assumptions like Warner's that food procured in urban areas is superior to dishes from rural regions.

Appalachian writer Jeff Mann showcases similar instances of culinary resistance and pride in his 2005 memoir/poetry collection, *Loving Mountains, Loving Men*. In this text he discusses the reality of living as an openly gay man in Appalachia, and he claims that "being gay and being Appalachian sometimes feel to me like mutually exclusive states of identity" (102). Yet mountain food seems to bridge such identity gaps, or at least to begin a path between those two disparate points. In an essay titled "Ephemera," Mann writes about a young man named Justen who plans to move to Los Angeles because "he was openly gay in his home county and now feels that he cannot return there safely" (127). At the end of the essay, Mann warns Justen to be careful in Los Angeles, extending him a standing invitation to visit in West Virginia: "If you come home missing West Virginia food, you don't have to go back to Boone County to get it. Fuck Boone County, or at least those in Boone County who were cruel to you. Come here, and we'll feed you brown beans and cornbread, chowchow, wilted lettuce, new peas and potatoes, ramps and creecy greens, biscuits and gravy" (132). Not only does Mann celebrate mountain food as do many other Appalachian authors, but he also uses it as a way to heal wounds inflicted by prejudice.

In the same way that Denise Giardina's descriptions of food in *Storming Heaven* provide a resistant response to descriptions found in Warner's *On Horseback*, so too do certain scenes in *Loving Mountains, Loving Men*. When Warner and the Professor arrive in Asheville, Warner demonstrates an obvious bias for city living and the food it provides. Almost one hundred and twenty years later, Mann overturns such bias when contemplating the food options available to urban Appalachians living in metropolitan areas like Washington, D.C.: "I have a sudden, painful vision of expatriate queer Appalachians in their tiny, overpriced apartments yearning for good biscuits, barbecue, and bowls of greens. Beet greens, collard greens, mustard greens, turnip greens, kale. My father has grown them all. They are the sort of rough, filling, healthy, cheap food that poor people eat. True folk food" (147). Mann's assertion that such greens are the "cheap food that poor people eat" indicates no shame based on class status but instead venerates such food and people. The fairly recent craze over such local, healthy food has plenty of middle- and upper-class Americans emulating the ways of "the folk." Perhaps as Emily Satterwhite suggests in *Dear Appalachia*, doing so helps these consumers imagine "Appalachia as an enchanting place apart, a world protected from the worst aspects of contemporary and commercial life" (219). Thus by partaking of the food associated with the region, consumers can at least partially soothe concerns that permeate the postmodern condition.

In the final section of *Loving Mountains, Loving Men*, Mann features several poems about food, including pieces titled "Ramps," "Creecy Greens," and "Chowchow," that may be read as an antidote for the detached relationship many Americans have with the food that they eat. In a poem called "Goldenrod Seeds" the narrator reveals,

Feasts are what
I remember most, dinner tables where
good food was love made solid
offered by those too shy or proud to speak it. (lines 5–8)

Later in the poem he lists buttermilk biscuits, country ham, and blackberry
cobblers as examples of the "good food" he references, but Mann's food poems
extend beyond praising mountain foods; they stand as a testament to the
necessity of such food, both for physical and cultural sustenance. In "Civilization Comes to Summers County," the speaker asks, "Our grandparents
used to gather ramps / and creecy greens, boil down sorghum, / can tomatoes,
peppers, chowchow, beans. / Who needs all that now?" (11–14) Considered
together, the poems assert that readers all need that now, whether Appalachian or not. Readers need it to remember the history of the mountain South
and also to preserve the mountains and their culture for future generations.
In "Maple Syrup," the speaker realizes the importance of such syrup, because
while "[a]t fourteen maple syrup was nothing special," as an adult the speaker
realizes that it is a "costly" and "precious" commodity, one that allows him to
"bite into . . . history" (1.8, 1.24, 1.27). And in "Ramps," the speaker contends
that "ramps remember the wild asleep / beneath our skin, a rich green wild
/ we hungrily take in and taste again, / while another Wal-Mart goes up, /
another well runs dry, draglines slice off / the breast of another mountaintop"
(25–30). In this poem, Mann introduces the issue of Mountaintop Removal
(MTR), implying that while ramps "remember" the "rich green wild," if coal
companies continue to blow up mountains at such an alarming rate[3], ramps—
along with numerous other plant and animal species, not to mention home-
steads and the streams that support them—will vanish. Thus Mann not only
celebrates Appalachian food, but he also uses food descriptions to emphasize
the importance of the literal mountains that sustain these Appalachian culinary traditions.

The dynamics explored in this essay occur numerous times in Appalachian literature, and it seems that for every instance of shame associated with
food, authors provide yet another example of stubborn pride and resistance,
with an invitation for readers to join them at the table. Interestingly, this praise
for traditional mountain foods is finding its way into mainstream Americana,
and it is being celebrated. Imagine my surprise, for example, when I stum-
bled upon ramps for sale at a Whole Foods in Baton Rouge in 2006. They
were $19.99 a pound. Numerous other examples abound, including morels,
ginseng, and so on. The Appalachian Sustainable Agriculture Project (http://
www.buyappalachian.org) contains pages of information for consumers in

southern Appalachia who want to shop at tailgate markets, join a CSA, buy local baked goods, and support restaurants that serve local fare.

Some cities in Appalachia are gaining reputations as culinary destinations, yet as folklorist Lucy Long points out, the popular restaurants in these towns do not appear to "celebrat[e] Appalachian food so much as [they celebrate] food being created in a specific and unique area of Appalachia" (15). She goes on to posit that "the emphasis on local produce does not attempt to connect that produce with the cultural heritage of the area. In fact, that heritage seems to be forgotten so that neither the hillbilly stereotype nor the romanticized Elizabethan ancestor image is referenced in this celebration" (15). In her analysis of Asheville, North Carolina, as a "foodscape," Long perhaps too optimistically concludes, "[C]ulinary tourism has created a public identification of Appalachia as a distinctive cultural region that is no longer 'Other' to mainstream America, but a potential centering for a new American identity" (18). Yet careful analysis of current media images of Appalachia coupled with recent literary portrayals of the food made available to many Appalachian people—especially those who occupy lower positions on the class hierarchy—reveals that Appalachia still firmly occupies the position of Other to both the South and the rest of the nation, and food still plays an integral role in that Othering.

Diane Sawyer's 2009 *20/20* special, "A Hidden America: Children of the Mountains," for example, coined the stigmatizing term "Mountain Dew Mouth" to describe the cavity-laden teeth of many central Appalachian children. Although sugary soda hardly comprises part of a healthy diet, many Americans believe that consumption of such products also says something unsavory about the consumer. As scholar and Appalachian Shannon Brooks attests, mountain people are well aware of the social judgments associated with food preference, and she explains that when she went to college she "managed to rub out [her] accent, replace Flatt and Scruggs with Mozart and Bach, and [give] up Mountain Dew for white zinfandel" (159). Brooks's statement indicates that she had some level of control over the food choices she made, but not all Appalachians can assimilate their preferences.

Ron Rash's 2010 short story collection, *Burning Bright*, includes a story called "The Ascent" about a little boy named Jared whose parents are addicted to methamphetamines. Because his parents are focused solely on acquiring their next high, Jared subsists on cereal, the kind "with a green leprechaun on the front" and milk (83). Another story in the collection, "Back of Beyond," depicts a similar plotline about a western North Carolina couple whose meth-addicted son has made them afraid to return to their home. As a result, they live in an unheated trailer where a relative named Parson finds "cereal boxes, some open, some not, [and] a half-gallon milk container, its contents frozen solid. The room's busted-out window help[s] explain why" (28). The characters Rash describes, people who are literally living on cereal, are not portrayed as ignorant hillbillies unaware of proper nutrition. Instead, Rash renders them as individuals whose lives are being destroyed by a family member's addiction. In these stories readers will not find celebratory descriptions of culinary resistance or depictions of locavores selecting kale at the weekly tailgate market, but instead grim descriptions of the food made available to people who live with addiction while also subsisting near or below the poverty line. Rash's portrayals do not deny the association between food, social class, and mountain people, but unlike past implications that suggest some inherent character flaw based on food preference, Rash's stories point to the much larger social issues of addiction, poverty, and their food-related consequences.

A kind of reversal has happened during the last century. Petit and Stone scoffed at traditional foods and encouraged "technologically advanced" soda bread and biscuits, but now processed foods socially place mountain people in the same way that traditional foods once did. Consuming large quantities of processed foods does not support a healthy lifestyle, but the judgments about mountain people that accompany these products date back to the late 1800s, suggesting that those bent on criticizing Appalachian people have long relied on a rotating menu of Appalachian foods to do so. From travel writers and local colorists whose writing supported such judgments to mid-late twentieth century Appalachian authors whose work rails against them to contemporary writers whose portrayals lay bare the sometimes painful details that explain particular food choices, examining how authors depict food in Appalachian literature reveals a troubling narrative, one that helps explain the national insistence on putting Appalachia in its place.

Notes

1. For a brief listing of such work, see *Appalachia in the Making: The Mountain South in the Nineteenth Century; Backtalk from Appalachia: Confronting Stereotypes; Hillbilly: A Cultural History of an American Icon.*

2. For more information about the history of the American Missionary Association and their coining of the term "mountain white," see Chris Green's *The Social Life of Poetry: Appalachia, Race, and Radical Modernism.*

3. For more information about MTR, see www.ilovemountains.org; there are also multiple other scholarly publications available on this topic.

Works Cited

"A Hidden America: Children of the Mountains." *20/20* ABC. 10 Feb. 2009. Television.

Appalachian Sustainable Agriculture Project. *Appalachian Sustainable Agriculture Project.* 2011. Web. 2 Jul. 2011.

Arnow, Harriette Simpson. *The Dollmaker.* 1954. New York: Perennial, 2003.

Batteau, Allen. *The Invention of Appalachia.* Tucson: U of Arizona P, 1990.

Billings, Dwight, Gurney Norman, and Katherine Ledford, eds. *Back Talk from Appalachia: Confronting Stereotypes.* Lexington: UP of Kentucky, 1999.

Brooks, Shannon. "Coming Home: Finding my Appalachian Mothers through Emma Bell Miles." *NWSA Journal* 11.3 (1999): 157–71.

Cunningham, Rodger. "Writing on the Cusp: Double Alterity and Minority Discourse in Appalachia." *The Future of Southern Letters.* Eds. Jefferson Humphries and John Lowe. New York: Oxford UP, 1996. 41–53.

Engelhardt, Elizabeth S. D. *A Mess of Greens: Southern Gender and Southern Food.* Athens: U of Georgia P, 2011.

———. "Beating the Biscuits in Appalachia: Race, Class, and Gender Politics of Women Baking Bread." *Cornbread Nation 3: Foods of the Mountain South.* Ed. Ronni Lundy. Chapel Hill: U of North Carolina P, 2005. 32–46.

Fox, John, Jr. *The Little Shepard of Kingdom Come.* New York: Grosset & Dunlap, 1903.

———. *The Trail of Lonesome Pine.* New York: Charles Scribner's Sons, 1908.

Frost, William Goodell. "Our Contemporary Ancestors in the Southern Mountains." *The Atlantic Monthly* 83.497 March (1899): 311–19.

Giardina, Denise. *Storming Heaven.* New York: W.W. Norton & Company, 1987.

Green, Chris. *The Social Life of Poetry: Appalachia, Race, and Radical Modernism.* New York: Palgrave Macmillan, 2009.

Harkins, Anthony. *Hillbilly: A Cultural History of an American Icon.* Oxford: Oxford UP, 2004.

Harney, Will Wallace. "A Strange Land and a Peculiar People." *Lippincott's Magazine* 12 October (1873): 429–38.

iLoveMountains.org. *iLoveMountains.org.* Web. 3 Jul. 2011.

Kingsolver, Barbara. *Animal, Vegetable, Miracle: A Year of Food Life.* New York: Harper Perennial, 2007.

Leach, Eugene E. "Charles Dudley Warner's 'Little Journey in the World.'" *The New England Quarterly* 53.3 (1980): 329–44. Web *JSTOR*.12 June 2012.

Long, Lucy M. "Culinary Tourism and the Emergence of an Appalachian Cuisine: Exploring the 'Foodscape' of Asheville, NC." *North Carolina Folklore Journal* 57.1 (2010): 4–19.

Lundy, Ronni, ed. *Cornbread Nation 3: Foods of the Mountain South.* Chapel Hill: U of North Carolina P, 2005.

Mann, Jeff. *Loving Mountains, Loving Men.* Athens: Ohio UP, 2005.

Miller, Jim Wayne. "From Oats to Grits, Mutton to Pork: North British Foodways in Southern Appalachia." *Cornbread Nation 3: Foods of the Mountain South.* Ed. Ronni Lundy. Chapel Hill: U of North Carolina P, 2005. 59–71.

———. *Newfound.* New York, NY: Orchard Books, 1989.

Pool, Maria Louise. *In Buncombe County*. New York: Duffield & Company, 1906.

Pudup, Mary Beth, Dwight B. Billings, and Altina L. Waller, eds. *Appalachia in the Making: The Mountain South in the Nineteenth Century*. Chapel Hill: U of North Carolina P, 1995.

Rash, Ron. *Burning Bright*. New York: Ecco, 2010.

Ray, Janisse. "Syrup Boiling." *Cornbread Nation 3: Foods of the Mountain South*. Ed. Ronni Lundy. Chapel Hill: U of North Carolina P, 2005. 144–48.

Reusing, Andrea. "Asparagus and Ramp Skillet Soufflé." *The Wall Street Journal*, 28–29 May 2011, Cooking & Eating: D7.

Satterwhite, Emily. *Dear Appalachia: Readers, Identity, and Popular Fiction Since 1878*. Lexington: UP of Kentucky, 2011.

Shapiro, Henry. *Appalachia on Our Minds: The Southern Mountains and Mountaineers in the American Consciousness, 1870–1920*. Chapel Hill: U of North Carolina P, 1978.

Smith, Lee. *Oral History*. 1983. New York: Ballantine Books, 1984.

Warner, Charles Dudley. *On Horseback: Tour in Virginia, North Carolina, and Tennessee, with Notes of Travel in Mexico and California*. Boston: Houghton, Mifflin, and Company, 1888.

Williams, Cratis. "The Southern Mountaineer in Fact and Fiction: Part I–IV." *Appalachian Journal* 3.13.4 (1975–76): 8–61, 100–162, 186–261, 334–92.

Chapter Nine

INVISIBLE IN THE KITCHEN
Racial Intimacy, Domestic Labor, and Civil Rights

DAVID A. DAVIS

In the homes and lives of middle-class white southerners through the middle of the twentieth century, black women were both ubiquitous and invisible. Other than field work, domestic labor was the occupation most readily available to black women, and generations of black women, from the earliest days of slavery to the last days of the civil rights movement, worked in the homes of white families. Many white children formed powerful maternal attachments to their black domestic workers that rivaled, if not displaced, their attachments to their actual mothers. Black domestic workers provided food, childcare, domestic stability, and maternal presence for white households, but the relationship was usually unilateral because domestic workers received little money, respect, or genuine affection from the families they served. The asymmetrical intimacy in these relationships has been frequently portrayed in literature, and some of the most iconic characters include Aunt Chloe in *Uncle Tom's Cabin* (1852), Dilsey in *The Sound and the Fury* (1929), Mammy in *Gone with the Wind* (1936), and Calpurnia in *To Kill a Mockingbird* (1960). In each of these novels written before the civil rights movement, the black domestic worker is the invisible center of the white family, and the character contributes substantially to the book's plot, but the character's condition does not change from the beginning to the end of the book. They are part of the book, but the book is not about them—they are ubiquitous and invisible.

Three contemporary novels by white southern women, however, focus specifically on the relationships between white families and black domestic workers. In Ellen Douglas's *Can't Quit You, Baby* (1989) Cornelia O'Kelley eventually realizes after her husband dies and her children leave home that her most meaningful relationship is with her cook, Julia "Tweet" Carrier, with whom she has silently shared a kitchen for decades. In Minrose Gwin's *The*

Queen of Palmyra (2010), young Florence Forest, whose father is a Klansman and whose mother is emotionally unstable, finds comfort in her grandmother's kitchen from the cook, Zenobia Johnson. And in Kathryn Stockett's *The Help* (2009), Skeeter Phelan interviews domestic workers in Jackson, Mississippi, to embarrass the racist Junior League and to further her writing career. These books reimagine intimate relationships between white women and black domestic workers during the civil rights movement, making black domestic workers visible during a period of racial tension and bringing a social movement into the white domestic space. By making the invisible visible, they challenge the established trope of the black woman in the white kitchen.

Intimate Kitchens

Can't Quit You, Baby opens with Cornelia and Tweet sitting together in the kitchen preparing fig preserves and carrying on a conversation. If the two women were white, then they might have been equals and friends, but "there is no getting around [...] that the black woman is the white woman's servant. There would have been no way in that time and place—the nineteen sixties and seventies in Mississippi—for them to get acquainted, except across the kitchen table from each other, shelling peas, peeling apples, polishing silver" (4–5). The proximity of white and black women in the kitchen was the closest form of interracial contact (with the exception of interracial sex) in the segregated South. In *Black and White Women of the Old South*, Minrose Gwin calls the relationship between black domestic workers and their white women employers a "peculiar sisterhood." The sisterhood emerged in the fraught mistress and slave or servant relationships of the nineteenth-century South, and "in modern fiction they become the *idea* of the terrible duality in human nature, the mysterious connection between human need for recognition and human desire to reject that need" (171). The dynamics of these intimate but unequal relationships is the product of a labor arrangement, a legacy of racism, and a vestige of slavery.

The roles that black domestic workers played in twentieth-century southern homes and the complex dynamics that defined their relationships evolved from the duties of slave house servants "who lived and worked intimately with their white folks in the Big House," as Eugene Genovese explains in *Roll, Jordan, Roll* (332). Within the plantation household, house servants performed laborious domestic tasks. On small farms, they worked side by side with the white family, sometimes going into the fields when necessary and often sleeping on pallets in the family's living quarters. On larger plantations, tasks tended to be more specialized, and a cook might have dominion of a large kitchen and a cadre of assistants and might challenge the plantation mistress's authority over the household (Fox-Genovese 160). The most enduring image of the house servant is the mammy, an essentialized figure with exaggerated maternal features who selflessly nurses white children and who is embedded in the southern imagination (Wallace-Sanders 2). Twentieth-century domestic workers, like their nineteenth-century predecessors, worked every day in direct proximity to a white family, usually under the direction of a white woman employer and with responsibility for most domestic labor, including many maternal chores. These roles generated a set of complicated intimate attachments because black domestic workers shared physical space with whites and performed tasks that required personal contact—cooking food, cleaning bedrooms and bathrooms, washing clothes, changing diapers, and sometimes wet-nursing babies.

Through the second half of the twentieth century, the kitchen in the homes of white southerners tended to be a gendered and racialized space, a room within the white home where an African American woman performed domestic labor. The kitchen is a culturally significant space because, as Diane Spain argues in *Gendered Spaces*, architecture conveys social status and "gendered spaces shape, and are shaped by, daily activities" (28). From colonial times through the 1970s, the kitchens in southern homes were typically small, utilitarian spaces at the back of the house, at the margins of the domestic space, and they were designed for food preparation, not as public spaces for entertaining guests. John Vlach explains that antebellum kitchens were moved out of the home partly for practical reasons of fire suppression and temperature control and partly because "moving such an essential home-making function as cooking out of one's house established a clearer separation between those who served and those who were served" (43). Technology made the detached kitchen less practical over time, but it did not change the essential function of the kitchen as a locus of domestic labor. Southern kitchens were a black space within the white home.

Black and white women came into close contact in the kitchen, which generated a complicated set of social bonds based on proximity and intimacy. Because black women performed many of the domestic tasks ordinarily fulfilled by a wife or mother, the black domestic worker often destabilized the traditional structure of the nuclear family, acting as a surrogate mother to the children, a surrogate wife to the father, and as an employee and challenger to the wife. Patricia Yeager comments that "this created a series of 'mercenary' extended families, 'kinlike' affiliations that [. . .] operated outside the constraints and freedoms shared by blood kin [and] created relations of unmitigated complexity" (188). These relations were complex because the color line operated within the white home, relegating black domestic workers to inferior status even as they asserted authority over many aspects of the family. Literary critics often focus attention specifically on the role of black domestic workers as maternal figures, but the fundamental role of most black domestic workers was as food preparers who interacted with the white family primarily from their space in the kitchen. According to Trudier Harris, "the kitchen is the 'natural' place for the domestic to be, for surely cooking is a major and time-consuming duty. But the kitchen is also the one room in the house where the white woman can give up spatial ownership without compromising herself [...] passing that particular space on to the domestic is a royal decree of her subservience and inferiority" (15).

These contemporary novels about domestic race relations feature the kitchen as the most intimate space within the home. "Entering the kitchens of contemporary southern women's narrative," Minrose Gwin writes in "Sweeping the Kitchen," "means exploring a space which has been physically, psychologically, and culturally confining for women—a tight squeeze" (56). This tight squeeze can be understood as a form of asymmetrical intimacy. Lauren Berlant argues that the intimate sphere couples the bourgeois public sphere with the domestic private sphere in a set of relations that are dynamic and asymmetrical, and she asserts that this coupling is evident in the traditionally gendered division of labor, which, although based on a Victorian fantasy, continues to organize social and spatial division. Berlant's notion, while useful, does not factor in the additional complication of racial difference in the segregated South, which amplifies the problems of the domestic sphere because of the inherent inequality between the women sharing the space. Susan Stanford Friedman's theory of the cultural geography of the encounter between women at different levels of stratification "requires acknowledging how privilege and oppression are not absolute categories but rather shift in relation to different axes of power and powerlessness" (40). The intimate relations within the kitchen of the white home were inherently not reciprocal; black domestic workers often learned the most private details of their employers' lives and sometimes earned the trust of their employers, but the domestic worker was on the outside margins of the family's domestic sphere. White families frequently described their domestic workers as "like one of the family," to borrow the title of Alice Childress's collection of stories about black domestics, but the word "like" is a crucial qualifier in this statement—no one else in the family ate alone in the kitchen.

The segregated kitchen was the site of complex social dynamics and racial hierarchy governed by a delicate set of rules and mores. The editors of *The Maid Narratives* enumerate these rules (15), but usually, these rules were unstated, and Minny Jackson's mother in *The Help* explains them to her when she takes her first job. They include staying out of the white lady's business; "don't you ever let that White Lady find you sitting on her toilet"; "when you're cooking white people's food, you taste it with a different spoon"; "you use the same cup, same fork, and same plate every day"; "you eat in the kitchen"; "you don't hit on her children"; and "no sass-mouthing" (38–39). The rules she outlines enforce deferential behavior within the white household to maintain social hierarchy and physical separation between the races within the intimate space of the kitchen. They reflect the "contradictory desires among whites striving to distance themselves from an 'inferior' race, but dependent upon the very same people to perform the most intimate labor in their homes" (Hunter 105).

This asymmetrical intimacy belies the fact that the white southern domestic sphere is the product of black labor. Crisp white sheets, starched and pressed shirts, gleaming polished silver, sparkling bathrooms, platters of fried chicken and pork chops, every imaginable vegetable simmered with smoked ham hocks, decadent cakes and pies, and all of the other markers of middle-class status in the South are the result of black women's work, so to recognize class status in the South is to encounter the ubiquitous invisibility of black women. This issue is particularly clear in regard to food because eating food prepared by a domestic worker is literally consuming her labor, relishing the products of a supposedly inferior person. In addition to maintaining social hierarchy by enforcing racial deference, the protocols of the kitchen contained the contradictory appetites and revulsions of the white family toward the black domestic worker, the simultaneous urge to project maternal or familial attachment onto her and to see her as an inferior other. Lillian Smith recalls learning "to use a soft voice to oil my words of superiority" toward the domestic worker who cooked for her family and raised her (29). By veiling the exploitation inherent in the relationship, though, soft words protect her more than they protect the domestic worker.

These three novels, however, hinge on the white protagonist's realization of inequality in the kitchen. Florence Forest in *The Queen of Palmyra*, for example, describes Zenie as entering the kitchen and putting her apron on "like you'd harness an ox to a plow. The apron isn't part of her; she hates it" (90). She recognizes that Zenie labors and that she has a sense of self beyond being a domestic worker. Like most domestic workers, when Zenie serves the family a meal, she sits in the kitchen while the family eats, and after she clears the table, she eats alone in the kitchen. Florence comes to the verge of realizing the bitterest irony of kitchen intimacy, that domestic workers, as Rebecca

Sharpless explains in *Cooking in Other Women's Kitchens*, "were good enough to prepare food but not good enough to eat it in the company of their employers" (143). Of all the rules Minny's mother taught her, most of them concern maintaining a cordon sanitaire between her food and the family's food. The prohibition on commensality was the most sacred rule in white homes; to violate it would have been unthinkable.

Black domestic workers did, though, find ways to resist the rules of hierarchy. Psyche Williams-Forson explains in *Building Houses Out of Chicken Legs* that black women were able to use their cooking ability outside of white homes to assert their economic agency, but such entrepreneurial opportunities were often scarce, and many black women had no choice but to work in white homes. Domestic workers in white homes typically wore masks, to use Frantz Fanon's term from *Black Skin, White Masks*, to project an appearance of deference while repressing their inner state of mind. Because of their proximity to the white family, they could often create a small sphere of agency to manage or negotiate their employers' expectations, and they could also use their limited economic agency to quit an unacceptable position. Stockett's novel depicts an outrageous act of resistance in which Minny Jackson bakes a chocolate custard pie for her employer's devious daughter, Hilly Holbrook, that contains her own shit, and she violates the cordon sanitaire so dramatically that Hilly cannot retaliate without humiliating herself. Minny's act of resistance, however, does not prevent her from being fired from her job and neither does it change the asymmetrical intimacy of domestic work.

Domestic Civil Rights

In *Domesticity and Dirt*, Phyllis Palmer offers a couple of startling statistics about domestic workers in Jackson, Mississippi, in 1940: 81 percent of white households employed a domestic worker and more than 60 percent of black women were employed as domestic workers. The numbers in Jackson could have been higher than average, but even allowing for variations across the South, the majority of southerners were involved in the employer and servant relationship, and most white southerners, with the exception of the poorest families, shared their kitchens with a black woman. During the civil rights movement, kitchens were an important space because they were the point of the most intimate racial contact in the segregated South. Conflict in the public sphere often raised tension within the domestic sphere, placing domestic workers in an extremely precarious position. Sit-ins focused national attention on the prohibitions on commensality in public, but although some domestic workers actively supported marches and demonstrations, they were not often able to agitate within their employers' homes, so they continued to eat in the kitchen.

These three novels are set in Mississippi during the movement, possibly the most violent and most dangerous state for African Americans, and the tension plays a crucial role in the plot development. *The Help* mentions several important events, including James Meredith integrating Ole Miss, the March on Washington for Freedom and Jobs, and the assassination of Medgar Evers. None of these events are directly involved in the book, but they place the story in context. *Can't Quit You, Baby* is set a bit later, and the assassination of Martin Luther King, Jr., leads to a pivotal confrontation between Cornelia and Tweet, but Tweet is not an activist. *The Queen of Palmyra* places the movement at the center of the text, and the major confrontation in the novel pits Florence's Klansman father against Zenie's activist niece, Eva, colliding the public sphere with the domestic sphere.

Setting the novels during the movement destabilizes the social hierarchy in the kitchen, but the crucial destabilization affects the white characters more than the black characters. The spectacle of black people asserting their rights in public leads the white protagonists to realize that their privilege requires the exploitation of black people, specifically their domestic workers. Skeeter in *The Help* pitches her book of interviews with maids by explaining to her editor that "we love them and they love us, yet [...] we won't even allow them to use the toilet in the house. [We] glorified [the] Mammy figure who dedicates her whole life to a white family. Margaret Mitchell covered that. But no one ever asked Mammy how she felt about it" (106). Her book would ostensibly contribute to the movement by telling how "Mammy" felt, but it is even more significant to the plot of the novel that Skeeter has broken with her social clique to recognize that the domestic workers are exploited within the white household. On the night of Medgar Evers's murder, Florence in *The Queen of Palmyra* goes to Zenie's house, where Zenie's niece, Eva, suggests that Florence's father may have been involved in the murder and tells her to go away, which finally makes clear to her that her father's racial antipathy is deadly and causes her to withdraw from him.

Florence goes to Zenie's home on several occasions, but she is a child and has a greater degree of social mobility than most white people. Ordinarily, white people rarely entered black homes, and even then only by necessity. Susan Tucker explains that after Emancipation black domestic workers, who had normally lived in the homes of their employers, preferred the arrangement of living out, where they occupied a home separate from the white family and where they could establish a relative degree of autonomy. This arrangement created entirely separate spheres between black homes and white homes, and Tucker comments that, although blacks knew all of the intimate details of white home life, "whites knew little of black home life" (73). White people in black homes distorted the dynamics that governed the presence of black women in white homes. Skeeter enters the home of Aibileen Clark to interview her for the book because she cannot interview her in her employer's kitchen. When Skeeter comes to her home, Aibileen wears a formal dress, serves tea formally in the living room, and trembles with nervousness because she has "never had a white person in [her] house before" (144). Aibileen, who has internalized the culture of deference, cannot negotiate the change in dynamics, the intimacy of a white person in her own home. After a short exchange, Aibileen is overcome with fear and goes to the bathroom to vomit.

Aibileen likely feels that her home has been violated, even though she invited Skeeter to be there. Rebecca Sharpless explains that "for many African American women, their own homes represented an autonomy that living in their employers' households simply did not afford" (90). She cites bell hooks's idea from *Yearning* that home ownership for blacks had a radical political dimension because it allowed blacks a space of personal agency and self-determination outside the white domestic sphere (hooks 41–50). Zenie and her husband, Ray, saved their money to purchase a Jim Walter home, a prefabricated structure assembled on site. Although the home came without interior doors, Zenie and Ray are proud of the accomplishment it represents, a domestic sphere on par with her employer's home. The emergence of a black domestic sphere was one of the most significant consequences of Emancipation, although it was sometimes subject to white intervention. Creating space for black agency within the public sphere was the challenge of the civil rights movement.

Can't Quit You, Baby pivots on the intersection of the black domestic sphere and the white domestic sphere. Cornelia barges into Tweet's house on the day of Martin Luther King's assassination intending to share her condolences in a clumsy way. It proves to be a pivotal moment not because it brings Cornelia and Tweet together, but because Cornelia sees a barrette Tweet stole from her "on the coffee table, gleaming like a round gold target, like the bauble a hypnotist uses to subdue his subject's will" (99). The barrette comes as a shock. This is the first scene in the book where Cornelia enters Tweet's home, although the book says that she has been "in Tweet's house many times," and she forces her way in without waiting for an invitation (99). Most likely, on all the other occasions she had come into her house, she came as an employer there to pick up or drop off Tweet. She adopts the same pose of authority when she comes to commiserate over King's assassination, projecting the white authority onto the black domestic sphere, and Tweet cannot even acknowledge her. The fact that she came there to console Tweet over the death of Dr. King, the symbolic end of the civil rights movement, yet still asserts authority over Tweet's home indicates the rigid nature of asymmetrical intimacy.

Challenging the social hierarchy of the white domestic sphere required a broad spectrum of outside forces. In *The Help*, Skeeter publishes a book of interviews with the maids of Jackson who tell intimate stories about life in white households that embarrass many of the white families. She publishes the book anonymously, gives the maids pseudonyms, and blackmails the town's most malicious junior leaguer, Hilly Holbrook, to protect the maids who shared their stories. Ostensibly, the book is supposed to contribute to the civil rights movement in some way, but its actual impact is negligible, partly because of the book's anonymity. It misses an opportunity to bring the white domestic sphere into the public sphere. Protests, sit-ins, marches, and demonstrations had exposed the living and working conditions of African Americans in the South to the rest of the nation, which yielded some tangible results, but Skeeter's book has no results other than to get Aibileen Clark, the domestic worker who helped her most, fired from her job.

The civil rights movement did have a major impact on black domestic workers but not in a spectacular way. Beginning with the integration of war industries in World War II, more employment opportunities became available to black women, starting a trend of black women leaving white kitchens to work in factories or government service. The Civil Rights Act of 1964 outlawed discrimination in hiring practices and opened the labor market to black women, and thousands left their domestic jobs for opportunities elsewhere. Many of the new jobs were menial and low paying, but former domestic workers preferred the relative freedom of hourly employment in public to working in the confining intimacy of the white kitchen. The number of black women working in white households dropped precipitously in the second half of the twentieth century: 60 percent in 1940, 36 percent in 1960, and 7 percent in 1980 (Sharpless 179). There were no demonstrations in the kitchen, but when the opportunity emerged, the domestic workers left.

Transgressive Friendships

The social dynamics of the civil rights movement contribute to the plots of these three novels, but that does not entirely explain why the authors chose to set the books during the movement. The books were all published long after the movement ended, so none actually contributed to racial equality, except for creating a contemporary dialogue about race. These books allow both the authors and the readers to revisit, reimagine, and revise life in the southern home during the civil rights movement by creating relationships between white and black women that transgress the established racial hierarchy. In *Advancing Sisterhood?*, Sharon Monteith argues that these interracial friendships, which occur frequently in contemporary southern fiction, "work microhistorically to expose the context in which friendship may be seen as transgressive, trespassing the borders of what is socially expected or countenanced" (2–3).

These transgressive friendships follow a common motif in southern literature, one made paradigmatic in *Adventures of Huckleberry Finn*, but these novels shift the racial dynamics from slavery to civil rights, move the setting from a raft on the Mississippi River to kitchens in Mississippi, and change the characters' gender from men to women. Like Huck Finn, however, the white female protagonists are all marginalized from the white hegemony, some by will and some by force. Cornelia's friendship with Tweet actually begins after her husband dies and she leaves the South, Skeeter is the only unmarried member of her social circle, and Florence is a poor white girl with middle-class grandparents. Because of their marginalization, they can identify with the domestic workers, but only after they first recognize their own marginalization. Also like Huck Finn, the white characters are the protagonists, and the key theme in each of the novels is their developing racial attitudes. The transgressive interracial relationships in these novels are more transgressive for the white characters than for the black characters, although the relationships put the black characters at greater risk. Because these transgressive friendships challenge the social hierarchy, both parties are subject to retributive consequences, and the black domestic workers suffer more than the white women. At the end of the novels, the black domestic workers are fired, maimed, or dead.

The transgressive friendship, however, releases the white protagonists from the racist, masculinist hierarchy that marginalizes them. In *Can't Quit You, Baby*, Cornelia lapses into deep depression after her husband dies because she realizes that she spent her life following her mother's expectations that she replicate the roles of housewifery and motherhood that were appropriate for southern women. She yearns for the romance and adventure that she expected to find with her husband but that eluded her. While living with her daughter in New York, she hears Tweet's voice in her head, the voice that she deliberately ignored for decades, and it helps her find mental clarity. A couple of days later, she gets a phone call from Tweet's daughter who tells her that she has had a stroke in her own home and has burned her hand badly in a pot of greens she was cooking, and the same day Cornelia has sex with a man for the first time since her husband's death. The bizarre juxtaposition of Tweet's injury and Cornelia's release is part of a recurring pattern. In *The Help*, Aibileen Clark is fired from her job at the same time that Skeeter Phelan gets a job offer in New York that allows her to leave her stifling life in Jackson. In *The Queen of Palmyra*, Florence leaves Mississippi to live in New Orleans, where she represses the memories of her childhood, and Zenie dies while she is away. She recovers the memory of her childhood one day while teaching when she diagrams a sentence that Zenie's niece, Eva, taught her. She remembers that her grandmother took her to New Orleans because her father murdered Eva and that she witnessed the murder.

The Queen of Palmyra does not resolve neatly. After Florence realizes that she witnessed Eva's murder, she has complicated feelings of rage, guilt, and remorse. She confronts her elderly father, who symbolizes the patriarchal, racist South of her childhood, and she also realizes that she has been indirectly complicit in the hierarchy that he embodies, which leads her to contemplate suicide. She considers driving into the Gulf of Mexico as a hurricane approaches, but she decides against it, choosing instead to find a way to continue living. Her experience of intimacy in the kitchens of her childhood has extreme consequences, but the key point is that it does not have a happy ending for either the white or the black characters. The ending for Florence may have been happier if she found a way to keep her memories sublimated or if she learned how to commit herself to racial hierarchy, but she cannot. Because she recognizes that her most meaningful relationships are embedded in a matrix of racism, exploitation, and violence, the transgressive friendship has painful consequences for Florence even as it releases her from the region's social hegemony.

The transgressive friendships based on asymmetrical intimacy within the southern social hierarchy are too fraught to lead to happy endings because release from hegemony does not mean freedom. It means recognizing one's complicity with the systematic exploitation of domestic workers, which undercuts the sincerity of the relationship and causes feelings of guilt in the white protagonist. It also means rejecting the privileges of whiteness in the segregated South. At the end of *Can't Quit You, Baby*, Cornelia and Tweet achieve a form of rapprochement based on equality, but it takes place long after Tweet has left Cornelia's kitchen, ending the employer and servant relationship that had determined their lives together. The book culminates with Tweet and Cornelia admitting that they hate each other: "Hated you, Tweet says. She rocks back, leans forward in her chair. You ain't got *sense* enough to know I hated you. I hate you all my life, before I even know you. [. . .] I hate you, hate you, hate you. And I steal that gold barrette to remind me of it, in case I forget" (254). Cornelia responds, "Damn you, then. I hate you, too" (254). For a black domestic worker to hate her white employer is not unusual. In *From Mammies to Militants*, Trudier Harris discusses several stories in which domestic workers imagine killing their employers, but the hatred and the violent imaginings usually stay sublimated because the power dynamic will not tolerate disruption. The fact that Tweet and Cornelia can voice their feelings for each other and that they can temper their mutual animosity with a degree of mutual respect and genuine affection signals the possibility of equality between the women. The social hierarchy still privileges Cornelia, of course, and the equality exists primarily because Cornelia has voluntarily and temporarily subordinated herself, but it still suggests a possibility. Notably, this exchange does not take place in Cornelia's kitchen, a space in which Tweet would never have the agency to tell Cornelia that she hated her, so technically, the kitchen as a white domestic space is not integrated in this book.

The Help also has a complicated resolution, but it deviates significantly in its depiction of the problems the transgressive friendship creates for the white protagonist. With the encouragement of Aibileen and Minny, Skeeter accepts a job offer in New York, and Aibileen feels "so happy for" her to be beginning her life over in the city (437). Meanwhile, in Jackson, Minny's husband is fired, leading them to separate, and Hilly Holbrook forces Elizabeth Leefholt to fire Aibileen. This conclusion indicates that the transgressive friendship has not altered the social hierarchy, and, in fact, none of the transgressive friendships portrayed in these novels actually change the dynamics of domestic labor. Transgressive relationships require opposing the established hierarchy, which has personal and deleterious repercussions for both parties in the friendship. But *The Help*, unlike the other two books, allows the reader to imagine a relatively happy ending for the white protagonist. The ending has made it attractive to mainstream audiences and contributed significantly to the book's success, but it undercuts the actual dynamics of transgressive friendships between black and white women that developed in the kitchen by presenting a revision of the civil rights movement that invites readers to imagine relationships between white women and domestic workers as meaningful and mutually beneficial.

The initial printing of *The Help* includes a postscript in which Stockett describes her relationship with Demetrie, her family's domestic worker. She reminisces about talking to her in the kitchen while she fried chicken and waiting anxiously while she ate separately from the family. When her parents divorced, Demetrie filled in as her ersatz mother, and she recalls herself as believing that Demetrie "was lucky to have us" (448). When writing the book, she explains that she felt like she was "crossing a terrible line," she claims that she does not "presume to think that [she] knows what it really felt like to be a black woman in Mississippi," and she mentions that her favorite line in the book is "we are two people. Not that much separates us. Not nearly as much as I thought" (451). These points suggest that she understands the complicated dynamics of intimacy in the kitchen, but her apprehension is well founded. Stockett understands the dynamics of asymmetrical intimacy in the white domestic sphere, but she misrepresents the effects of transgressive interracial friendships. Ablene Cooper, a maid who works for Stockett's sister-in-law in Jackson, sued Stockett for $75,000 for appropriating her likeness for "commercial purposes, namely to sell more copies of *The Help*" (Miller). The case had overtones of familial resentment because Stockett's sister-in-law appears to be a model for Elizabeth Leefholt, which created a scandal in Jackson. A judge dismissed the case because the suit was filed after the statute of limitations expired (Robertson). Regardless, the differential between the maid's case for monetary damages and the fortune Stockett has made on the book and the film based on the book reinforces the asymmetrical power relations between black domestic workers and white women, and the case undercuts the message of the book within the novel—a white woman helping black domestic workers to tell their own stories. Stockett has, instead, represented their stories as she would imagine them without asking the black domestic workers what they think. The most telling line in the book is "white people been representing colored opinions since the beginning of time" (128). The movie based on the book generated some controversy, including a condemnation from the Association of Black Women Historians, who claim that "*The Help* distorts, ignores, and trivializes the experiences of black domestic workers."

Stockett commits the same fault that her protagonist Skeeter hoped to correct, telling a black domestic worker's story without asking her "how she felt about it" (106). Gwin and Douglas manage to avoid the fault by deeply considering the effects of an interracial friendship between women in the white domestic sphere and portraying the consequences of transgression. Minrose Gwin has spent her career as a literary critic studying race, gender, memory, and space in southern literature. She brings her scholarship to bear on her depiction of Florence and Zenie, and both her fiction and her criticism are influenced by her childhood in Mississippi. She dedicated the novel to Eva Lee Miller, her babysitter with whom she maintained a lifelong relationship, and whom she calls "a model for me" (5). Douglas dedicated *Can't Quit You, Baby* to Mathelde Griffin, who was her family's domestic worker when she was a young woman. She admitted that she saw herself in Cornelia because she is a "southern white woman who has lived in this world and seen injustice and been a party to injustice, been a party to blindness, party to deafness all my life" (Jordan 58). She implicates herself in the process of not hearing the voices within earshot, of overlooking the human relationships immediately within her domestic sphere, beginning with Mathelde Griffin, who "had Tweet's voice" (Jordan 55). Writing the book, for Douglas, is a process of reexamining her relationship with Griffin, in particular, and with black people, in general, and of recognizing her own complicity with the system of racist and sexist hierarchy that defined her life in Mississippi. Gwin and Douglas are more reflective about the effects of friendships between white women and domestic workers than Stockett.

These novels reimagine the kitchens of white southern homes as a site of the struggle for social equality during the civil rights movement. Because domestic spaces were outside the public sphere, they tell a story about the movement that is otherwise impossible to understand. Sit-ins in public restaurants drew media attention to the prohibition on interracial commensality in public, but segregation within southern kitchens was more difficult to address. The domestic sphere where asymmetrically intimate relationships developed was shielded from publicity and demonstrations and not subject to court rulings or federal legislation, so the movement's effects in the kitchen were indirect and complex. Southern kitchens were not integrated; they were automated. David Katzman documents that in the first half of the twentieth century "the development of technology lagged significantly in the South, where black women provided the bulk of domestic labor" (130). Southerners resisted investing in labor-saving appliances while labor was cheap, but as black women found employment opportunities outside white homes, they were replaced with washing machines, dishwashers, and frozen dinners.

No longer merely ubiquitous invisible black maternal figures in the kitchen, the domestic workers in these novels are complex, nuanced characters who challenge the trope of the mammy. Sherrie Inness argues that books about food and cooking are "a venue for social and political change" (4). These novels about the southern kitchen portray changes taking place in the region's social and political hierarchy, and they allow contemporary readers to reimagine and critically reconsider the relationships between black domestic workers and white women in the domestic sphere. In *Of Woman Born*, Adrienne Rich, who grew up in segregated Baltimore under the care of a domestic worker, wrote in 1976 that black and white women "have been mothers and daughters to each other; and although, in the last few years, black and white feminists have been moving toward a still-difficult sisterhood, there is little yet known, unearthed, of the time when we were mothers and daughters" (253). Slowly, novels such as these excavate the intricate and intimate relations between black and white women that were forged in southern kitchens.

Works Cited

Association of Black Women Historians. "Open Statement on *The Help.*" http://www.abwh
.org/images/pdf/TheHelp-Statement.pdf. August 21, 2011.

Berlant, Lauren. "Intimacy." *Critical Inquiry* 24.2 (Winter 1998): 281–88.

Douglas, Ellen. *Can't Quit You, Baby.* New York: Penguin, 1988.

Fox-Genovese, Elizabeth. *Within the Plantation Household: Black and White Women of the
Old South.* Chapel Hill: U of North Carolina P, 1988.

Friedman, Susan Stanford. *Mappings: Feminism and the Cultural Geographies of the Encounter.* Princeton, NJ: Princeton UP, 1998.

Genovese, Eugene. *Roll, Jordan, Roll: The World the Slaves Made.* New York: Vintage, 1976.

Gwin, Minrose. *Black and White Women of the Old South: The Peculiar Sisterhood in American Literature.* Knoxville: U of Tennessee P, 1985.

———. "Sweeping the Kitchen: Revelation and Revolution in Contemporary Southern Wom-
en's Writing." *Southern Quarterly* 30.2–3 (Winter–Spring 1992): 54–61.

———. *The Queen of Palmyra.* New York: Harper Perennial, 2010.

Harris, Trudier. *From Mammies to Militants: Domestics in Black American Literature.* Philadelphia: Temple UP, 1982.

hooks, bell. *Yearning: Race, Gender, and Cultural Politics.* Boston: South End Press, 1999.

Hunter, Tera. *To 'Joy My Freedom: Southern Black Women's Lives and Labors after the Civil
War.* Cambridge: Harvard UP, 1997.

Inness, Sherrie A. *Secret Ingredients: Race, Gender, and Class at the Dinner Table.* New York:
Palgrave, 2006.

Jordan, Shirley. *Broken Silences: Interviews with Black and White Women Writers.* New
Brunswick, NJ: Rutgers UP, 1993.

Katzman, David M. *Seven Days a Week: Women and Domestic Service in Industrializing
America.* Urbana: U of Illinois P, 1981.

Miller, Laura. "The Dirty Secrets of *The Help.*" *Salon.com.* February 26, 2011.

Monteith, Sharon. *Advancing Sisterhood?: Interracial Friendships in Contemporary Southern
Fiction.* Athens: U of Georgia P, 2000.

Palmer, Phyllis. *Domesticity and Dirt: Housewives and Domestic Servants in the United States,
1920–1945.* Philadelphia: Temple UP, 1989.

Rich, Adrienne. *Of Woman Born: Motherhood as Experience and Institution.* New York: Norton, 1976.

Robertson, Campbell. "A Victory in Court for the Author of *The Help.*" *New York Times*
http://artsbeat.blogs.nytimes.com/2011/08/16/a-victory-in-court-for-the-author-of
-the-help/. August 16, 2011.

Sharpless, Rebecca. *Cooking in Other Women's Kitchens: Domestic Workers in the South,
1865–1960.* Chapel Hill: U of North Carolina P, 2010.

Smith, Lillian. *Killers of the Dream.* New York: Norton, 1961.

Spain, Daphne. *Gendered Spaces.* Chapel Hill: U of North Carolina P, 1992.

Stockett, Kathryn. *The Help.* New York: G. P. Putnam's Sons, 2009.

Tucker, Susan. *Telling Memories among Southern Women.* Baton Rouge: Louisiana State UP,
1988.

Van Wormer, Katherine, David W. Jackson, and Charletta Suddath. *The Maid Narratives: Black Domestics and White Families in the Jim Crow South*. Baton Rouge: Louisiana State UP, 2012.

Vlach, John Michael. *Back of the Big House: The Architecture of Plantation Slavery*. Chapel Hill: U of North Carolina P, 1993

Wallace-Sanders, Kimberly. *Mammy: A Century of Race, Gender, and Southern Memory*. Ann Arbor: U of Michigan P, 2008.

Williams-Forson, Psyche A. *Building Houses Out of Chicken Legs: Black Women, Food, and Power*. Chapel Hill: U of North Carolina P, 2006.

Yaeger, Patricia. *Dirt and Desire: Reconstructing Southern Women's Writing, 1930–1990*. Chicago: U of Chicago P, 2000.

Chapter Ten

EATING IN ANOTHER WOMAN'S KITCHEN
Reading Food and Class in the Woman-Loving Fiction of Ann Allen Shockley

PSYCHE WILLIAMS-FORSON

A s a human activity, food habits, rituals, behaviors, and choices, along with the reasons behind them, are fundamental to understanding social inter- actions. In literature, food practices—including the acquisition, prepa- ration, presentation, and consumption of food—help to define characters, illuminate cultural and regional specificities, and shed light on the develop- ment of women's identities. Some writers deliberately employ food themes as a literary device for both visual and cultural impact. Others use food inciden- tally as part of the ongoing, natural flow of the narrative. Still others do none of this. Rather, they use food in their literary work to mark time and place and to reveal disparities of race, class, gender, and ideology. Such is the case with the literature of southern fiction writer Ann Allen Shockley, a literary critic, archivist, and librarian who has authored an award-winning anthol- ogy, several short stories, and three novels. My own introduction to her work occurred when I was a graduate student studying nineteenth-century African American women. During my research, I came across Shockley's *Afro-Ameri- can Women Writers, 1746–1933: An Anthology and Critical Guide* (1988). Later, I happened upon her second novel, *Say Jesus and Come to Me* (1982), in a used bookstore and quickly determined that the authors were one and the same. It was not until years later, however, when furthering my research on Shock- ley that I learned of her substantial publication record. But for one compre- hensive study by S. Diane Adams Bogus, a bibliography compiled by Rita B. Dandridge, and a few articles, her literary contributions have been grossly underrecognized and ignored due in no small part to adversarial reviews and lack of publicity (among other factors).[1]

First published in 1974 and now considered a classic, *Loving Her* has been called "groundbreaking" because it is the first novel by an African American author to deal explicitly with an interracial woman-loving relationship and the first to feature a black lesbian as its central character (Lane v).[2] In all her work, Shockley shows evidence of concern for women (and men) including the ways they negotiate race, gender, and sexuality in their everyday lives. Given that the sexual lives of black women have always been shrouded in a culture of dissemblance and self-imposed secrecy, it is no wonder that literature exploring their same gender relations would stimulate a great deal of conversation.[3] But this focus has been almost to the exclusion of other subject matters that reveal black female gender definitions, power negotiations, and character development. Left unremarked upon, for example, is the immense amount of time that Shockley spends in all of her novels and many of her short stories detailing commonplace aspects of women's everyday lives using material and expressive culture, particularly food. Though Shockley maintains that symbolic meanings "[do] not enter the picture," food, dining rituals, and customs pervasively serve as subtexts for larger issues. By associating her women characters with a variety of foods, Shockley challenges linear models of female identity.[4]

Some of these foods are clearly identifiable as southern: butter beans and corn, collards, kale, and other greens (with vinegar), fried chicken, chitlins, and pork chops, and sweet potato pie with whipped cream.[5] But in addition to these she also includes lamb chops, buffalo meat, ham and rye, Hamburger Helper, and beer, as well as scotch, coffee, and hot tea. This array of foods and their persistent presence in her work leads one to ask in what ways are foods utilized in Shockley's novels and what meanings can we glean from their use? How is food used to reveal tensions between people of different races, genders, and sexual orientations? And lastly, how does Shockley use food to confront race, gender, and class ideologies that are used to suppress and oppress? A close reading of *Loving Her* illustrates how this overlooked theme not only reveals elements of African American southern cultural identity, but also female self-expression and gender development and the conflicts that often exist beneath the surface of human relationships.

Originally titled *A Love So Bold* until changed by publisher Bobbs-Merrill, *Loving Her* centers on Renay Davis, a musician, who marries her boyfriend Jerome Lee after his forcing her to have sex on their first date results in pregnancy. Seven years later, Renay finds herself in a loveless marriage to a repeatedly unemployed and abusive alcoholic. The novel opens with Renay fleeing her violent home in the wee hours of the night. With her daughter, Denise, in tow asking questions about her mother's swollen face, the two make their way to shelter—the home of Terry Bluvard, a wealthy white female writer whom Renay met while playing piano at a local supper club. Almost immediately, we learn that the housing arrangements will be one where they hide their true relationship from Renay's daughter. Renay tells Terry that they have to be careful, "like married people" (4). Very soon, the makings of a routine are disclosed:

> Before the night came, they made a game with Denise of unpacking the suitcases and filling drawers. Because they were hungry and Terry didn't like to cook, Renay dug deeply into the kitchen cabinets and huge refrigerator for food. She came up with a dinner of broiled lamb chops, canned peas, instant mashed potatoes, and pear salad. They ate with undisguised delight. It seemed like a banquet. (4)

With this brief scene, we learn right away that Renay will be assuming the role of primary food preparer since "Terry didn't like to cook." In one of the few critiques of the novel wherein food is considered, Stefanie Dunning argues:

> One of the most obvious ways [race arises to constantly stage Renay's and Terry's racial difference] is that Renay assumes all the domestic duties in the house as soon as she moves in with Terry. Her first act upon fleeing her relationship with Jerome Lee is to make a meal. In actual practice this differs little from the way she was expected to cook for Jerome Lee. Though the force of Terry's query about dinner differs greatly from Jerome Lee's abusive commands . . . the domestic space she occupied with Jerome Lee is similar to the one she occupies in Terry's house . . . ostensibly the narrative goal is to move Renay from a vexed domestic space to a liberatory one; yet the history of servitude which marks black and white women's relationships resonates with Renay's assumption of domestic duties. (76)

While Dunning makes a valid point in that the histories of black women's kitchen servitude cannot be disregarded, she also limits all black women's abilities to cook for their interracial partners as circumscribed by racial history. As Dunning argues, this history cannot be overcome by household variation or the ways in which feeding work helps to create gender, sexuality, ethnic, racial, and class identities. But much more is to be considered in examining the food work Renay does. In the novel, she is a full-time homemaker, part-time piano player at the Peacock Supper Club, and a mother. More than once, mention is made that Terry and Renay begin eating after Denise says, "Mommy, I'm hungry." In this context, it makes sense that Renay would assume the cooking role. In fact, Terry mentions in this same scene that "[Cooking is] too much trouble" (5). Reading the novel in the way Dunning suggests may foreclose seeing Renay's cooking as a viable contribution to the household. Moreover, it reduces the inclusion of foodways and dining rituals to signifiers of race and gender, since Renay takes on the traditional female roles of cooking and mothering.

Candace West and Don Zimmerman explain Renay's work as "doing gender" (140). In their conceptualization, gender is about relationships and social interactions rather than a set of traits one embodies. As the primary meal planner, Renay is knowledgeable about the invisible work involved in feeding others not because she is a woman but because she is accustomed to performing this task. Christopher Carrington reinforces this point in his study on lesbigay families. Borrowing from the work of noted sociologist Marjorie DeVault, author of *Feeding the Family: The Social Organization of Caring as Gendered Work*, Carrington writes:

> Feeding actually consists of a number of distinct processes including planning, shopping, preparation, and management of meals. Planning presumes the possession of several forms of knowledge about food, about the household, about significant others, and about cultural rules and practices toward food. In most lesbigay families . . . one person emerges as a fairly easily identified meal planner . . . Planning for most families means thinking ahead, perhaps a day or two or even a week, but in many cases just a few hours before a meal. (260)

This "social and interactional" kind of work that Renay employs is directly tied to her desire to please her friend and lover, Terry. Though Terry's writing brings in much more money than Renay's piano playing, we cannot assume that their household functions under a patriarchal model of hierarchy. The power here is ambiguous.[6] Theirs is a practical arrangement in which Terry offers her home, kitchen, and occasional financial resources, and Renay—in part because she has a child—provides nurturing, partly in the form of meals. The feeding work, then, should probably be read as more complex and consequential.

To be sure, that is one element of food's functionality—it is capable of highlighting complexities of gender, but also race, class, and sexuality. Perhaps anticipating the kind of criticism levied by Dunning, Shockley sought to emphasize Renay's skills and expertise in order to disturb the notion that she has simply substituted one space of servitude for another. To accomplish this, Shockley sets up the meals early in the novel. A skilled cook can usually often pull together a satisfying meal in a short period of time with a few ingredients, hence Renay's ability to scrounge around in the kitchen to compose a balanced meal of broiled lamb chops, peas, mashed potatoes, and pear salad. In this new family configuration, Renay is given the chance to confront directly what Alycee Lane describes as "the repressive implications of the so-called black aesthetics of her day." Though Lane is referring to Jerome's dismay that Renay seems unable to play the kinds of "funky" music he likes, her observation has salience to food (xv). By allowing Jerome to castigate Renay's piano playing—and by extension her cooking—with the intent to demean and hurt, Shockley is exposing the ways in which black women's aesthetic work is often unnecessarily criticized, belittled, and disregarded. In the foreword to the novel, Lane goes on to write, "[N]ot only does Shockley take issue with black cultural nationalism's narrow definitions of what constitutes *black* art, but more critically reads black aesthetics as a masculinist, heterosexist discourse, one that constrains black women's creativity" (xiv). Renay is a southern migrant to the North, so one might assume that she is conversant only in the particular set of foods that constitutes "black cuisine." But Shockley defies this limited characterization by giving Renay the ability to generate breakfasts of fried country ham slices, eggs sunny-side up, round German fried potatoes, and tomato salad. And though we are not given to know where Renay has learned her culinary skills, whether from watching, practice, or formal training, we are told she can whip up dishes that are quite elaborate. For example, once when Terry has an unexpected business guest to visit, Renay uses leftovers to create turkey and wild rice casserole, candied sweet potatoes with a "dash of rum," and string beans "floating in a savory cream sauce" (102, 115). Through food preparation, Renay is given an opportunity to exercise improvisational riffing in the kitchen and, in doing so, to give and also to receive pleasure.[7]

As opposed to reading Renay's meal preparation as household drudgery or reinscribing her as a domestic, it is possible—and maybe even necessary—to see Renay's cooking as empowering, full of creativity, and offering a space of "embodied politics of resistance" (Johnson 3). This kind of resistance, often manifest in vernacular traditions, including food and foodways, stems from E. Patrick Johnson's concept of "quare" (3). The concept of quare acknowledges ready differences among gays, lesbians, bisexuals, and transgendered people of color, while simultaneously recognizing how "racism and classism affect how the world is experienced and theorized." Quaring "queer" validates ways of knowing as both "discursively mediated and as historically situated and materially conditioned." Of importance to this analysis is Johnson's emphasis that "as a 'theory in the flesh' quare necessarily engenders a kind of identity politics, one that acknowledges difference within and between particular groups" (3). Renay, then, quares the kitchen space at Terry's because her black queer/lesbian identity challenges ideas of compulsory heterosexuality that is comfortable with women cooking intimate dinners only for men, not other women. Furthermore, Renay's character rejects the controlling image that presents black women who cook in fancy kitchens as merely "the help."

Renay continues to bend, violate, and break gendered norms of embodiment by hungrily consuming the food she has prepared. The adults are uninhibited in their food consumption as they eat with "undisguised delight." But there is a double entendre here that surrounds hunger and newness. In a household where only one person works, and then intermittently, lamb chops probably would have been a luxury item for Renay. In Terry's house, not only does Renay find new foods that quell her physical hunger, but also a new kind of lovemaking to fulfill her sexual needs. Renay is able not only to express these hungers and appetites, but also to have them fully satiated. In discussing the work of Elsbeth Probyn and her research on sex with food, Arlene Avakian and Barbara Haber remind us that both engage surfaces that "tingle and move." They write: "When eating and sex are commingled rather than added to each other, they may have the potential to disrupt assumptions, make new lines of connection, increase the possibility for pleasure, and promote new ethics" (16). The tingling to which Avakian and Haber refer is found here in the pleasure of eating good foods and in Renay's ability to eat without male constraint and control. It is a feeling that gives way to the sheer giddiness she expresses while consuming a basic evening meal.

Critics have noted that themes of religion are as pervasive in Shockley's work as race and gender. Bogus writes, "[W]hether explored as an explicit topic or drawn upon implicitly by the interjection or allusion to God or Christ, the theme of religion, its helpfulness and hypocrisy are inextricably woven into the fabric of many of Shockley's stories" (175, 167). Religious food symbolism and metaphors reinforce the emphasis on new beginnings and revitalization. Lambs were ritually used in Judeo-Christian religious sacrifices, and it was roasted lamb that was eaten during Passover—the celebration of deliverance and the exodus/escape. Lamb was also eaten during the Last Supper prior to the crucifixion of "the perfect lamb," and lamb is often among the foods that make an appearance at Easter dinner celebrations following the period of fasting and abstinence. Given this context, the dinner of lamb chops, peas, mashed potatoes, and pears can be read as symbolizing resurrection and renewal, the newness of life and relationship, revival, and a raising of the dead (in this case, dormant female sexuality). Most of all, the dinner celebrates a deliverance from "evil." Reading a simple weekday dinner through this quared/queered lens "erases the distinction between the heterosexual female cook who sustains her family with food and the lesbian who satisfies her sexual needs by making love with women. Blurring the culinary boundaries between straight and queer women."[8] Despite Shockley's insistence that her symbols are not conscious, it is nonetheless curious that her inclusion of the pear seems to pay homage to Zora Neale Hurston's *Their Eyes Were Watching God*. As Hurston's protagonist Janie lay beneath the pear tree, "she saw a dust-bearing bee sink into the sanctum of a bloom; the thousand sister-calyxes arch to meet the love embrace and the ecstatic shiver of the tree from root to tiniest branch creaming in every blossom and frothing with delight. So this was marriage!" (11). This scene in *Their Eyes Were Watching God*, which marries the bee and the bloom, is fitting here because Renay too is embarking upon a "marriage" full of passion and optimism. Adding the pear salad to the lamb chop dinner metaphorically, then, allows the women to ingest an idealism that their union seems to represent. It is a seemingly perfect moment, full of bliss and harmony. It is also a falsely idyllic moment—for Renay as much as it was for Janie.

The peace of mind that accompanies Renay's consumption of these foods and her new sexual awakening continues through the weekend and well into Monday morning after she drops off her daughter at school. By the middle of the novel, this equanimity is cemented by the routine of making Denise's breakfast of fruit, cereal, and milk, and then Terry's grapefruit juice, eggs, toast, and black coffee. But on the return trip from Denise's school after that first Monday morning, Renay stops at a supermarket near Terry's house and buys food with money "Terry had carelessly stuffed into her purse" (7). Though this imprudence gestures toward Terry's role as financial provider in the union, this is not necessarily the case. Renay makes it clear that she works, even if part-time, because she *has* to work. In the narrative voice Shockley writes, "Yes, she *did* have to *work*. To let Denise know she was contributing to their keep, and to preserve her independence" (41). So while Terry's extra money expands Renay's ability to be experientially and experimentally free, Renay is careful to pull her weight. While grocery shopping, Renay is captivated as "she took her time wheeling the cart slowly up and down the sparkling aisles, noting the contrast between this market and the markets where she usually shopped" (7). It is more than the physical landscape that is contrasted—clean as opposed to dirty floors, fresh versus decayed scraps of produce and wilted vegetables, red meats rather than those "tinged with brown"—it is also the symbolic representations of blackness (7). And the descriptions of the kind of grocery stores that Renay left behind signify more than just the landscape and the foods. They also serve as stand-ins to the life of doom and gloom that Renay has escaped.

This symbolism of difference actually begins with that first dinner. Though the ingredients may have been different, the meal itself was more reminiscent of Renay's upbringing where food seems to have been plentiful, provided for by her hard-working mother and deceased father's pension. A decidedly well-structured meal, the lamb chops, peas, potatoes, and pear salad was characteristic of a middle-class orderly dinner—consisting of meat, vegetable, starch, and dessert—which came into vogue on the post–WWII homefront, especially in suburbia. Many of these meals were made all the more accessible in grocery stores and supermarkets because instant and frozen/canned foods offered conveniences for women who had gone to work during the war and had no desire to return to kitchens and hot stoves.[9] Terry's instant potatoes and canned peas are soon replaced, however, by more slow-cooking ingredients that Renay finds at the supermarket. Alongside lettuce, tomato, root vegetables, and meats, Renay finds herself drawn to "the exotic food section, picking up caviar, terrapin stew, turtle soup, and rattlesnake meat . . . Bristol Cream . . . and dainty pink and white frosted cupcakes sprinkled with nuts" for her daughter (8). It is important here that Shockley does not include foods that are considered stock representations of southern African American culture—fried chicken and fish, ham, candied yams, lima beans, greens, macaroni and cheese, succotash, watermelon, cornbread, and so on. It is not so much that Shockley imbues her character with disdain for blackness; instead, she fills Renay with a desire for more than the life of blackness that she was living had to offer. The plethora of new and unusual canned foods represents different choices and options in Renay's life. In this, the much-expanded grocery store with its many possibilities enables Shockley to portray Renay as capable of *wanting* more opportunities for herself and her child and of being unafraid of experimentation. In reference to Johnson's formulation of "quaring," the grocery store, like the kitchen at Terry's, can be read as more than simply a repository for foodstuffs. It may be read as a space that allows Renay to transgress the black community's food norms, quaring her race, gender, and food culture. At the very least, in that space and even if for a brief time, Renay is also able to return to and/or perform an upper-middle-class status. Johnson explains that "there exists a politics of taste among African Americans that is performed so as to dislodge fixed perceptions about who one is or where one is from . . . performing a certain middle-class style has enabled African Americans to 'pass' in various and strategically savvy ways."[10] The supermarket and Terry's kitchen become conduits for different manifestations of self-expression.

On the surface it might appear that Shockley allows her character to disavow her culinary cultural heritage because Renay seems to accept without question all that the white world has to offer. But, before the reader can make this assumption, Shockley makes it clear that Renay has not forgotten her culinary roots. Nowhere is this better exemplified than when Terry and Renay decide to move to the country so they can have more privacy, be delusionally free from prejudice, and give Denise more freedom to run around. To christen their new digs, Renay cooks a special dinner—a chitterling dinner—which Shockley introduces this way:

> "What's that I smell?" Terry asked, wrinkling her nose.
> "I'm introducing you tonight to what is commonly referred to as soul food. That there what y'all is smelling is known as black folks' delight—hog nuts, or Kentucky oysters. Depend on where you are from and what you want to call them. We're also having turnip greens, potato salad and cold-water cornbread like my mother used to make." (86)

By invoking her mother and sharing this food, Renay brings Terry closer to learning more about the inner workings of some black communities. As they eat, Renay instructs Terry on how to chew chitlins and how to season them—"You know, there's really an art to cooking . . . You have to cook them slowly with onions, celery stalks and a dash of lemon." After Terry tastes them and frowns, Renay coaches her to "put some mustard vinegar and hot sauce on them. They help to bring out the flavor" (86). These acts are significant for what they suggest about cultural bridging and are weighted all the more because the women eat by candlelight on a table set with fine linen and silver. Reflecting a time-honored tradition of eating chitlins on china, the dinner companions also sip champagne, prompting Terry to remark "cryptically," "First time I've ever had champagne" (86).

Renay's culinary performance is interesting for its revelations and its disruptions as much as for Shockley's placement of the scene. The chitterling meal occurs after the couple has moved into a new living space, but it also occurs after Terry's recurring housekeeper mistakes Renay as the new maid. After Renay tells Terry about the incident and Terry apologizes, Renay mockingly replies, "No need, ma'am. Y'all got you' cleanin' woman right h'yar wif y'all, and sho' nuff!" (54). With the chit'lins and champagne dinner, Shockley may be pushing back against those stereotyped images of black women as maids by allowing Renay to engage in what E. Patrick Johnson calls a "performance of self" (11). Johnson explains that "a performance of self . . . has the potential to transform one's view of the self in relation to the world. People have a need to exercise control over the production of their images so that they feel empowered. For the disenfranchised, the recognition, construction and maintenance of self-image and cultural identity function to sustain, even when social systems fail to do so" (11). It is a Janus-face performance, always looking forward while simultaneously looking backward; hence, the chitlins and the champagne do the work of both "reify[ing] oppressive systems" but also "contest[ing] and subvert[ing] dominant meaning systems" (11).

The champagne disrupts the soul food/southern/nationalist paradigm. At the same time, the chitlins disrupt the respectability implied by a dinner by candlelight on white linen tablecloth with champagne. The chitlins actually bring tension to this perfectly ordered scene, serving as a threat to the precariously formulated union. The symbolism of ingesting filth and a sparkling wine usually reserved for special occasions may be an articulation of Shockley's ambivalence about Renay and Terry's relationship, especially in the racially charged era in which they are living. The chitlins serve to remind Terry that Renay *is* black and that she is aware of her blackness and what it means for her in this relationship. If at any given moment Renay can be mistaken for Terry's maid, then her life is more circumscribed by racial politics than either of them is willing to acknowledge.

Another way of reading what Shockley is doing here is to consider that she is allowing black women the space—within the limited social dictums of the black pride movement—to self-define and to subvert race, class, gender, and sexuality norms. This way of reading allows for multivariate interpretations of *blackness*. The 1960s and early 1970s, the time period in which the novel was both set and published, witnessed the heterogeneity of blackness being called into question in many areas, not the least of which was in the kitchen. By situating the novel during this era, Shockley draws our attention to a tumultuous time in American history when a multiplicity of definitions and discourses surrounded what it meant to be a woman, black, and/or gay. Embroiled in these polemics on identity politics are also those of cultural misappropriation, namely the contested term of soul food. Written in response to the statement that African Americans had no distinctive foodways patterns, LeRoi Jones (Amiri Baraka) in his collection of social commentaries titled *Home: Social Essays*, described most of what we know today as "down home southern food": grits, hoppin' John (black-eyed peas and rice), fried fish and chicken, buttermilk biscuits, dumplings, lima beans and corn, string beans, okra, smoky hot barbecue, and most anything coming from the pig, from neck bones to maw to pork chops and fatback. Sweet tea or lemonade and a large wedge of sweet potato pie round out the description. Pushing back against Jones were, among others, Elijah Muhammad and Dick Gregory, both of whom rejected the diet as unhealthy and evocative of slavery.[11]

Many lives were circumscribed by ideologies of the black power movement that, according to bell hooks, "made synonymous black [with] liberation and the effort to create a social structure wherein black men could assert themselves as patriarchs, controlling community, family, and kin" (98). Shockley seems to be using food to push back against this misogynistic and homophobic diatribe that relegated women to a subordinate status. Wahneema Lubiano points to the often-inherent hypocrisy of black nationalism, arguing that "even as it functions as resistance to the state on one hand, it reinscribes the state in particular places within its own narratives of resistance. That reinscription most often occurs within . . . narratives of the black family" (68). Through Renay, Shockley challenges black women as reproducers of the next generation of warriors, cultural bearers, and supporters of male needs. Given this reasoning, it would be easy to read Terry as a white savior, but a better interpretation may be to see her as the vehicle by which Renay is finally able to expand her undeveloped, but long-hidden, desire for other women. Early in the novel, Renay's proclivity is made evident when her roommate Marissa chides her for not immediately returning Jerome Lee's advances. Though she "hated" the kiss of a man, she carried out expected gendered performances of desire by "superficially acting out the woman's role she thought she was expected to play in the context of their relationship" (15). With Terry, Shockley suggests that black women have the right to choose whom they want to love and simultaneously speaks back to the politics that require black women to be submissive to hierarchical masculinist constructions of family. This politics is apparent in the novel during the scene where Renay cooks dinner for Jerome and his friend.

Jerome is prone to disappearing for days and weeks on end. So frequent and erratic is his behavior that Renay is forced to find a part-time job. After one of Jerome's especially long absences, he arrives at home with a friend, Stew, who is dressed in "a pink knit suit, pink tie, and white shirt." Despite the outrageous outfit that implies an affinity for things feminine, Stew asks Jerome, "Man, how'd you git such a good-looking woman?" Ignoring his friend, Jerome demands his wife make them a home-cooked meal rather than the TV dinners she has warmed. Hurrying to the store, Renay returns to cook a fried chicken dinner, but by the time dinner is ready, Stew leaves, and Jerome passes out (23–24). In the scene immediately following this one, Renay heads to the supper club for work, and, later, Terry offers her a ride home. It is the first night that Renay and Terry sleep together and the first time Renay has an orgasm (28).

Shockley provocatively places Jerome's brutish behavior concerning the chicken dinner in direct opposition to the sexual climax Renay experiences with Terry. In doing so, she problematizes the idealized heterosexual family model that many nationalists espoused. It could easily promise black women a life of violence and subservience instead of harmony and bliss. In an ironic twist, Jerome actually destabilizes the Norman Rockwell "Freedom from Want" myth by turning his back on the family meal. Food here gets deployed to wage a commentary on the narrative of a stable (read heterosexual) black family. Renay's decision to cook a fried chicken dinner for Jerome and Stew fits with the soul food/southern food cultural debates that took place within black nationalist discourses. On the other hand, it is an impractical food to make at a late hour because it required her to visit a grocery store and because it is labor intensive. Recognizing that domestic violence and abuse come in all forms, Jerome's late night request for a meal is an assertion of patriarchal power. As Carole Counihan reminds us, "[C]ontrol of money and food purchases is a key index of husband-wife balance of power. Men may wield power by controlling food purchases and claiming the authority to judge the meals women cook. They can disparage the food or demand certain dishes. Men can refuse to provide food or to eat. Husbands often legitimate wife abuse by citing meal failures" (11). Jerome's inability to eat because he is too drunk only heightens his emotional mistreatment, reinforcing his balance of power. What could have been an intimate act between Jerome and Renay—sharing a food loaded with cultural significance—falls flat as the act of subservience pervades the scene. In contrast to the earlier portion of the novel when Renay and Terry eat in "undisguised delight" and nurturing is a central part of that experience, here food serves as a metaphor for unsatisfied hunger. Here, fried chicken, a food considered the cornerstone of black and southern cultural heritage, destabilizes the heterosexual family configuration and highlights the discord therein. When Jerome was home, Renay was supposed to obey or succumb to violence designed to keep her in line. An example of that obedience is forcing her to cook a meal that conforms to the prescribed black aesthetic—fried chicken.

In opposition to Jerome's disavowal of the meal, Shockley positions Renay's heightened intimate sexual moment. It is when Renay reaches outside her race and her patterned sexual behavior that she finds freedom and equality. In her foreword to the novel, Lane suggests it is the precisely the equity between the two that "makes the sex between Renay and Terry so good" (x). Unlike Jerome, who saw the bedroom as a kingdom over which he ruled, Terry cares about Renay's needs. With this displacement of marital bliss—and using food and sex—Shockley rearticulates the nationalist ideal suggesting how relationships can be experienced. She furthers this rewriting in one of the final scenes in the novel that takes place in a kitchen.

When Jerome figures out Renay's living arrangement, he breaks into their house and confronts her with his revelations about her newfound sexuality. During the argument, Renay suggests that Terry takes better care of their daughter than he did, which enrages him. In the midst of the turmoil, Renay tries to soothe her demoralized husband with a drink of Terry's Ambassador Scotch, which he immediately rejects as "bulldagger's booze" (131). Jerome strikes the proffered drink from Renay's hand, after which he brutally beats her to compensate for his feelings of inadequacy and his deflated spirit. Shockley depicts the brutality of this scene as ironic by several different means. First, kitchens are often the space of familial bonding, so the kitchen provides an adequate setting to highlight the ways Renay has taken both the culinary and sexual sustenance away from Jerome and given it to Terry. Second, now that Renay has denounced the notion that heterosexuality is the only option for black women, the kitchen represents the rupture of black (heteronormative) families. This affront is extended when Renay offers Jerome Terry's "bulldagger" scotch, a drink that may well have been out of his economic reach. Suggesting such a salve for his injured ego was like rubbing salt in a wound. Lastly, kitchens are notorious for being landscapes where jealousies exist—from formal cooking competitions to other culinary kinds of rivalries. In most cultures, when a man eats in the kitchen of a woman not his wife it can be read as a form of adultery.[12] When a woman *eats* in another woman's kitchen—outside of a platonic relationship—it can be considered profane. For these reasons and more, the kitchen is often a site of disruption, fracture, and violence.

Renay survives the beating and decides to convalesce at her mother's house in Tilltown, Kentucky. Prefaced in the novel with simply the word "home," it is a place that holds conflicting memories for Renay. An "insular" town surrounded by tobacco and farms, it is "steeped in long-time black poverty and rigid white provincialism" (141). Despite any misgivings Renay may have about returning to the "one-story green frame house on dusty, unpaved Booker Street" in "colored town," it is the only time in the novel when Renay is described as eating two helpings of food at one meal. It is also only the second time that we see Renay embracing southern/soul cuisine, this time more than the last when she ate the chitlins and champagne dinner. Her mother prepares her favorite meal: clove-studded baked ham, sweet potato pudding, garlicky collard greens with ham hocks, cornbread, and chocolate cake. The dinner is consumed in surroundings that are familiar and memory-filled. Yet, even in this place of relative security, Renay is discomforted and disquieted. She can reveal only so much to her family and friends about the life she has with Terry, despite her daughter's repeated references to her new auntie. When Renay's mother asks about Terry, Renay simply replies, "She's a writer and a good friend of mine. I live with her." Later, when Renay's friend Fran asks why she wants to live with Terry instead of her, Renay simply replies,

"I *like* her. We get along" (146). In the narrative voice, Renay ponders: "How do you explain to your best friend that you are a Lesbian? One declaration would end their closeness, for Fran would always view her in the new light. She would secretly fear her, mistakenly looking upon herself as a sex object and fear being labeled the same because she was her friend. Renay couldn't take the gamble. Fran was the link to her home and her people" (146). Renay's dis-ease is further grounded when Fran insists Renay accompany her on a double date. After much hesitation, Renay agrees to hang out with her childhood friend. In a scene reminiscent of a blaxploitation film, the four—Renay, her blind date, Bob, Fran, and her boyfriend, Lazarius—head to the Ebony Lounge where jive is the order of the day. Renay's discomfort is palpable, and it intensifies when a gay man passes their table and Fran disgustedly mutters, "*fag,*" to which Renay remains silent (153). Her uneasiness is furthered when, following the party, someone suggests they get soul food.

Ma's Stewpot reportedly had great food despite being a "small room [of] dingy gray with cracked linoleum, a curved, scarred counter with sticky mustard and catsup shakers, and wooden tables that looked abandoned from various kitchens" (156). Like any dive that smelled of "leftover food, grease, and coffee," Ma's was the place to be after a long night of partying. When the group decides to order the requisite chitlins, coleslaw, cornbread, and ribs, Renay clearly shows her displeasure by opting for a hamburger and coffee, prompting Fran to remark, "*Now* she wants to put the fire out" (157). This food event stands in contrast to the one in Renay's mother's dining room where a different kind of southerness was on display. In this setting, soul and southerness are pitted against one another as signified both by the food and the locations in which each is served. At her mother's, Renay felt relaxed, surrounded by her family and the perceived comforts of home. This sense of relief and contentment is reflected in her hearty appetite for the home-cooked southern meal. In the setting of Ma's Stewpot, however, she is forced to play the role of the heterosexual. Earlier in the evening, while at the club, one of Lazarius' friends comes to the table and, between dashikis and afros, givin' dap, and soul talk, the friend queries Lazarius on his dedication to the cause. Having firsthand knowledge of how the contradictory ideologies of "the cause" almost cost her life, Renay looks on in silence. This muteness continues at the hole-in-the-wall eatery until a young black man sporting a black power t-shirt enters with a white woman. While Fran complains, "talk black—sleep white," the men appreciate the union on the basis of their own sexual interests, and Renay finds a sense of kindred with the interracial coupling (158). A tense moment follows when Bob and Lazarius learn from Fran that Renay's empathy is due to her relationship with Terry. The strain is disrupted only by the arrival of their food.

Renay's hamburger stands out all the more as a cultural signifier of difference amidst the platters of "chit'lins," "strips of red-brown barbecued ribs," "round bowls of coleslaw and square pieces of cornbread" (158). Her burger, though food, is neither southern nor soul, and, in this setting, is an anomaly. That she does not conform or acquiesce to the pressure around her to eat the same foods as her dinner companions speaks to Renay's increased personal growth. Her rejection of the black nationalist narrative, here exemplified by the food, quares/queers the space, making it a site of transgression. Renay's decision to speak in support of the interracial couple and to order the hamburger instead of the soul food can also be read as a critique of essentialism. Soul food is a signifier for blackness and Ma's Stewpot a place for community building, but only if you fit the standard definition of "community." This is signaled by Fran's reference to Renay as "putting out the fire" because she orders a burger instead of the ribs and cornbread. Fran "delimits the possibilities of what blackness can be" even as Renay employs a performance of disidentification, valuing the cultural rituals of black food consumption, yet resisting its insistence (Johnson 14). Thrust into this space where heteronormativity is privileged, Renay transforms it by neither totally aligning herself with the cultural norms nor absolutely rejecting them. Just because she agrees to the blind date does not mean she has to acquiesce totally and go "all the way" by enjoying the foods she is supposed to consume in a soul food shack. She furthers her transgressions when she rejects Bob's sexual advances. In so doing, she effectively closes the door on what could have been a chance to help to rebuild the race.[13] Despite being with her own people, Renay sees herself as belonging with Terry and thus in the liminal space between a black and white world, belonging wholly to neither. Renay's refusal to eat the soul food serves as a rejection of all the things that others consider deviant—loving Terry and leaving Jerome to be with her, among them.

As a cultural signifier, food helps to challenge notions of a particular kind of black experience and an essentialist black female body. In *Loving Her*, as in most of Shockley's fictional writings, women in a variety of same gender relationships represent broad spectrums of female sexualities. One critic suggests that such presentations "compel readers to reexamine restrictive, stereotypical images of black womanhood and lesbian identity" (Keating). It has been my contention in this essay that food helps to achieve this goal. While there are more food events than those addressed here, the point is to illustrate the richness that is obscured when food is not considered among the important themes in Shockley's fiction. Food serves to articulate and express varying meanings of black female identity and most of all to allow women to construct different versions of their lives.

Acknowledgments

This essay benefited immensely from comments and suggestions by Kenyatta Graves, Carole Counihan, Kimberly Nettles, Pauline Adema, Christina Hanhardt, and graduate students Darius Bost and Jessica Walker.

Notes

1. S. Diane Bogus makes the interesting point that the publication of *Loving Her* "took critics by surprise." As a result, no one knew much about Shockley or her prolific publication record, when the novel was published. The lesbian-themed book jacket arrived seemingly in a vacuum. This, coupled with vitriolic reviews like the one written by well-respected male critic Frank Lamont Phillips, who called the novel "bullshit that ought not to be encouraged," and feminist critic Jeanne Cordova's appraisal of the book as "a bad lesbian novel," along with Shockley's long interims between writing meant negative publicity clouded her work. Bogus also explains that Shockley refuses to discuss her work or give public interviews, none of which necessarily bodes well for positive audience reception. See S. Diane Adams Bogus, "Theme and Portraiture in the Fiction of Ann Allen Shockley." Diss., Miami University (1988), in particular chapter 2 that details the critical reception of Shockley; *Ann Allen Shockley: An Annotated Primary and Secondary Bibliography* (1987), compiled by Rita B. Dandridge; and Jewelle Gomez's, "A Cultural Legacy Denied and Discovered: Black Lesbians in Fiction by Women" (1983). More recent contributions include: Yakini Kemp's "When Difference Is Not the Dilemma: The Black Woman Couple in African American Women's Fiction" (1999) and Trimiko Melancon, "Disrupting Dissemblance: Transgressive Black Women as Politics of Counter-Representation in African American Women's Fiction." Diss., U Mass Amherst (2005).

2. I use the term woman-loving or same-gender loving because it is widely used by African American scholars in responding to the request by Johnnetta Cole and Beverly Guy-Sheftall to take into consideration the "cultural specificity of Western categories when speaking of same-gender sexual and emotional bondings among persons of African descent on the continent and in the African diaspora." Trimiko Melancon explains that same-gender loving is "pragmatic" because it offers "insight into the specificity of certain sexualities" desires, intimacies, and eroticism within a racialized context. For more on this, see Cole and Guy-Sheftall, *Gender Talk: The Struggle for Women's Equality in African American Communities*, p. 165; also see Melancon, "Towards an Aesthetic of Transgression: Ann Allen Shockley's *Loving Her* and the Politics of Same-Gender Loving," p. 643 and fn 2, 3, and 4 for more on the term as an analytic.

3. See Hine's now classic essay, "Rape and the Inner Lives of Black Women in the Middle West," where she coins the phrase "culture of dissemblence" to explain the ways in which black women developed a "cult of secrecy" to protect and guard the inner workings of their personal lives.

4. Arguably, any of Shockley's texts could have been selected for this analysis, including her most recent novel *Celebrating Hotchclaw*. However, given the amount of attention levied upon *Loving Her*, I thought it a compelling point of entry into the ways food can be called into play to disrupt assumptions, increase the possibility for pleasure, and provide alternative ways of reading race, gender, and sexuality in a text. For a reading of some of the ways food operates in *Say Jesus and Come to Me*, see Williams-Forson, *Building Houses Out of Chicken Legs*, chapter 5.

5. For a more detailed description of traditional African American foods, see Whitehead and Williams-Forson, "African American Foodways," pp. 425–37.

6. I thank Carole Counihan for this insight.

7. Sometimes Terry refers to Renay as "chef," an accolade that well elevates Renay above a common cook. A good article illustrating this point is Brett Williams's "Why Migrant Women Feed Their Husbands Tamales: Foodways as a Basis for a Revisionist View of Tejano Family Life."

8. Searching Google will reveal that lamb chops are a noted favorite among "manly meals." Jessamyn Neuhaus confirms popular opinion in *Manly Meals and Mom's Home Cooking: Cookbooks and Gender in Modern America*. Early cookbook guides reveal that peas and asparagus are a usual companion to the chops, making the presence of the pear salad all the more conspicuous in its appearance. On queering foods and foodways, see Julia Ehrhardt, "Towards Queering Food Studies: Foodways, Heteronormativity, and Hungry Women in Chicana Lesbian Writing."

9. In a conversation with Rafia Zafar, I was reminded of how socioeconomics is also reflected in this food scene. Zafar remarks, "[T]hat one dinner you single out speaks much to issues of middle-class access (and love for) 'convenience' ingredients (e.g., boxed mashed potatoes); as much as we today might shiver at the thought of canned peas—they represented something beyond a serving of vegetables." E-mail correspondence with the author, September 9, 2011. A good read on the role of convenience foods in expanding women's choices is Sherrie Inness, "34,000,000,000 Work Hours Saved: Convenience Foods and Mom's Home Cooking," 17–38.

10. This point may well be true for Renay given the description of her childhood home as possessing the furnishings of a middle-class life. It was only after Jerome sold her prized possession, the old piano given to her by her mother—the holder of her "childhood hopes and adult dreams in one treasured package"—that Renay felt a dramatic line had been crossed and she therefore fled her less-than-ideal marriage. See *Loving Her*, p.29; Johnson, fn 15, p. 21.

11. Amiri Baraka, "Soul Food"; Doris Witt, *Black Hunger: Food and Politics of U.S. Identity* does an especially good job of teasing out the complexities of understanding the term "soul food" and several of the competing discourses and interpretations that surround it, then and now. See her chapter "Eating Chitterlings Is Like Going Slumming: Soul Food and Its Discontents."

12. For more on this phenomenon, see Williams, "Why Migrant Women Feed Their Husbands Tamales"; Carole Counihan, "Mexicana's Food Voice . . ."; Gracia Clark, *Onions Are My Husband*; and Psyche Williams-Forson, "Other Women Cooked for My Husband."

13. That being said, Bob is written off as less than the epitome of a *strong, black man*. When Lazarius' friend, Alunkah, questions why he has not been to the revolutionary meetings, the friend directs his comments only to Lazarius. After Lazarius reminds Alunkah of Bob Stewart's presence and name, Alunkah acknowledges knowing Bob, but also associates "Mr. Stewart" with the white establishment (154–55).

Works Cited

Avakian, Arlene, and Barbara Haber. *From Betty Crocker to Feminist Food Studies: Critical Perspectives on Women and Food*. Amherst: University of Massachusetts Press, 2005.

Baraka, Amiri (LeRoi Jones). "Soul Food." *Home: Social Essays*. London: MacGibbon & Kee, 1968. 121–24.

Bogus, S. Diane Adams. "Theme and Portraiture in the Fiction of Ann Allen Shockley." Diss., Miami University, 1988.

Carrington, Christopher. "Feeding Lesbigay Families." *Food and Culture: A Reader*. 2nd edition. Edited by Carole Counihan and Penny Van Esterik. New York: Routledge, 2008. 259–88.

Clark, Gracia. *Onions Are My Husband: Survival and Accumulation by West African Market Women*. Chicago: University of Chicago Press, 1995.

Cole, Johnnetta B., and Beverly Guy-Sheftall. *Gender Talk: The Struggle for Women's Equality in African American Communities*. New York: Ballantine, 2003.

Counihan, Carole. *Anthropology of Food and Body: Gender, Meaning, and Power*. New York: Routledge, 1999.

———. "Mexicanas' Food Voice and Differential Consciousness in the San Luis Valley of Colorado." *Food and Culture: A Reader*. 2nd edition. Edited by Carole Counihan and Penny Van Esterik. New York: Routledge, 2008. 354–68.

Dandridge, Rita B. *Ann Allen Shockley: An Annotated Primary and Secondary Bibliography*. Westport, CT: Greenwood Publishing, 1987.

Dunning, Stephanie. "(Not) Loving Her: A Locus of Contradictions." *Queer in Black and White: Interraciality, Same Sex Desire, and Contemporary African American Culture*. Bloomington: Indiana University Press, 2009. 61–83.

Ehrhardt, Julia. "Towards Queering Food Studies: Foodways, Heteronormativity, and Hungry Women in Chicana Lesbian Writing." *Food & Foodways: History & Culture of Human Nourishment* 14.2 (April–June 2006): 91–109.

Gomez, Jewelle. "A Cultural Legacy Denied and Discovered: Black Lesbians in Fiction by Women." *Homegirls: A Black Feminist Anthology*. Edited by Barbara Smith. New Brunswick: Rutgers University Press, 2000. 110–24.

Hine, Darlene Clark. "Rape and the Inner Lives of Black Women in the Middle West: Preliminary Thoughts on the Culture of Dissemblance." *Signs: Journal of Women in Culture and Society* 14.4 (1989): 912–20.

hooks, bell. *Race and Representation*. Cambridge, MA: South End Press, 1999.

Hurston, Zora Neale. *Their Eyes Were Watching God*. 1937. Urbana: University of Illinois Press, 1978.

Inness, Sherrie. "34,000,000,000 Work Hours Saved: Convenience Foods and Mom's Home Cooking." *Secret Ingredients: Race, Gender, and Class at the Dinner Table*. New York: Palgrave Macmillan, 2005. 17–38.

Johnson, E. Patrick. "Quare Studies or (Almost) Everything I Know about Queer Studies I Learned From My Grandmother." *Text and Performance Quarterly* 21.1 (2001): 1–25.

Keating, Ann Louise. "African American Literature: Lesbian." In *GLBTQ: An Encyclopedia of Gay, Lesbian, Bisexual, Transgender and Queer Culture*. Edited by Claude Summers. (March 2010). http://www.glbtq.com/literature/african_am_lit_lesbian,4.html, March 12, 2011.

Kemp, Yakini. "When Difference Is Not the Dilemma: The Black Woman Couple in African American Women's Fiction." *Arms Akimbo: Africana Women in Contemporary Literature*. Edited by Yakini Belinda Kemp and Janice Liddell. Gainesville: University Press of Florida, 1999. 75–91.

Lane, Alycee. Foreword to *Loving Her* by Ann Allen Shockley. 1974. Lebanon, NH: UPNE-Northeastern Library of Black Literature, 1997. v–xvi.

Lubiano, Wahneema. "Black Nationalism and Black Common Sense: Policing Ourselves and Others." *The House that Race Built*. Edited by Wahneema Lubiano. NY: Vintage Books, 1998. 232–52.

Melancon, Trimiko. "Disrupting Dissemblance: Transgressive Black Women as Politics of Counter-Representation in African American Women's Fiction." Diss., U Mass Amherst, 2005.

———. "Towards an Aesthetic of Transgression: Ann Allen Shockley's *Loving Her* and the Politics of Same-Gender Loving." *African American Review* 42.3–4 (Fall/Winter 2008): 643–57.

Miller, Lisa, Paul Rozin, and Alan Fiske. "Food Sharing and Feeding Another Person Suggests Intimacy." *European Journal of Social Psychology* 28.3 (May/June 1998): 423–36.

Neuhaus, Jessamyn. *Manly Meals and Mom's Home Cooking: Cookbooks and Gender in Modern America*. Baltimore: Johns Hopkins University Press, 2003.

Shockley, Ann Allen. *Loving Her*. 1974. Lebanon, NH: UPNE- Northeastern Library of Black Literature, 1997.

———. "The Black Lesbian in American Literature: An Overview." *Conditions* (1979): 133–42.

———. *Say Jesus and Come to Me*. New York: Avon, 1982.

———. *Celebrating Hotchclaw*. Rehoboth Beach, DE: A & M Books, 2005.

West, Candace, and Don Zimmerman. "Doing Gender." *Gender and Society* 1.2 (June 1987): 125–51.

Whitehead, Tony, and Psyche Williams-Forson. "African American Foodways." *Encyclopedia of Food and Culture*. Edited by Solomon Katz and William Woys Weaver. NY: Thomson Gale, Inc., 2002. 425–37.

Williams, Brett. "Why Migrant Women Feed Their Husbands Tamales: Foodways as a Basis for a Revisionist View of Tejano Family Life." *Ethnic and Regional Foodways in the*

United States. Edited by Linder Keller Brown and Kay Mussell. Knoxville: University of Tennessee Press, 1984. 113–27.

Williams-Forson, Pysche. *Building Houses Out of Chicken Legs: Black Women, Food, and Power.* Chapel Hill: University of North Carolina Press, 2006.

———. "Other Women Cooked for My Husband: Negotiating Gender, Food, and Identities in an African American/Ghanaian Household." *Feminist Studies* 36.2 (Summer 2010): 435–61.

Witt, Doris. "Eating Chitterlings Is Like Going Slumming: Soul Food and Its Discontents." *Black Hunger: Food and Politics of U.S. Identity.* NY: Oxford University Press, 1999. 79–101.

Chapter Eleven

CONSUMING MEMORIES
The Embodied Politics of Remembering in Vietnamese American
Literature of the U.S. South

LISA HINRICHSEN

> ... the smell and taste of things remain poised a long time, like souls, ready to
> remind us, waiting and hoping for their moment, amid the ruins of all the rest;
> and bear unfaltering, in the tiny and almost impalpable drop of their essence,
> the vast structure of recollection.
>
> —**Marcel Proust,** *Swann's Way, Remembrance of Things Past, Volume I*[1]

Since Marcel Proust first consumed his famous madeleine, food has been
powerfully linked with the enigma of memory. As Proust claimed, food
has the power to revive "lost time," to awaken nostalgia, and to resurrect
involuntary memories. Drawing on food's mnemonic function, this essay
analyzes the complicated interplay between food's consumption and trauma's
assimilation in two novels by Vietnamese American writers: Lan Cao's *Monkey Bridge* (1997) and Monique Truong's *Bitter in the Mouth* (2010). In foregrounding cultural similarities between the U.S. South and the Global South,
these novels process complicated questions of historical trauma, diasporic
identity, national and regional identity, cultural assimilation, and neocolonialism through their fixation on material practices of food production and consumption. In underscoring the embodied politics of remembering, Cao and
Truong not only recall the fraught incorporation of Asians into the American body politic in the wake of the Vietnam War, but also forecast the role
that taste and diverse foodways play in enabling and sustaining the affective
and corporeal aspects of American multiculturalism. While underscoring the
overlap between Vietnamese and southern culture's traditional emphasis on
food, family, place, and the past, these texts also reveal the affective pressures

that are part of diasporic identity, and articulate the political and personal "bitterness" that often underlies the experience of globalization.

In positioning food and questions of taste as material links between complex political histories of globalization and displacement and personal affective histories, both *Monkey Bridge* and *Bitter in the Mouth* recall the history of Vietnamese immigration to the U.S. during the 1970s. In focusing on South-South axes of displacement and migration, this literature reflects the widespread dispersal of Vietnamese immigrants to southern locales such as Fort Smith, Arkansas; Clarkston, Georgia; Charlotte, North Carolina; Falls Church, Virginia; and Bayou La Batre, Alabama. And in centering on the production and consumption of food, Cao's and Truong's texts implicitly mirror how, as immigrants settled in the U.S. South and elsewhere, the food industry became a source of employment for many new arrivals. The restaurant business formed a way of maintaining cultural practices, as well as a great deal of personal independence, while earning a living, and Vietnamese restaurants began to appear in cosmopolitan centers throughout the U.S. after the end of the Vietnam War in the 1970s. Many Vietnamese immigrants also became engaged in other aspects of the food industry, such as shrimp and crab catching and processing along the Gulf of Mexico and ownership of specialty grocery stores. Indeed, the widespread availability of Vietnamese food throughout the U.S. is a marker of both the scope of immigration and the centrality of food to Vietnamese culture and immigrant entrepreneurship.

While the history of Vietnamese American literature, and especially Vietnamese American literature set in the U.S. South, is a relatively brief one—published writings before 1995 were almost exclusively rooted in authorial biography—its focus on food, family, and the presence of the past in the present resonates with long-standing tropes of southern literature.[2] As Maureen Ryan writes, Vietnamese American literature "offer[s] both a challenge to and a reinforcement of traditional southern perceptions of place, history, and family" (240), and she notes that this body of literature offers "fertile material for an exploration of that southern story of what Edward Ayers calls 'unresolved identity, unsettled and restless, unsure and defensive'" (252). While we must be careful not to limit our reading of Vietnamese American literature to southern tropes, flattening cultural and historical particularity, we can, as Ryan suggests, see key linkages with the intergenerational and intersubjective cultural politics that inform southern literature. Notably, however, the South frequently appears different when analyzed through the matrix of a transnational rather than national narrative.[3] Its allegedly exceptional cultural heritage is diminished or obliterated, and the South is instead often seen as American. In blurring the mythic boundary of North-South distinctiveness, and in dissolving conceptions of southern homogeneity, Vietnamese American literature suggests revised connections between the local and the national and the local and the international, reconfiguring historical and ideological narratives.

As I suggest here, culinary representations play a key part in this remapping, for they materialize a context of intercultural exchange and increasing global mobility and, importantly, become tropes linked with the desire to negotiate identity and memory in new transnational spaces. Specifically, Cao's and Truong's texts tie the consumption of food not only to processes of cultural assimilation but also to the struggle to work through historical and personal trauma. Highly conscious of both the body politic and the corporeal body, these writers utilize food as a way to return to the politics of materiality and physicality that shaped American reception of Vietnamese immigrants in the wake of the Vietnam War, while refuting the paradigms of essentialism, racism, and nationalism that were—and often continue to be—projected onto the refugee body.

Set in Falls Church, Virginia, Lan Cao's *Monkey Bridge* is a bildungsroman told in double time, interweaving a daughter's American experience in 1978 with her mother's 1968 Vietnamese experience in order to explore the intergenerational effects of trauma and its sociocultural construction. As *Monkey Bridge* links Mai Nguyen and her mother, Thanh, in a web of shared history, culture, affect and grief, and physical blood, bone, and body, the narrative complicates and questions the limits, wholeness, and consistency of identities. The double-layered, cross-generational plot of *Monkey Bridge* plays with collapsed time lines and confused temporal frameworks, oscillating back and forth between Vietnam and Virginia, but consistently positions the body as a physical topos for absorbing and conveying the psychological and material impact of violence. Here, it is a scarred "battlefield" that mirrors the devastated landscape of Vietnam (7). The text's insistence upon bodily memory and mimetic repetition in the form of bodily symptoms also gestures toward the central trauma of the tale: namely, the decision by Mai's grandmother to prostitute herself to the family's landlord to save the family's tenuous claim to farm his land, an action that irreparably fractured the family with "sin, illegitimacy, and murder" (228). Notably, Mai inherits not only a set of psychic and spiritual beliefs from her mother, who, marked by "single-minded conviction" and reluctance to assimilate to U.S. culture, commits suicide after preparing an elaborate ritual feast, but also a set of materialized practices and culturally specific rituals that largely revolve around food (204).

Central to the text's emphasis on the body as a political and psychic space is its overt concern with food as both a mnemonic and a cultural experience.

Mai notes that the American culture of disposability and consumer-driven taste problematizes the longevity of memory: "There was nothing to hold on to there. Nothing could stick in such a place" (92). Coming from a culture where the consumption of food functions as a way of marking time and entrenching memory—"I could tell the seasons of the year from her food" (219)—Mai and her mother now find themselves struggling with how to "stick" in time and place. Within an American culture that prizes packaged foodstuffs and throwaway convenience, which means dinner is served with "plastic spoons and knives, picnic plates and Ziploc bags, tin foil and Styrofoam cups" (92), Mai and Thanh utilize the production and consumption of Vietnamese food as a ritual practice in their attempts to suture past and present. Unlike friends who choose to "consume" America in the form of high fructose sweets, Mai and her mother find comfort in familiar tastes that replay history through sensation. The practice of everyday life takes on a strategic importance because the daily practices of cooking and culinary consumption become a localized, materialized means to work through the trauma of displacement. Drawing on the way that Vietnamese food revolves around the search for a balance of yin and yang properties—all but lost in American food culture—Mai and her mother seek to utilize food as a way to "commemorat[e] the luminous link that binds the dead and the living" in a culturally specific manner (219).[4]

The novel's emphasis on the quotidian materiality of life has a dual function: first, to present the "tender, vital, and most important mundane parts" of Vietnamese life (127); and, second, to offer a bodily politics of memory crucial to understanding diasporic Vietnamese identity. The "mundane parts" of Vietnamese life—here localized in the baking, simmering, and stuffing that goes on in the kitchen—play a political as well as descriptive role, offering a counternarrative to popular American conceptions of Vietnamese life that obscure or forget the everyday in favor of the spectacular trauma of wartime experience. Cao, like Mai herself, wants to tell an American public that it "was not all about rocket fires and body bags" (127). Her means of doing this is to descriptively "walk [us] to the bakeries, where bakers pulled from their oven trays of moon cakes, fat with stuffings of cashews, lotus and watermelon seed, round duck-egg yolks, and raisins" (127–28). Thick description here becomes more than mere literary indulgence. Within the politics of early Vietnamese American fiction, it forms the very means to engage with the politics of representation and historiography. The "urge to reveal something palpable," as realized in the signifying power of food, becomes a way to ground and localize history against the distortions of abstraction, generalization, and historical distance (127).

Food also becomes a signifier connected to the representation of racialized identity. As Anita Mannur argues in *Culinary Fictions: Food in South Asian Diasporic Culture* (2010), "the use of food is more than an a priori affirmation of palatable difference; it is also a way to undermine the racialized ideologies that culinary discourse is often seen to buttress" (7). The culinary is, as she positions it, a site of affirmation and resistance, marking community against diasporized realities and forming a means of resisting the way that identity is always readily available for consumption and commodification. Cao delivers extensive passages cataloging food that at first seem to offer merely "nostalgic gestures," or what Frank Chin (1981) calls "food pornography,"[5] a mode of representation that underscores the "exotic" aspects of ethnic foodways, marking eating and sensory taste as signs of cultural and national difference: "Huge hunks of dough humbled into delicate star-shaped dumplings, a complication of intestines and goose liver baked into precise loaves of pate [...] hand-whipped chocolate mousse laced with Chantilly cream, caramel custard inspired by my mother's Providence School days, lotus-seed pudding in a rock-sugar concoction, and the most delicate dish of all, a porridge of rare swallows' nests" (222).[6] Underscoring the impact of French colonialism on the national palate, Cao plays with taste as a record of both cultural history and individual experience. Yet *Monkey Bridge* repeatedly emphasizes the historical Vietnamese process of absorption, adaptation, refinement necessitated by colonial rule, which inherently troubles any easy definition of a national Vietnamese cuisine, and Cao reveals how this hybridity is realized in food culture: pate is served alongside dumplings, mousse alongside lotus-seed pudding. Cao's prose thus both performs and parodies orientalizing myths, strategically revealing the complications of national identity in the wake of colonialism and deconstructing American stereotypes about cultural and racial otherness as simultaneously consumable and indigestible.

Such connections between the consumption of food and the process of cultural assimilation link the body and the body politic in significant ways, raising key questions about cultural and historical memory even as they complicate simplistic paradigms of nationalism. As a young Vietnamese girl in the U.S. South, Mai suffers the double pressure of being both "invisible and at the same time awfully conspicuous" in a region where race has long been seen only along the limited binary of black and white, and her world largely takes place within the homoethnic enclave of Little Saigon (42). In her work on Asian American cultural politics, Lisa Lowe argues that the post-1965 Asian immigrant came to be seen as the return of the repressed memories of American neocolonialism in Asia. The Asian American immigrant's presence, according to Lowe, dramatized a threat to a U.S. identity founded upon repressing and forgetting that history, and as such, their bodies form a sign of historical trauma. The material body of the immigrant takes on the burden of cultural and historical memory, becoming, in Cao's words, the "custodian of a loss everyone knew about but refused to acknowledge" (64).

Sensing this, Mai initially believes that she and her mother "would have to go through the motions and float harmlessly as permanent guests, with no more impact on our surroundings than the mild, leisurely pace of an ordinary day. We would have to make ourselves innocuous and present to the outside world a mild, freeze-dried version of history" (42). That Cao draws on culinary language here—"mild, freeze-dried"—highlights the relationship between culinary practices and the affective and psychic pressures of racial assimilation, especially acute in the U.S South. Mai feels she must be easily consumable as a racial subject, her "otherness" made digestible to southern palates. The words she uses ring also of the mechanization of American food production, in which food is not harvested so much as it is manufactured, and this resonance underscores the relationship between culinary practices, the performative pressures of identity, and the construction of memory. Michael Lambek, for example, stresses how Western memory production "freezes words and images [. . .] puts frames around them; and [. . .] render[s] remembering mechanical and impersonal" (238). Cut off from both the land and from a shared historical sensibility, and under pressure to conform to new performative ways of being, Mai "float[s]," affectively and bodily discombobulated.

The ghostly social presence of the immigrant in the U.S. South is offset here, however, by the groundedness of culinary practice, the materiality of food that Cao cannot resist repeatedly cataloguing: "candied coconuts sliced into paper-thin strips, ginger diced into thick cubes and coated with rock sugar, tamarinds dipped in syrup to give them a succulent sour taste that tickled the tongue" (48). Against the "freeze-dried" American public sphere, Vietnamese food culture is here materially unleashed in an explosion of rich materiality, and the lyrical assonance and consonance of Cao's prose elevates food to the level of the poetic, linking the tongue and acts of linguistic production with moments of culinary consumption. That the richest descriptions of culinary practice lie inside Thanh's diary, which Mai peeks into as a way to communicate with her often silent mother, further adds to the relationship between a certain linguistic materiality and the tangibility of the meals she describes. *Monkey Bridge* thus asks what it means not only to "carr[y] the landscape of the delta in her flesh" (115), as Mai's mother does, but to consume, as Mai does, cuisines that reconfigure—and reground—the relationship between flesh and land via culinary consumption.

The grocery store becomes a loaded site for this cultural and culinary exchange. Throughout *Monkey Bridge*, Cao contrasts Mai's sense of the American A & P market's "fluorescent aisles," "sharply chilled air," and offerings of "cans of Coke," "chicken and meat sealed in tight, odorless packages" with Saigon's outdoor "sky markets" marked by the "sharp acrid smell of gutters," the "fat, heavy scent of guavas and bananas," and "barrels of live crabs and yellow carps and booths of duck and geese" (32–33). The A & P's "unexpected abundance" mirrors a mythic American excess. Mai and her mother are drawn toward "fruits so beautifully polished and waxed that they looked artificial" (33) and items wrapped in "dazzling packaging" (33). Like the fluorescent supermarkets in Don DeLillo's *White Noise* (1985), Cao's A & P marks the transactional economy of capitalism as well as the blandness fundamental to the logic of exchange and mass production. With its open spaces, goods of all kinds, meticulous designs, and seductive spectacles, the American supermarket becomes a mesmeric place that marks the "complete absence of identity, of history" (41). Under the fluorescent light of the A & P, everything is rendered hygienic, inoffensive: Mai finds "chicken and meat sealed in tight, odorless packages" (33). America here is, as Mai's mother declares, "the great brand-new" (60), and this "newness" takes the form of erasure. Cut, sealed, and packaged, the meat's origins are concealed, and any sign of earthiness or animal life is washed away. Any recognition of local produce or regional cuisine is invisible. The A & P, a grocery store with New York origins, epitomizes how Cao dissolves conceptions of North-South distinctiveness. Transnational food sales and chain stores usurp the presence of the particular and the local.

Even the Mekong Grocery in Falls Church's Little Saigon, where both Thanh and Mrs. Bay work, offers its own form of simulacra, providing a place of "fabricated [. . .] familiarity" (64) that lures in both Vietnamese and American GIs through offering up "frozen pulps of jackfruits and durians; the burlap sacks of dried arnica and lemon-grass stalks; the apothecary jars of eucalyptus oil, rice wine, and medicinal fluid steeped in hundred-year-old herbs; even the vats of nuoc mam, salted fish compressed for four months to a year into a pungent, fermented liquid" (64–65). Cao's prose emphasizes how food culture is tied to the impulse of many Little Saigon residents "to hang onto their Vietnam lives, caressing the shape of a country that was no longer there" (255). Whereas the A & P offers the comfort of both order and excess, the Mekong Grocery provides its own stabilizing familiarity, for it functions as a place where shoppers can forget about the U.S. South that surrounds them. For the GIs that frequent the Mekong Grocery, it provides a space to reconnect with the material world they simultaneously inhabited as well as destroyed. If the Vietnam War, according to Mrs. Bay, represents a "consuming complication of allegiances" (65), those commitments linger, *Monkey Bridge* indicates, in experiences of taste, or in what we might think of as modes of "culinary citizenship" that are not necessarily equivalent to national citizenship (Mannur 20). As Mrs. Bay states, "Those who had been in Vietnam, the vets and us, were forever set apart from everyone else, who hadn't" (65).

Monkey Bridge's final commentary on food culture comes in a description of Thanh's final feast, which she prepares before committing suicide. This meal both realizes and definitively concludes the commentary on the power of food to awaken cultural and individual memory. Suffering from the "common contagion of nostalgia" (212), Thanh ritualizes the extravagant preparation for her feast. In the midst of this frenzy of activity, Mai feels "part of something immaculate and sweet, a domestic order that comforted and consoled" (217). Instead of feeling like an adult, translating English and helping her mother navigate American culture, Mai, in the warmth of a kitchen simmering with delicious smells, feels like "a child whose mother cooked" (222). In consuming the meal, Mai feels linked with a lost time and place, and Cao underscores the potential of food to bridge time and space, opening up the "could have been" of history: "We could have been in our brick courtyard in Saigon some time before April 30, 1975, and I could have been surrounded by an intact family" (218).

Yet Mai realizes only belatedly that this "week-long four burner feast" serves as "a death mask or a funeral arrangement" (256). The ritual of food preparation, which she thought promised "the virtue of a clean beginning" and a "sense [of] order," actually marks an end, and the cultural function of the culinary to be the "monkey bridge" between past and present, here and there, takes on a haunting resonance as Mai realizes the personal intent behind her mother's elaborate feast (225). Food stands in here as an offering, a surplus that counterbalances the lack of spoken language between mother and daughter, putting closure not only to Thanh's life but to the unresolved familial past. As Thanh notes in her diary, the feast she prepares "is exactly the feast I would have prepared for your grandmother years ago had we not been caught in the cross fire between the elephant and the fleas" (254). Like writing, food becomes a way of communicating what cannot be said directly. The feast becomes a way of saying, as her mother writes, that "it is all yours, the nerve tissue of your family's past, the labor and loop of your mother's life, and the blood that pumps its own imperishable future through the chambers of your heart" (254). Food is linked with flesh, futurity, and inheritance, and this meal, in which trauma is both produced and consumed, brings together the familial and the feminine, evoking the haunting power of the grandmother's bodily transgressions and the sustenance of the mother's heart and breast.

The primary mother-child bond is rehearsed and recemented in this final funeral feast; heart and mouth are repeatedly fused and food and affect are intertwined. Mai eats to fill her hunger for "emotional attachments that carried the length and depth of time and space" (226). In filling her appetite both for the past and for the future yet to come, Mai's mother attempts to leave her with an experience of shared taste that becomes a way of "commemorating the luminous link that binds the dead and the living" (219). The delicate, spindly nature of food as "monkey bridge," however, is positioned in ambiguous terms, as Mai is left still struggling to digest what happened, to balance the tastes of the final feast with the bitter sensation of loss.

Sensations of bitterness and loss likewise linger in Monique Truong's *Bitter in the Mouth* (2010). Published thirteen years after *Monkey Bridge*, *Bitter in the Mouth* provides an updated account of Vietnamese American experience in the U.S. South and gives a much clearer picture of regionality. Truong, the author of the best-selling *The Book of Salt* (2003), revisits Cao's tropes of family, food, and memory, but she also underscores—and exudes skepticism about—crucial changes in the diversity of southern identities and, more broadly, in an American sense of taste. *Bitter in the Mouth*, like *Monkey Bridge*, engages both with far-reaching geographic politics and with the localized space of the body, transforming questions of physical and cultural displacement into multifaceted sensory experiences, but it more insistently reflects the way contemporary Asian American literature responds to the discourses of postmodernism, post-structuralism, and issues of diaspora, transationalism, and postcolonialism. Though centrally concerned with Vietnamese identity in the South, *Bitter in the Mouth* offers none of the lush cataloguing of Vietnamese food that makes up the bulk of *Monkey Bridge*. Instead, Truong works through the politics of difference by presenting the costs of sameness in the form of homogenized and mass-manufactured food that is now as global as it is American. Preoccupied by the relationship between the universal and the particular or local, Truong focuses on the problem of how both taste and language are constituted, established, and mobilized in relation to the racialized subject.

Like *Monkey Bridge*, *Bitter in the Mouth* is a bildungsroman, and Truong tells the story of Linda Hammerick's upbringing in Boiling Springs, North Carolina. Truong sets her tale of Linda's transition into adulthood during the 1970s and 1980s, a time when, as Linda states, the world no longer "routinely bypassed" the tiny town of Boiling Springs: instead, "South American magnolias and JC Penny catalogs came to Boiling Springs. New cars from Detroit and plastic hair barrettes from Taiwan came [. . .] Ersatz pizzas and all-you-can-eat salad bars came to Boiling Springs. De facto segregation and dead-end jobs came to Boiling Springs. Queers, Jews, Chinks, Japs, and Gooks came" (213). In stressing the Americanization of Dixie—namely, how Boiling Springs has become "like any other American city, only smaller and duller and with less crime" (213)—Truong asks us to think about the consequences of the globalization of capitalism and the proliferation of "free" markets on everyday life in the South. As she stresses through her harnessing of a string of epithets, consumer diversity does not find an equivalent in a corresponding sense of racial and ethnic diversity. Instead, the suturing of the South to the Global South through capitalism's exportation abroad has only further entrenched structures of exploitation. Furthermore, the excess that is produced in "America, a country of abundance" and "North Carolina, a state of plenty" (34), here materialized in an everyday sense as food culture, the gluttony of the "all-you-can-eat" buffet is undermined by being linked to the "ersatz," or the fake and inferior, highlighting the presence of cheap foodstuffs that often fill such buffets, and spotlighting the contemporary South itself as a site of artifice.

In this world of inferior excess, the "real"—whether that be the "real South" or real food—is not only hard to get ahold of, but it is often no longer even desired. In place of nutritious food, there are instead incomplete meals that substitute for real cooking; mention of artificial sweeteners like vanillin used in "instant, industrialized baked goods" like "Nilla Wafers, Chips Ahoy!, Lorna Doones" (76); and commentary on "the endangered art of baking" (267). Every night Linda's mother "dependably" pulls out a casserole for dinner—"chicken a la king, tuna noodle, beefy macaroni" (34)—made from prepackaged goods that predictably taste the same: "No matter the recipe, a can of condensed cream of mushroom soup, the all-American binding agent of disparate foodstuff, was mixed in" (35). Through terming this can of mushroom soup "the Great Assimilator" (34) and later labeling Bisquick as the "American Dream" ("With it, we could do anything" [75]), Truong links domestic materiality with American national identity, offering a wry commentary on the loss—of flavor, of diversity, of distinction—that accompanies a certain facile notion of how to mix things (and people) together. An American food culture that tries to appeal to all through the diminishing of distinctive notions of taste ultimately appeals, Truong suggests, to no one. Truong thus investigates the unacknowledged ways that race continues to structure and define both the public sphere and the private sphere, and positions taste, something that is both intimate and socially determined, as a way to think about both of these categories.

In positioning unremarkable daily meals as assertions of bland American dreams and values and linking homogenized taste with the contemporary realities of agro-industrial food production, Truong's text resonates with Amy Kaplan's insights on "manifest domesticity," or the ways in which "international struggles for domination abroad profoundly shape representations of American national identity at home, and how, in turn, cultural phenomena we think of as domestic or particularly national are forged in a crucible of foreign relations" (1). The kitchen is a transactional site for the flows of transnational capitalism, as practices of quotidian material life subsidize corporate growth abroad, and with this expansion, the corresponding exportation of national ideologies. Though the food cultures she presents are often more American than they are southern, Truong's text traces the presence of regional identities and food cultures much more assertively and explicitly than Cao's novel, suggesting that as the narrative of globalization unfolds, locality paradoxically plays a more pronounced and important role than it ever has.

Engaging with southern archetypes, histories, foodways, and literature, from its opening epigraph from *To Kill a Mockingbird* (which Linda reads, likening her father to Atticus Finch) to repeated mentions of Linda's idolization of Dolly Parton, *Bitter in the Mouth* both draws on and troubles southern culture and history. Truong underscores how regional foodways and traditional cuisines play an important role in materializing southern culture, and the text is littered with mentions of sweet tea, sweet potato fields, pimento cheese, Cheerwine, mint juleps, red velvet cake, peach cobbler, and buttermilk biscuits. Southern culture seems to be the only place where "the endangered art of baking" (267) survives, and where, though still hardly nutritious, the food is made from recipes rather than boxes. Truong describes, for example, Boiling Springs as a place where "[b]arbecue was as great a divider as religion" (65) and where "renouncing pork was the equivalent of renouncing God" (234), revealing the relationship between food cultures and community formation. Yet while southern foodways are celebrated—the allure of Bridges Barbeque Lodge's extraordinary vinegary sauce and pulled pork sandwich stands out vividly against "Pizza Inn, Waffle House, Arby's, Roy Rogers, and Hardee's" (39)—southern history, especially its history of racial intolerance, is resolutely problematized. But there are interpersonal divides more significant than barbecue in Boiling Springs. Indeed, Truong implicitly suggests, the pressure to reassert forms of "southern living" might even reentrench patterns of division, if not structures of racial alienation.

Curiously, only belatedly does the text fold in racial issues. This belatedness is both a strategic move to mirror the cultural whitewashing of Linda's Asian heritage in the South and a reflection of her own delayed knowledge of the true facts of her parental history. Linda's Vietnamese background is revealed to the reader midway through the novel at her graduation from Yale when her name is called as "Linh-Dao Nguyen Hammerick" (158). We later learn that she was orphaned in a traumatic fire, which she cannot remember, and subsequently adopted by the very southern Hammerick family (their uppercrust background stems from making their money in cotton, "another way of saying they had made their money in slaves" [55]). Within *Bitter in the Mouth*, race is explored as a disjunction, a split between "being" and "looking": "I was often asked by complete strangers what it was like to grow up being Asian in the South. You mean what was it like to grow up *looking* Asian in the South" (169). Linda's grandmother Iris, a traditional southern belle, makes her understand that they are "close in the way Maine and Hawaii were close," couching race in the language of geography, and Linda comes to think of herself as "a mirror that failed to produce an exact image," and thus "an "aberration," for the "body, especially that of an offspring, was best when it was a reflective surface" (133). With her body turned into a blankness acknowledged by nobody, she hides behind a model minority identity of being "the Brain," a prosthetic intellectual self, or what she terms the "disembodied" "Smartest Girl" in the room (173). Truong thus insistently critiques the politics of contemporary American colorblindness, which is marked by a refusal to see difference and to acknowledge race. In exposing the contradiction between aspirations to universality and the diminishing of difference and particularity, Truong's novel builds upon *Monkey Bridge*'s situation of Mai's body as "invisible and at the same time awfully conspicuous," to provide a critique of the type of neoliberal "freedom" and community built on the strategic forgetting of race, exposing the affective and psychological cost of assimilation in our putatively postidentity age (42).

Amidst and against this racial and historical forgetting, Truong positions the sensation of taste, presenting a mode of hybridity that is internal rather than, like race, in the realm of the visible. In deferring a direct address of Linda's multiculturality until the midpoint of the text, Truong instead centers on multisensory experience, for Linda realizes the world in synesthetic terms: "When my teacher asked, 'Linda, where did the English first settle in North Carolina?' the question would come to me as 'Linda*mint*, where did the English*maraschinocherry* first*Pepto-Bismol* settle*mustard* in Northched-darcheese* Carolina*cannedpeas*?'" (21) The multisensory and multicultural are linked through the way that transnationalism can be conceptualized as processes through which "immigrants forge and sustain multi-stranded social relations that link together their societies of origin and settlement" (Basch et al. 7). Here, Truong explores these "multi-stranded social relations" as sensory or neurological networks.

Via her synesthesia, Linda finds that, like food itself, "the word could also fulfill and satisfy," filling her with sensation (75). Language can be craved: "I would long for the word like it was a spoonful of peach cobbler, the kind that Bridges served only on Saturdays" (102). Indeed, the taste of words is often more appetizing than her mother's disastrous dinners:

> I, a skinny eleven-year-old, sat on the edge of the bathtub and blurted out, "Notagain*pancakenosyrup*."
>
> There it was. Sustenance. Simple. Without sauce.
>
> Each repetition of "again" was a revelation. The faster I said it, the more intense and mouth-filling the taste became. Each repetition was a restitution for past meals suffered. Each repetition was an inoculation for future meals to be endured. I wanted to see how many times I would have to say the word in order to approximate the feeling of being full. (75)

In positioning taste here as "sustenance," and in locating it directly in contrast to "future meals to be endured," Truong charts out an alternative aesthetics of consumption. As Bourdieu theorizes, taste functions as both an aesthetic and a moral category, and as a means of distinction because "good taste" is acquired through acculturation into a certain social position. Taste thus both groups and separates individuals. Though Linda speaks a common tongue, her language is an idiolect of its own, fundamentally connected with a sensation of taste that cannot be adequately communicated. The specific links between language and taste that she experiences are hers alone, a private speech rooted in the body. Though filled with "intense and mouth-filling" sensation, Linda's taste is not equivalent with the "good taste" of social belonging.

Instead, these tastes, which she terms her "incomings" (23), are so strong and distracting that they only further contribute to her social isolation in her small southern community. She tries to diminish her multisensory experience of the world through dipping tobacco, smoking cigarettes, and drinking alcohol: "I smoked my way into an attention span that matched my academic potential" (24). In her need to concentrate on the meanings of the words she hears in class and in social situations—the focus necessary to acquire "good taste"—she has to "neutraliz[e]" the idiosyncratic taste that accompanies each signifier (29). Yet the novel also explores what happens when Linda does the reverse, as when she "disregard[s] the meanings of the words" in order to "enjoy what the words could offer me" (74). Here, the disconnection between signifier and signified, *langue* and *parole*, is freeing, for its arbitrariness produces its own kind of pleasure, even as Linda lets go of the safety of intelligibility. In bringing together empiricism and theory, and in linking post-structuralist accounts of language with theories of taste, emphasizing the mouth as a site for both ingestion and utterance, Truong likens the exchange of food and the sensation of taste to the trafficking of signs and the speaking of a tongue. With the locating of taste as a cognitive problem, a fissure or friction of matter and spirit, signified and signifier, Linda's synesthesia raises key questions about the relationship between the social and the private. Because taste is here linked—arbitrarily but significantly—to language, Truong suggests that foodways (and what we might think of as "tasteways") are connected with the production and retention of cultural and personal narratives. In setting Linda's idiosyncratic, heterogeneous sense of taste against an increasingly homogenous, bland, "tasteless" American food culture, Truong plays with the tension between particularity and universality, and asks what is lost when we diminish the eccentricities of taste.

Intriguingly, like *Monkey Bridge*, *Bitter in the Mouth* suggests that taste becomes its own form of historical documentation, functioning as a mnemonic device rooted in the body. As Ann Cvetkovich has suggested, affect might be considered a form of history itself, with the potential to reconfigure conventional understandings of identity and representation. Like the production and consumption of food, which Cao's *Monkey Bridge* positions as fundamental to the transfer of culture, taste is an ineffable part of the structure of feeling that underlies lived experience. Here, emotional and affective life *is* political life. As with the trailer fire that killed Linda's biological parents, all that might be left is the "taste of bitter" (117), a kind of residue in the body: "The trailer on fire might not have existed. There were no photographs and no history, official or anecdotal. There was only my memory: coffee left too long on the burner, an uncoated aspirin caught in the throat, how a drop of mercury might taste on the tip of the tongue" (117). Linda notes that her lexical-gustatory synesthesia, which she calls her "secret sense," functions, precisely because of its fundamental heterogeneity, as "an inborn mnemonic device" (115). Synesthesia becomes a form of cognitive cryptography for the trauma she was not able to assimilate as a young child, here manifested as a "bitterness in the mouth" for which she cannot find language. It is a form of cognitive hybridity that performs cross-cultural and cross-sensorial work, enacting what Sneja Gunew provocatively calls the "mouthwork" of memory processing, and Truong ultimately offers a complex vision of neurological cosmopolitanism that contests typical arrangements of identity and experience and reconfigures them, effectively remapping cognitive and geopolitical space.

For in centering on the mysterious sensation of a bitterness impossible to adequately name, Truong suggests that sensation exceeds the language that we have to name it. The narrative that emerges from the "mouthwork of memory" can only approximate the way trauma is registered in the body. The word triggers sensation but is not equivalent to the taste, and Truong leaves us with questions of how to symbolize lack and how to bring it from private affect into public consciousness. In the absence of language, taste lingers, marking trauma's void and making its absence present. The radical subjectivity of taste, Truong suggests, is forgotten in universalizing narratives, and the mysterious eccentricities of the body—its appetite for not only food, but, as the novel elsewhere indicates, for sex—are erased in favor of dominant paradigms of social experience.

Here, the multisensory nature of synesthesia, which has no "master" narrative, is mobilized against paradigms of homogeneity. In the small community of Boiling Springs, which stands in for the South as a whole, the uniformity of taste, race, and historical narrative are challenged and dismantled by Linda's particular mode of sensing and feeling the world. The hybridity intrinsic to synesthesia intensifies the affective dimensions of language but also creates alienation. Taste, Truong indicates, makes language strange. In reclaiming what she terms "unrelated" sensations, her synesthesia initiates an investigation into how the multicultural imaginary powerfully renders whiteness—and its dominant modes of feeling, evaluating, and tasting—uncanny (21). In contrast to her white southern household's aesthetic of sameness—her mother's frequent use of cans of mushroom soup ("the Great Assimilator") and packages of Bisquick (the "American Dream")—Linda reimagines the world as otherwise, asserting what Lisa Lowe terms the "heterogeneity, hybridity, and multiplicity" that function in Asian American texts not just as rhetorical moves but as "the material conditions that characterize Asian American groups" (67).

As Truong subtly underscores, multicultural environments are by nature synesthetic, interweaving different smells, cultural styles, music, and colors. We daily cross "monkey bridges" between mind and body, present and past, self and culture, here and there, you and me. Our individuality is always crossed, mediated, and yoked together by culture, history, family, and taste. Thus, Truong builds upon and updates the framework that Cao offers for the exploration of memory, providing a more nuanced conception of the relationship between food and culture in Vietnamese and southern culture. As novels obsessed with questions of taste, food production and consumption, and cultural difference and assimilation, Lan Cao's *Monkey Bridge* and Monique Truong's *Bitter in the Mouth* form provocative entry points for a discussion of the role that food plays in diasporic cultures, including an increasingly diverse U.S. South, and in the construction and retention of cultural and individual memory.

Notes

1. P. 37.

2. See Janette, 105–6.

3. For more on the South and globalization, see James C. Cobb's and William Stueck's edited collection *Globalization and the American South* and James L. Peacock's *Grounded Globalism: How the U.S. South Embraces the World.*

4. As Sari Edelstein writes, yin is "whatever is cold, fluid, humid, passive, somber, interior, deficient, and feminine in essence like the sky, moon, night, water, and winter" (328). Yang is linked to "whatever is hot, luminous, active, exterior, excessive, and masculine in essence like the earth, sun, fire, and summer" (328).

5. The term "food pornography" comes from Chin's play *The Year of the Dragon* (86).

6. Notably, Cao explicitly defines "pho," a staple of Vietnamese food, as "white noodles in a beef broth with a faint touch of cinnamon and anise, cilantro and parsley floating on top" (68), marking this as a text that has the white American reader in mind.

Works Cited

Basch, Linda, Nina Glick Schiller, and Cristina Szanton-Blanc. *Nations Unbound: Transnational Projects and the Deterritorialized Nation-State.* New York: Gordon and Breach, 1994.

Bourdieu, Pierre. *Distinctions: A Social Critique of the Judgment of Taste.* Trans. Richard Nice. Cambridge, MA: Harvard UP, 1984.

Cao, Lan. *Monkey Bridge.* New York: Penguin, 1998.

Chin, Frank. *The Chickencoop Chinaman / The Year of the Dragon: Two Plays.* Seattle: U of Washington P, 1982.

Cobb, James C., and William Stueck, eds. *Globalization and the American South.* Athens: U of Georgia P, 2005.

Cvetkovich, Ann. *An Archive of Feelings: Trauma, Sexuality and Lesbian Public Cultures.* Durham: Duke UP, 2003.

Edelstein, Sari. *Food, Cuisine, and Cultural Competency for Culinary, Hospitality, and Nutrition Professionals.* Sudbury, MA: Jones and Bartlett, 2010.

Gunew, Sneja. "'Mouthwork': Food and Language as the Corporeal Home for the Unhoused Diasporic Body in South Asian Women's Writing." *The Journal of Commonwealth Literature* (June 2005) 40: 93–103.

Janette, Michele. "Vietnamese American Literature in English, 1963–1994." In *Asian-American Writers.* Ed. Harold Bloom. New York: InfoBase Publishing, 2009. 105–22.

Kaplan, Amy. *The Anarchy of Empire in the Making of U.S. Culture.* Cambridge, MA: Harvard UP, 2003.

Lambek, Michael. "The Past Imperfect: Remembering as Moral Practice." In *Tense Past: Cultural Essays in Trauma and Memory.* Ed. Michael Lambek and Paul Antze. London: Routledge, 1996. 235–54.

Lowe, Lisa. *Immigrant Acts: On Asian-American Cultural Politics*. Durham: Duke UP, 1996.

Mannur, Anita. *Culinary Fictions: Food in South Asian Diasporic Culture*. Philadelphia: Temple UP, 2010.

Peacock, James L. *Grounded Globalism: How the U.S. South Embraces the World*. Athens: U of Georgia P, 2007.

Proust, Marcel. *Swann's Way, Remembrance of Things Past, Volume I*. Trans. C.K. Scott Moncrieff. Teddington, Middlesex: The Echo Library, 1922.

Ryan, Maureen. "Outsiders with Inside Information: The Vietnamese in the Fiction of the Contemporary American South." In *South to a New Place: Region, Literature, Culture*. Ed. Suzanne W. Jones and Sharon Monteith. Athens: U of Georgia P, 2002. 235–52.

Truong, Monique. *Bitter in the Mouth*. New York: Random House, 2010.

Chapter Twelve

THE ECONOMICS OF EATING
Native Recipes for Survival in Contemporary Southern Literature

MELANIE BENSON TAYLOR

In his introduction to an American Indian–themed special issue of *Southern Cultures*, editor Harry Watson ends with the reminder that "'Native American' is as southern as succotash" (5). Unfortunately, for most southerners, that realization generally comes as a side order rather than the main dish, and as metaphor or memory more than reality. The Native American roots of southern heritage are frequently recognized (or invented), while the still-thriving indigenous branches of the regional family tree are far more rarely and incidentally acknowledged. Indeed, in the South more than anywhere else in the nation, it is commonplace and desirable to claim a remote Cherokee princess grandmother who provides colorful dinner conversation but little else of enduring cultural import.[1] As Watson's succotash metaphor implies, the occluded legacy of American Indian southerners extends even to the region's distinctive and celebrated foodways. In fact, appreciating the indigenous elements of the southern table shines an especially intimate and revealing light on the foundational, sustaining, and largely unnoticed origins of the regional character. As Joe Gray Taylor and John T. Edge state at the outset of the *Foodways* volume of the *New Encyclopedia of Southern Culture*, "The first white men to come into the South ate what the American Indians ate . . . They had to learn these lessons to survive and later push their way westward" (1). All over the continent, it seems, the same ironic pattern held: the Indians' gifts of corn and succotash provided the means of survival that fueled westward expansion and the birth of a nation—and paradoxically, ensured the slow destruction and occlusion of the Natives' own crops, cultures, and lifeways.

That "destruction" is complete only in the national imagination, though, where indigenous influences tend to exist as historical relics rather than actual, living presences. In the South especially, the assumption that local

Indians vanished after Removal is nearly universal, and so far, the burgeoning, multiethnic field of southern foodways has failed to offer evidence to the contrary. Beyond token acknowledgments of Indians' prior inhabitance and culinary tutelage to the first settlers, "No Indian claims to a rightful place within southern foodways [have] surfaced," Rayna Green laments, "and no one has made any claims on Indians' behalf"—not even Indians (123). A Cherokee southerner herself, Green posits her own plea for visibility in this vacancy:

> The story (and the action that needs to follow a good story) is missing in the South, where Native food might bring good news. And with that news could come a cultural construct that might be surprisingly useful—a region of the mind called "Native South"—a good name, perhaps, for the chain of restaurants that could appear in Indian casinos. The food served there would be shockingly familiar, albeit a tad underseasoned, to all good southerners, and once again Indians will welcome everyone to eat. (124)

Green vitally touts the inestimable benefits of unveiling a "Native South" that extends far beyond the buffet table and well into the regional imaginary. Such a project, begun haltingly in literary and historical studies, has yet to enjoy widespread recognition and acceptance. What would come along with that development, however, is not necessarily auspicious: as Green tacitly implies, the indigenous feast table will once again be open for consumption by all, just as we have seen their innate cultural goodwill and hospitality exploited repeatedly throughout the colonial saga. In these contemporary iterations, moreover, the reclamation of indigenous culture is manufactured within the walls of casinos and branded franchises, where the daily special differs little from the overprocessed, undernourishing dish shared—and sold—by all the hungry inhabitants of postcolonial, capitalist America.[2]

A Place at the Table: Making Room for Native Southern Studies

Published in 2007, the *Foodways* volume of the *New Encyclopedia of Southern Culture* begins with a nod to the foundational influence of the American Indian diet in southern food culture, but the attention to indigeneity ends there. Along with entries for things like "biscuits," "chitterlings," and "lunch counters," the volume includes sections on African American, Appalachian, Cajun, Hispanic American, and Jewish foodways—essentially, every and any ethnic, racial, and geographical sect *but* Native American Indians. Sprinkled sparsely throughout the collection, the reminder of indigenous presence

provides a faint hint of flavor on the margins. In many ways, this oversight—
or, more accurately, peripheral repression—is symptomatic of the persistent
marginalization of Native southern studies in the South's academic and cultural landscapes more broadly. For most, the reality of the southern Indian is
simply an oxymoron or an anachronism, where southerners typically assume
that local Natives live on only in bloodlines and place names rather than as
an ongoing, vital presence. Indeed, the Native South is a space rarely considered an active geography within Indian country at all, even by Native scholars.[3] As Mick and Ben Gidley suggest in a recent essay, "The eradication of
Indian tribes in the Southeast was probably more wholesale than in any other
culture area," and the narratives accompanying those efforts only intensified
its effects (167). Following Andrew Jackson's sweeping Removal efforts of the
1830s, the idea of a southeastern Indian became swiftly and virtually obsolete,
emblematic of "an entire vanished way of life" (Peterson 4). Today, Natives
are popularly assumed to be clustered in the Southwest, in Oklahoma, on the
plains—not in the grits-and-gravy territories of the Deep South.

Yet the often surprising fact is that many Indians *do* remain, either having resisted Removal or returned in later decades to reunite with families and
lands left behind. But for a variety of reasons, these groups fly low on the radar
of both "official" recognition and quotidian contact. Of the 564 tribes currently recognized by the federal government, only a fraction reside in southern states. Many more have state recognition, and others persist in informal
but highly organized and enduring communities.[4] It is true that Removal
accomplished the radical diminution of tribes in the area, not simply at the
moment of eviction but in the subsequent struggle to survive in a region that
labored to forget its indigenous history. For the generations who survived
in the South beyond Removal, preserving Native identity in the region was
further fraught by the strict biracial politics of Jim Crow. Loretta Leach, a
Wassamasaw Indian, grew up in 1950s South Carolina unable to admit or
even inquire about her heritage: "People around us would say we were too
dark to be white and too light-skinned to be black. So what were we?" she
wonders. When her own children are born, she documents them officially as
"white," well schooled in the lessons of her parents that "it was too hard to be
Indian because you would be cast out of the community," but claiming to be
black was worse, "because you might be lynched. Best not to claim anything
at all" (213). For many other Indians, even this feeble choice of omission was
preempted by social oversight and administrative fiat: in the "paper genocide" of the South's Natives, the most notorious "murderer" was Walter Ashby
Plecker, a Virginia physician who served as registrar of the state's Bureau of
Vital Statistics. In this capacity, he devoted thirty-four years to "reclassifying

Indian and mixed-blood Virginians" as "either black or white," using threats and coercion to train staff members to carry out his racist mission as well (Hobson et al. 1).

Indeed, those tribal groups that do obviously remain, such as the Mississippi Choctaw or the Florida Seminoles, are frequently deemed too "modern," mixed, and assimilated to qualify as "real" Indians anymore. Writing about the cinematic version of Forrest Carter's faux-Cherokee autobiography, *The Education of Little Tree*, one reviewer marveled that "Indians are no longer the indigenous people of the earth . . . they are just like the rest of us. They like to hunt, make moonshine, gather wild herbs in season, and have a close relationship with the earth. In short, they are a lot like the hill people in the Tennessee mountains, with Indian stuff added to their lives as a kind of cultural spice" (Marker 226). While I know many Tennessee folk who would object to this caricature of themselves, I know still more Cherokees who would vehemently protest being relegated to the spice rack of Appalachia. Put simply, American Indians are perhaps the only cultural group expected to remain forever unchanged and frozen in time. Partly, this phenomenon is the ugly stepchild of colonial guilt: it is much easier to suppress the demons of national settlement when its victims are no longer vital presences capable of asserting their proprietary rights and their legitimate, treaty-sanctioned claims to political sovereignty. Certainly, many contemporary tribal nations do persist in this way, holding fast to their embattled status as independent nations on ceaselessly shifting but wholly valid legal grounds—a reality that is supremely difficult for many Americans to acknowledge directly. Americans face the vestiges of black-white racism soberly (if often too sanguinely) because slavery and segregation are safely considered closed chapters in the errors of history. Confronting Indian affairs is far stickier because, given the ongoing crises and conflicts in Indian country and federal mismanagement, it is abundantly clear that no moral conflict has been surmounted or even acknowledged precisely. For the white South, any reminders that Indian removal strengthened—indeed, made possible—the entire plantation economy contravened regional myths of nativist autochthony, agency, and integrity. The notion that Indians deserve to be reckoned as central rather than peripheral figures in southern history and culture is an unsettling fact rarely acknowledged either within the region or beyond.

Rather than acknowledge their indebtedness to these indigenous forebears, Americans have proven far more likely to adopt mythical and anachronistic Indian analogues to serve their own more immediate purposes and crises. Specifically, in an age of expanding global capitalism and its corrosive effects, antimaterial alternatives such as those presumably embodied by Native cultures increase in popularity and need. At the same time, the supposed "savagery" of Native cultures has proven an irresistible vehicle for non-Native subjects to play out their own repressed fantasies of violence; this phenomenon takes explicit, visible forms as well as more subtle ones, such as in the development of regional barbecue as a "savage" expression of anti-European, nativist culture. Such borrowings allow Americans to participate viscerally in a "primitive" tradition and culture that their everyday lives and identities would otherwise negate or resist. Literally for centuries, the ideological Indian has shifted character and purpose along with the changing needs of the dominant national culture, absorbing its anxieties and desires like allegorical tofu.[5]

This claim to syncretism may seem distasteful or reactionary to some, as it appears to further elide rather than uncover the distinct Indian roots and traces in the regional fabric. Generally speaking, Native critics are not anxious to see indigenous culture further entrapped within the inhospitable borders of regionalism generally, and particularly within a historically impolitic and exclusionary field like southern studies.[6] To be sure, a continued emphasis on regionalism and regionalist studies constitutes for many a decidedly backward step in a field focused on moving beyond colonialist geographies and paradigms, yet this need not necessarily be the case, as a number of new "critical regionalist" perspectives has begun to elucidate. Despite the current proliferation of globalization's reach and impact, those studies argue, localism—another form of tribalism—becomes an increasingly vital, often reactionary and protective category of lived experience and ideology. In his *Critical Regionalism* (2007), for example, Douglas Powell acknowledges that region is inherently a "social invention," but as such, it "supplies critical regionalism [with] a language of possibility, rooted in the landscapes of particular communities viewed in terms of their vital connectedness to other places.... The function of critical regionalist cultural scholarship ideally should be not only to criticize but also to plan, to envision ... the construction of texts that can envision more just and equitable landscapes" (24–25). By reappraising the profound cultural connections among and within the South's disparate communities, we better understand the inherent constructedness of regional imaginaries at the same time that we imagine and invent new, "more just and equitable" containers of belonging—including the Native South "of the mind" that Rayna Green calls for. In *Reasoning Together* (2008), a volume produced collectively by several Native literary critics working toward tribally attuned theoretical models, Tol Foster (Cherokee) advocates an approach called "relational regionalism," which takes into account the profound transformative influence of indigenous cultures on surrounding non-Native communities, and vice versa. Looking beyond the immediate borders and traditions of a particular tribal context allows us to see the powerful ways in which those outside influences are imbricated in the community's life and evolution: the region beyond the tribe's borders does not just effect change on tribal groups but is in fact changed *by* them as well. Foster warns that such revelations are neither the uncritical, glorifying regionalisms of the past nor the idealized utopias of postcolonial models. "The regional frame traces contributions and collisions between communities as those events and practices become constitutive of the communities themselves," he explains (273). In the end, he argues, such an approach might actually prove "in a strange way tribally specific" (271, 270).

In the South especially, cries against invasive federal policies and meddling financial interests beyond the region bind both the post-Reconstruction southern and the Native ideologies in a common anti-industrial, anticommercial orientation. Both groups—with varying degrees of cause and complicity—perceive themselves to be victimized and exploited by a national economy on which they have long depended (and thus resented). Yet, despite their mutual protests and resistance, both groups reveal that they are, in fact, inextricable from what the contemporary South itself has necessarily become: a region committed to profit, strength, purity, and endurance more voraciously than any other American region. Attempts to embody the value-positive ideal of resisting capitalism's dehumanizing mechanisms fail to transcend figurative potential, and more often, southeastern Native writers attest to an ineluctable entanglement within the system that degrades and devalues them. More distressing, these efforts have the uncanny effect of driving cultural groups further apart and into isolation, and constructing a marketable fantasy of authenticity rather than the less appetizing goulash that it really is. The casino cafes that Rayna Green imagines would no doubt "sell" an image of authentic Native cuisine that feels both strange and familiar all at once, but it also constructs and markets a fantasy that does little justice to the vibrant and eclectic hybridity of the contemporary South, nor to the living indigenous cultures that have always been at its source.[7]

In many ways, tracing out the resurgence of Native foodways is one of the most apt and revealing ways to investigate this phenomenon. While we are better able to appreciate the rich fusions of the southern mix, we must also face the reality that the end result is rarely harmonious or unproblematic. In the same way that the Native example and type has been ossified and usurped by the American postcolonial imagination, so too are Indian contributions to the southern feast table consumed and exploited inequitably. The current trendiness of heirloom foods and "authentic" (read: unprocessed, clean, unmodified) foods necessarily turns the public gaze back to Native American models, but that process has been slow to infuse the South's food scene, presumably because there are fewer visible tribes and community gardens to headline such efforts. But I am less concerned here with uncovering precisely what those Indian influences are than with interrogating the import and implications of such attention. In what follows, I aim to show the pressures experienced by Native southerners in acknowledging that irrefutable hybridity borne of long regional association at the same time that they struggle to preserve, showcase, and "sell" their own distinctive cultural traits and contributions. The process has become a seemingly ineluctable feature of a global capitalist economy where culture is subordinate to commerce, and where survival depends not just on the sustenance we put into our bodies but how those foods often transform, sicken, and betray their makers. Far from being an ethnic curiosity on the cultural studies map, Native southern foodways has the unsettling potential of exposing the bitter fruits of regional cross-pollination and the discomposing hungers of contemporary global capitalism.

Hospitality, Hybridity, and Hominy: Survival and Adaptation in Native Southern Literature

In her 1994 work *Selu: Seeking the Corn-Mother's Wisdom*, Cherokee-Appalachian writer Marilou Awiakta attempts to reorient the American public's relationship to corn, the staple that indigenous peoples have long considered a repository of not just nourishment but of wisdom, teaching lessons of "adaptability, cooperation, unity in diversity" (9). By telling the story of Selu, the Corn Mother, who transformed herself into an ear of corn in order to feed her family, Awiakta shares a foundational Cherokee parable of indigenous peoples' hardiness, devotion, and cyclical renewal. While the story of Selu exists in similar forms among numerous tribal cultures, its significance has not, for the most part, been transmitted to the broader non-Native population along with the grain itself. "At an early age, schoolchildren learn that corn was a 'gift from the Indians' and that early settlers would have starved without it. But the recipients of the gift have always written the official history of America. In the minds of most descendants—and therefore, in the national mind—corn remains a grain only, an 'it' appropriated for their use" (20). Awiakta's purpose is to reintroduce corn to the common table of America on a broad scale, where citizens of all races gather and partake of this vital staple that is far "more than a food" (219). Her aim is not simply to remind us where the gift of corn originally came from. Rather, it is to emphasize the pervasive import and impact of that gift in ways that exceed both the tribally specific and the literal-physical dimension.

As a staple grain in the American and especially the southern diet, corn is very literally "in our blood." She writes, "[J]ust to name a few dishes calls up thoughts of home and heritage and comfort" (219). The dishes she goes on to list—"corn on the cob," "succotash, hominy, grits, polenta, tortillas, chips"— implicate multiple cultural and ethnic groups all at once. She mentions both "piki bread," a delicate blue-corn disc made by the Hopi, as well as the distinctly southern "cornbread rising fat in a cast-iron skillet" next to "hush puppies and fish fries." The list goes on deliciously so, enraptured of the dizzying, cross-cultural array of uses and tastes; deliberately, she balances distinctive cultural and regional dishes with others, such as Cracker Jack treats and movie popcorn, that have widespread appeal (219). Near the end, she even cites the corn used "in dressing with turkey, especially during holidays, when friends and family gather" (219). While the "holidays" featuring a dressed turkey are numerous, the most well-known would surely be Thanksgiving—a celebration of national origins and the apocryphal partnership between settlers and Indians that is nothing if not bitterly ironic for most Native peoples. But this delicate transcendence encapsulates the general mode of Awiakta's graceful presentation throughout the book. The common feast table has long been a pivotal, if painful, scene of nourishment and survival in the Americas, despite the grave imbalances in how each dish has been portioned and passed to each individual in the ensuing centuries. These days, Indians celebrate both national and Christian holidays along with the rest of the country, often with little sense of conflict or angst, as many consider their American citizenship or Christian ideologies compatible with their identity as Indians. Awiakta thus meets us in the complex, intermediary, cross-cultural space where we are, reminding us that as Mother Corn has survived so much tumult, interference, and processing, so too have the country's first inhabitants managed to persist—in evolving, hybrid, and sometimes deep-fried forms, but with a kernel of stubborn constancy remaining unchanged at the heart of it all. The "cross-pollination" and resulting diversity that both the grain and the people have undergone is generally a cause for antagonism and strife, particularly in the hyperbolic racial incubator of the South, but the binding comforts of home and hominy remind us of what unites rather than fractures us. "Americans eat corn every day. What if every time we encounter the grain, we remember the Corn-Mother—the law and wisdoms imbedded in her story?" Awiakta wonders. "What if we then create new harmony in ourselves, with each other and with Mother Earth?" (227). At a cultural moment when corn products saturate the American diet and typify the excessive, overabundant practices that contribute to the increasing national waistline, Awiakta's hopes for balance, respect, and harmony seem decidedly sanguine. But one of the most powerful recognitions of such work is the notion that something as integral and unifying as this staple crop might provide the seed for coming together more powerfully and thoughtfully around a regional common table.

To be sure, many Native southeastern writers are following Awiakta's lead in affirming their seamless presence and binding, sustaining energy within the South's persistently divisive social structure. That presence is often expressed deliberately as a hybrid, hyphenated one: Awiakta, for instance, proudly refers to herself not simply as Cherokee but "Cherokee-Appalachian." Similarly, Kathryn Lucci-Cooper (Cherokee) claims her "mixed heritage" as both a southerner and an Indian in the Smoky Mountains (3). With aunties and grandmothers who managed to be both "devout" Christians and Cherokee traditionalists, Lucci-Cooper experienced what she deems "a reasonable coalescing of Christian principle woven within the warp and weft of Cherokee storytelling and handed down as a basket of mountain tradition. We never knew anything was different about us. We thought all people were pretty much the same, just a mixture of cultural identities" (4). The family's main concern is simply surviving in "southern Appalachia's coalfields" with its "apple trees and cornstalks," home terrain that they are determined to protect and maintain at all costs (6). These constant references to safeguarding the earth's resources in southeastern Indian works return our gaze to the literal "common ground" of the region. While attunement with nature is an association made most readily with Native culture, in these works it is extended to map an inherently plural region, a territory where everyone is "pretty much the same." The focus returns deliberately and necessarily to the sources and staples of continued survival: Lucci-Cooper mentions both the "coalfields" and the "apple trees and cornstalks" of the Appalachian landscape, presumably because both have been exploited in the course of building and feeding an advancing civilization. Poet Karenne Wood (Monacan) similarly surveys her own Virginia homeland and sees the same confusion and waste: "we showed settlers our ways to grow plants, and a fever came to all of us: Virginia's alluvial bottomland greened—we cleared it all, even hillsides, not for food crops but tobacco." After the "greed spread like blight" and "the earth itself failed us," a new generation emerged that "became pickers of berries and fruit but were never the same" (21).

Southeastern Native writers commonly acknowledge and lament these original and ongoing devastations of their homelands—from the earliest colonial incursions to later industrial advances. While many do so in a way that binds rather than separates them from the broader culture, unity is far from a salve for the "fever" of progress that infects "all of us," as Wood admits, and leaves none unchanged. Again, the dinner table serves as a vital metaphor for both the gathering potential and sundering effects of this coeval struggle. In Dawn Karima Pettigrew's (Eastern Cherokee) debut novel, *The Way We Make Sense*, Manna, a young Eastern Cherokee woman from North Carolina's Qualla reservation, finds herself living in New Mexico with a Native veteran named Silas and his grass-dancing nephew. One evening, they have a guest over for dinner—a black woman from Mississippi—and Manna makes a special cornbread recipe handed down from her father on the back of a hardware store receipt. The African American woman "ate that cornbread and actually started crying. Sat there with her eyes running, calling it 'soul food.' Silas asked her why, and she said every bite reminded her of home" (125). The dish unites the Indian host and her black guest as kindred southerners far from home. They also share the meal with one of Silas's neighbors, Bill Lawton, a Lumbee carpenter originally from North Carolina, and the dish inspires him and Manna to muse together on the mixed soul of the South itself:

> [Manna remembers]: "Everybody kind of ended up all together. So when you're looking at a Creek Indian, a lot of times they're red, white and black all at once."
>
> Bill Lawton understands. "Us Lumbee are like that, too."
>
> "So maybe it isn't color or anything like that that makes good cornbread. Maybe it's knowing how to make the best of a bad situation, or getting a dollar out of fifteen cents."
>
> Manna pauses, looking into a world that Bill Lawton cannot see. "You know what? Southern food is all 'soul food.' You cook it, your soul knowing that no matter what color you are, if you live long enough, life will break your heart." (125)

While the moment reads initially as an affirmation of cross-cultural affinity, Pettigrew also reveals an insurmountable isolation and loneliness at the core of it all. What binds the black, Native, and hybrid southerners is not the cornbread per se but the survival instincts that go into the mix, that acculturated knack for making the most of meager ingredients. It is no accident, after all, that the original recipe is printed on the back of a hardware store receipt—both the bread and the building materials signify the lifelong efforts of the South's Cherokee and African Americans to reconstruct, maintain, and often purchase meaningful and sustaining lives. Yet it doesn't escape us either that Manna's father—the original holder of both the receipt and the recipe, which are near-homonyms for a reason—is long absent, having abandoned his pregnant wife, and that the displaced daughter struggles to survive her own "bad situation" far from home. The recipe brings her closer to the place and people that she has lost, but it cannot recover them any more than the receipt will trade for a stable home and family; the metonymy of "soul" and food is apparently a broken, heartsick one that induces tears, gestures of community, but no lasting satisfaction or recompense.

Indeed, throughout the novel, food routinely serves as a failed proxy for love and comfort. Fleeing North Carolina after losing her own true love, Manna finds herself picked up by a long-haired Indian stranger and taken to a filthy house where she is raped, discarded, and left starving. Alone and in despair, Manna discovers an abandoned baby. Together, she and the child scrounge for provisions, but they find only a single egg and outdated milk in the refrigerator. Manna gives the milk to the baby, but neither eats the egg. Again, the particular choice of the unpalatable food, juxtaposed with the lost and hungry children, suggests that they have suffered a radical disruption from their genealogical and maternal (and by extension, tribal) anchors. The search for food thus takes on an explicitly cultural dimension, but the prospect of filling their existential void seems bleak. The baby finds and begins chewing on a flyer advertising a local powwow. As she ingests bits of the flyer, we understand that she is swallowing a new and unfulfilling form of material consumption—the kind that has come to infiltrate Native tradition and ritual, converting it into pageantry and advertisements on glossy paper, "the color of weary goldenrods" that betrays its distance from nature and true value (83). Even after she is rescued by Silas, Manna remains unable to digest many foods, including milk, a vital link back to the mother and tribe from which she is estranged. "I should have stayed at home, / Eaten hominy," she realizes (79). Perhaps because hominy is a particularly indigenous form of corn, its memory signifies the constancy and fulfillment of home and culture. Baking cornbread in New Mexico can offer at best only an adapted, metaphorical comfort and a temporary sense of community, but perhaps, in the end, this *is* the paltry and unsatisfying diet of contemporary Indian life.

Full of It: Construction, Consumption, and the Insatiable Appetites of Advanced Capitalism

Indeed, what emerges most strikingly throughout southeastern Indian narratives is a deep, pervasive hunger for lost and missing cultural ties and traditions that seem increasingly unrecoverable in their "pure," unadulterated forms. Such losses seem markedly profound and distressing in the East, where tribes have struggled to maintain or rebuild distinctive senses of community and solidarity apart from mainstream culture. These pressures have been especially acute and transformative in the South, where claims to cultural distinctiveness have long been deeply rooted less in historical truths than nostalgic re-creations for all southerners, Native and otherwise. As Scott Romine recently articulated in his groundbreaking *The Real South*, the "fake"—that is, the "virtual, commodified, built, themed, invented, or otherwise artificial territoriality" of the region—eventually "becomes the real South through the intervention of narrative" (9). Similarly for American Indians, as Paul Chaat Smith attests, "the tacky, dumb stuff" invented *about* Indians by non-Natives has become "the real thing now" (6). Substituting what appears to be a "real"—if frequently "tacky" or "dumb" or invented—version of Indian identity becomes a crucial mechanism for maintaining cultural distinction in a world that equates indigeneity with anachronistic pageantry.

The fact that this phenomenon appears incessantly in works that center on traditional foodways is especially revealing. Turning on the dual notion of "consumption," these narratives expose Natives' indissoluble dependency on the very economies they mean to resist. Indeed, for many tribes, the entry into a broader consumer marketplace with the help of casino revenue and numerous other business ventures is precisely what has afforded them the opportunity to pursue and strengthen political viability and sovereignty. And yet, such capitulation presents an insurmountable problem for groups whose very identities center on antiestablishment, antimaterial, anticapitalist principles. Scholars like Alexis Celeste Bunten argue earnestly for a distinction between indigenous and nonindigenous tourism, suggesting that Native tourism subscribes to a specific brand of "'Indigenous capitalism' as a distinct strategy to achieve ethical, culturally appropriate, and successful Indigenous participation within the global economy" (285). Yet if we consider the possibility that "culturally appropriate" formations are themselves the product of commercial interests and projections—what John L. and Jean Comaroff call "ethno-commodification" in their wide-ranging study *Ethnicity, Inc.* (2009)—then such sanguine interpretations of the new market for "genuine" Indian experience must relinquish some of their potency. Defenders of Native "authenticity" and "indigenous capitalism" are not necessarily wrong; they are simply, for all the best, most hopeful reasons, downplaying the essential "triangulation of culture, identity, and the market" (20). In other words, the fetish of culture, often produced in well-intentioned, earnest efforts to both redeem and preserve tribal identity, becomes the reigning version of cultural legitimacy.

In Pettigrew's novel, for instance, Manna's regret over leaving home and "hominy" might compel us to read her eventual homecoming as a triumphal restoration of tribal community and fulfillment, yet that notion turns problematically on the radical commercial success of her ancestral cornbread recipe. In the final section of the book, Manna has returned to Qualla and becomes famous when her former lover, who had previously been changed into a tree, returns to human form:

> Manna and Thomas go on TV . . . A man calls from Toronto, wanting to make a feature film . . . Strangers mail them gifts. A car salesman from Ohio gives them a Volvo. A lady from Forrest City, Arkansas, sends them a cashier's check for $500,000. Manna uses the money to open up a café, right in the center of downtown Cherokee. "Bread of Life," they call it. People come from all over the world for Manna's cornbread . . . Of course, Manna doesn't do the actual baking. Famous people, like athletes and television personalities, send for special orders. (134)

The mystical event is obviously incredible, but through it, Pettigrew deftly conveys the mass appeal of such "miracles," particularly when they emerge from these seductively spiritual cultures. Put another way, Native mysticism sells, and that is something that the Eastern Cherokee, who host millions of tourists each year, know and capitalize on better than most. Begun in 1950, the long-running historical reenactment "Unto These Hills" replays the drama of the Trail of Tears to huge audiences and sizeable profits. Nearby, Oconaluftee Indian Village allows visitors to experience everyday life in an eighteenth-century Cherokee town. Joe Feather, one of the tribe's most popular performers, muses, "The people who come to see me know nothing about me. They want me to feed this monster they've got inside them, and it makes them feel better if they come here and give me a dollar. But we're in America, man, and we have to *survive*. And I will do anything to help my family survive" (Friedland 121). In a depressed Appalachian countryside where travel and tourism have replaced logging and hunting as primary forms of subsistence, the Cherokees adapt to the changes and play the role that will most help them to "survive." Significantly, that often means consciously skewing even the facts of their own culture and history. As Henry Lambert reports, these "Cherokee 'chiefs' soon realized that their income was tied to their exotic appearance," which non-Natives associated with Plains Indian stereotypes such as elaborate feathered headdresses rather than the less popularized and more modest Cherokee customs like buckskins. "If you are going into show business," one performer noted simply, you have to "dress for it" (Starnes 146).

An uncannily similar statement in Pettigrew's narrative alerts us to the sober pragmatism of the Indian's efforts to survive at all costs in contemporary

America. Living with Silas, his nephew, and the orphaned baby, Manna and her new "family" drink Kool-Aid and watch *The Lone Ranger* and *The Cosby Show* on television, and the routine becomes "their daily ritual" (91). Watching celluloid simulacra of their own culture, followed by celluloid simulacra of African American culture, Manna begins to worry that the baby might get "loaded down by negative stereotypes" (92), a danger underscored by their ingestion of a highly processed drink absent of nutritional substance and associated with the phenomenon of unquestioning capitulation to a seductive fantasy.[8] In a telling echo of the real-life Joe Feather, Silas shares his theory on the "economics of eating":

> Jay Silverheels got to be a millionaire talking about "kemosabe" this and "kemosabe" that. That's how we win this war. We beat the white man at his own game. Mumble and murmur and act half set back so they look the other way. When they do, throw up a casino or two and part them from their money. Sell them the cigarettes that cloud their lungs at discount prices. Finally, open an online pharmacy and sell them drugs while they wait to die. Tonto knew what he was doing. (92)

Initially, Manna questions his logic: "According to your theory," she protests, "Hattie McDaniel and Stepin Fetchit were geniuses."[9] Silas responds: "Cinema don't have nothing to do with it, young lady. We're talking about economics here. The economics of eating" (92). By the time she returns to Qualla, Manna has apparently internalized this lesson.

In Pettigrew's dramatization of the real-life Qualla theme park, Manna, too, engages in "show business" in order to survive. What is distressing is the way her success resonates distinctly with biblical deliverance—as does Manna's very name, which functions in the Old Testament as a kind of "bread" supplied by God to feed the starving, homeless Israelites. Clearly, both Manna and her "Bread of Life" become proxies for salvation in this world, precious commodities intended to feed and restore her bereft people. But the result is not precisely the victory it seems: she becomes a virtual Cherokee Paula Deen, a trademark and a signifier of the blessed, and yet merely a cardboard cutout of the real thing. Her bread, which she doesn't even bake herself anymore, becomes mere symbol rather than sustenance. It, and by extension, Manna herself, ends up being consumed hungrily by the masses from "all over the world," not just her own tribe. There are "Multitudes of people, crying, / Asking for manna and pleading for quail, / Shouting, reaching, pushing, shoving, / Salt and oil, flour and lard, / Eating is everything, pass your basket" (133). We might read the novel's ending cynically as a tongue-in-cheek parody of the "success" available to contemporary Natives who choose to sell their traditions for a mess of pottage. On the other hand, the notion that "eating is everything" troubles that critique by reminding us of the basic, kindred hungers that plague and bind Indians with other yearning "masses." Perhaps, for Manna, being able to fill others' baskets is an empathetic duty and a reward, one that few understand as acutely as the spiritually and culturally depleted Indian of the American Southeast.

It would be difficult, then, to condemn narratives that find genuine triumph and deliverance in endings like Manna's, as Pettigrew seems at least partially to do. In the profound impoverishment and invisibility of tenancy in a region long committed to displacing, appropriating, and devouring its indigenous traces, how can we critique the enormous appetites of the survivors who yearn for simple fulfillment? A longer look at the abundance of similar moments throughout southeastern Native writing would yield a startling but significant portrait: one of living cultures who exist on the margins of southern society, markedly apart and yet bound viscerally and economically to their regional kinfolk of all colors and stripes. The stories uncovered here are specifically indigenous ones, to be sure, but they are simultaneously southern, American, and global as well. Together, they testify to the gaping wounds inflicted by colonial processes and the ravishing hungers left in their wake. Alabama Creek poet Janet McAdams might be speaking for all of us when she confesses, "I'm licking salt from the long wound of history. / The blood is sweet and my mouth's full of it. / I'm milking this body for everything it's worth" ("News from the Imaginary Front").

Notes

1. According to a 1996 study by Theda Perdue and Michael Green, "no less than 40 percent of Southerners claimed Native ancestry, usually in the form of a 'Cherokee grandmother.'" The quotient is "considerably more than the 22 percent who claim descent from a Confederate soldier" or the mere 2 percent who can officially declare themselves "Indian" (147).

2. For a thorough historicizing of the ways that indigenous culture functions as a trope shared by all—and literally incorporated into the national consciousness through particularly "savage" interpretations of Native foodways—see Andrew Warnes's *Savage Barbecue: Race, Culture, and the Invention of America's First Food* (2008).

3. Notable exceptions include works by historians such as Theda Perdue, Michael Green, Malinda Maynor Lowery, and Katherine T. Osburn, as well as literary critics Eric Gary Anderson, Annette Trefzer, Kirstin Squint, and myself.

4. As of 2010, the following southeastern tribes have federal recognition (by state): Alabama: Poarch Band of Creek Indians; Florida: Seminole Tribe and Miccosukee Tribe of

Indians; Louisiana: Coushatta Tribe, Jena Band of Choctaw Indians, Tunica-Biloxi Indian Tribe, and Chitimacha Tribe; Mississippi: Mississippi Band of Choctaw Indians; North Carolina: Eastern Band of Cherokee Indians; South Carolina: Catawba Indian Nation.

5. By far the most persistent and revealing flavor bestowed on the all-purpose American Indian is the wise, romantic, ecological anticapitalist who protects the spirit and memory of our deepest national values particularly at the moments when we seem to be losing or forgetting them. Indigenous commitments to environmental justice and moderation became particularly attractive to many white Americans impatient with the burgeoning consumerism and militarism after World War II. As Iron Eyes Cody demonstrated enduringly in the popular television ad campaigns of the 1970s, paddling and weeping his way down a garbage-strewn river, Indians do not like littering, pollution, or multisyllabic expression. Never mind that Cody was actually an Italian-American actor "playing Indian" on screen (and equally fervently in his private life); such pageantry simply underlines that the Native American trope has become a fungible celluloid fantasy, a mirror held up to a society anxious to gaze upon its own inherent well of alternative value.

6. For compelling political and cultural reasons, Native sovereignty maintains an exceptional status within the realm of current academic and political discourse about globalization and multiculturalism. Whereas histories of nationalism tend now to headline a dark cautionary tale about imperialism and the destructive hegemony of the nation-state, in Native studies, conversely, nationalism is embraced as a necessary structure of survival. For many Indian critics, resisting the progressive critical trends means protecting and cultivating tribal sovereignty, both political and intellectual. Critics such as Elizabeth Cook-Lynn, Robert Warrior, Jace Weaver, Craig Womack, Lisa Brooks, and others have promoted (and in Womack's case, in *Red on Red: Native American Literary Separatism*, invented and performed) tribal-nationalist and pan-Indian modes of critical theory and interpretation.

7. The survival of southeastern Indian communities has lately been acknowledged in the realm of literary scholarship. There was no acknowledged "canon" of southeastern Indian writing per se, despite the remarkable work being published within its borders, until relatively recently—and inauguration aided by recent publication of a seminal anthology: *The People Who Stayed: Southeastern Indian Writing After Removal* (2010), edited by Geary Hobson, Janet McAdams, and Kathryn Walkiewicz. While some of the authors represented are respected voices in Native American literature, many others are new and virtually unknown figures, providing for critics a veritable treasure trove of new works and worlds to explore. Southeastern Indian writers include Louis Owens (Choctaw/Cherokee), Geary Hobson (Cherokee), LeAnne Howe (Choctaw), Karenne Wood (Monacan), Allison Adelle Hedge Coke (Cherokee/Huron), Marilou Awiakta (Cherokee), Dawn Karima Pettigrew (Cherokee), Drucilla Wall (Creek), and Janet McAdams (Creek), and, like the vast majority of mainstream America, virtually none of these writers claim just one heritage or cultural affiliation. These artists powerfully reimagine a contemporary southern homeland that is emphatically *not* a mythical, precontact, or preremoval one, but one always already plagued and succeeded by greed, desire, and territorial violence. In short, these southerners embody a culture—both southern *and* Native—fully and irreversibly colonized and hybrid, a fact often suppressed in word and performance but more difficult to conceal in the diurnal, hybrid dishes of the region's common table.

8. I'm referring, of course, to the 1978 Jonestown Massacre in which numerous Peoples Temple cult members were instructed by the prophet Jim Jones to drink a Kool-Aid type product laced with cyanide. The expression "drinking the Kool-Aid" now commonly refers to any act of blind faith and unquestioning adherence (*Oxford English Dictionary Online*).

9. Manna reminds us of two of the earliest examples of black cinema—both of whom achieved commercial success by embodying and furthering negative stereotypes: Hattie McDaniel, who famously played the stereotypical, loyal "mammy" figure in *Gone with the Wind* (1936), and Stepin Fetchit (screen name for the 1930s actor Lincoln Perry), who revived for the screen the minstrel show's bumbling, lazy slave persona who thrives on "putting on old massa—break the tools, break the hoe, do anything to postpone the work that was to be done." In fact, according to Perry's biographer Mel Watkins, "[T]he Fetchit character is actually a subversive trickster—he never got around to fetching *anything*" (quoted in Roy Hurst, "Stepin Fetchit, Hollywood's First Black Film Star").

Works Cited

Acoose, Janice, et al., eds. *Reasoning Together: The Native Critics Collective*. Norman: U of Oklahoma P, 2008.

Anderson, Eric Gary. "The Presence of Early Native Studies: A Response to Stephanie Fitzgerald and Hilary E. Wyss." *American Literary History* 22.2 (Summer 2010): 280–88.

Awiakta, Marilou. *Selu: Seeking the Corn-Mother's Wisdom*. Golden, CO: Fulcrum, 1993.

Bunten, Alexis Celeste. "More Like Ourselves: Indigenous Capitalism through Tourism." *The American Indian Quarterly* 34.3 (Summer 2010): 285–311.

Carter, Forrest. *The Education of Little Tree*. New York: Delacorte Press, 1976.

Comaroff, John L., and Jean Comaroff. *Ethnicity, Inc.* Chicago: U of Chicago P, 2009.

Cook-Lynn, Elizabeth. "The American Indian Fiction Writer: Cosmopolitanism, Nationalism, the Third World, and First Nation Sovereignty." *Wicazo Sa Review* 9.2 (Autumn 1993): 26–36.

———. "American Indian Intellectualism and the New Indian Story." *American Indian Quarterly* 20.1 (1996): 57–76.

Edge, John T., and Joe Gray Taylor. "Southern Foodways." In *New Encyclopedia of Southern Culture: Volume 7: Foodways*. Ed. John T. Edge. Chapel Hill: U of North Carolina P, 2007. 1–14.

Foster, Tol. "Relations and Regionality." In *Reasoning Together: The Native Critics Collective*. Ed. Janice Acoose et al. Norman: U of Oklahoma P, 2008. 265–302.

Friedland, Akiva. "Progess in the Land of the Cherokees?: Living and Dying by Tourism." In Issue on Race: Past Present and Future. *Oxford American Magazine* 64 (March 2009): 118–23.

Green, Rayna. "Mother Corn and the Dixie Pig: Native Food in the Native South." *Southern Cultures* 14.4 (Winter 2008): 114–26.

Hobson, Geary, Janet McAdams, and Kathryn Walkiewicz, eds. "Introduction: The South Seldom Seen." In *The People Who Stayed: Southeastern Indian Writing After Removal*. Norman: U of Oklahoma P, 2010. 1–20.

Hurst, Roy. "Stepin Fetchit, Hollywood's First Black Film Star." NPR (March 6, 2006). http://www.npr.org/templates/story/story.php?storyId=5245089 (accessed September 20, 2010).

"Kool-Aid, n." Third edition, December 2005; online version June 2012. http://www.oed.com/view/Entry/248277; accessed July 21, 2012.

Leach, Loretta. "Varnertown in the 1950s." In *The People Who Stayed: Southeastern Indian Writing after Removal*. Ed. Geary Hobson et al. Norman: U of Oklahoma P, 2010. 213.

Lucci-Cooper, Kathryn. "To Carry the Fire Home." In *Genocide of the Mind*. Ed. MariJo Moore. New York: Thunder's Mouth Press, 2003. 3–12.

Marker, Michael. "*The Education of Little Tree*: What It Really Reveals about Public Schools." *Phi Delta Kappan* 74:3 (Nov. 1992): 226–27.

Peterson, John H., Jr. "Introduction," Part One, "Setting the Stage: The Original Mississippians." In *Ethnic Heritage in Mississippi*. Ed. Barbara Carpenter. Jackson: Mississippi Humanities Council, 1992. 3–8.

Pettigrew, Dawn Karima. *The Way We Make Sense*. San Francisco: AuntLute Books, 2002.

Romine, Scott. *The Real South*. Baton Rouge: Louisiana State UP, 2008.

Smith, Paul Chaat. *Everything You Know about Indians Is Wrong*. Minneapolis: U of Minnesota P, 2009.

Starnes, Richard D. *Southern Journeys: Tourism, History, and Culture in the Modern South*. Tuscaloosa: U of Alabama P, 2003.

Trefzer, Annette. *Disturbing Indians: The Archaeology of Southern Fiction*. Tuscaloosa: U of Alabama P, 2007.

Warnes, Andrew. *Savage Barbecue: Race, Culture, and the Invention of America's First Food*. Athens: U of Georgia P, 2008.

Warrior, Robert. "Intellectual Sovereignty and the Struggle for an American Indian Future." *Wicaza Sa* 8.1 (Spring 1992): 1–20.

———. *The People and the Word: Reading Native Nonfiction*. Minneapolis: U of Minnesota P, 2005.

———. *Tribal Secrets: Recovering American Indian Intellectual Traditions*. Minneapolis: U of Minnesota P, 1995.

Weaver, Jace. *That the People Might Live: Native American Literatures and Native American Community*. New York: Oxford UP, 1997.

Weaver, Jace, Craig S. Womack, and Robert Warrior, eds. *American Indian Literary Nationalism*. Albuquerque: U of New Mexico P, 2006.

Womack, Craig. *Red on Red: Native American Literary Separatism*. Minneapolis: U of Minnesota P, 1999.

Wood, Karenne. *Markings on Earth*. Tucson: University of Arizona Press, 2001.

Chapter Thirteen

"GNAW THAT BONE CLEAN"
Foodways in Contemporary Southern Poetry

TARA POWELL

> I love you like barbeque
> You leave nothing on the bone
> ....
> You make me go hogwild honey
> Make me want to hurry home
> —**Kevin Young,** "Short End Blues"

ociologist John Shelton Reed suggests in *My Tears Spoiled My Aim* (1993) that one can "do worse" than to ask a southerner what "southern" means (53). The work of Reed, historian James Cobb, and other intellectual southwatchers suggests that young southerners' sense of regional identity is increasingly ahistorical and defined most clearly by cultural markers such as fashion, music, sports, and food. Yet, to entertain the idea of these markers as coverings for the "cultural nakedness" Cobb ascribes to the post-agrarian, post–Civil Rights era South, in some ways masks these choices' taproots in the region's racial and agricultural economic history (141). In imaginative literature, one time-honored strategy for evoking the home place is through representations of the kitchen table, and some of the South's finest contemporary poets representing the regional tabletop draw inspiration from the complexity of the relationship between food, identity, and history of place. Roy Blount, Jr.'s occasional humorous food poems; Michael McFee's uncollected series of food poems appearing in *Cornbread Nation, Southern Cultures, Edible Piedmont,* and elsewhere; James Applewhite's autobiographical meditations on longings associated with traditional southern foods; Kevin Young's blues odes to death-dealing comfort foods in *Dear Darkness* (2008); and collections by Nikky Finney and Honorée Jeffers exploring the history of preparing regional foods all suggest the preparation and tasting of food as a link between past and present regional life. That link continues over space and time to provide a sense of identity, even as the physical and intellectual landscape of the American South changes. Considered together and in the context of contemporary work in the broader field of southern studies, these poets lay the southern table as a place where, consciously or unconsciously, the texture of the past is as much in southern mouths as ever. Although for these poets the broad strokes of southern history are less interesting than their personal experiences of that history, in fact a closer look at the gustatory and culinary history of the South makes it possible to view their food poems as refractions of a specific moment of apparent cultural nakedness in the late twentieth-century American South.

Amidst a burgeoning latter twentieth-century academic interest in the sociology of food habits, there was also a resurgence of national interest in southern cuisine. In *Eating, Drinking, and Visiting in the South: An Informal History* (1982), Joe Gray Taylor points out that post–World War II America's fascination with the region's cuisine had been reflected in a variety of cookbooks and magazines. These popular sources often presented recipes and travel information alongside romanticized, *Gone with the Wind*-style portrayals of southern life. The ugly realities of the New South that emerged to a national audience during and after the Civil Rights Movement put a sudden halt to the national obsession with the region's cuisine that lasted for decades. Anthony J. Stanonis has observed that, in the Jim Crow South, "Food provided a powerful means of safeguarding white hegemony" (216) by way of cookbooks that "preserve[d] the region's mores and permit[ted their] recreation in kitchens everywhere," and also by "preserv[ing] eating practices, promot[ing] brand names (and slang), and patroniz[ing]restaurants that fortified [whites'] commitment to Jim Crow" (216–17). Beginning in the late 1970s, popular interest in southern food revived alongside academic interest in regional foodways. Among the most well-known nonfiction writers whose work during this critical moment would bridge popular and academic interest in southern foodways, partly by demonstrating how historical links between white and black foodways in the South are embedded in its present cuisine, has been journalist John Egerton, who helped to inspire a new generation of American and regional studies scholars to invest in the study of southern food as a way of thinking about identity. Though Egerton was able to observe in the 1980s that next to nothing had "been written about the importance of food in the social and cultural evolution of the South," that is, in part due to his own efforts, no longer true (4). Though still working its way into the academic mainstream in some ways, a relationship between food and cultural identity is now so accepted as to be a truism in most related fields. If food studies have yet to become entrenched in literary studies to that extent, certainly foodways is an essential and especially vibrant element of the field of southern studies. It has also become one of the most successful areas of crossover between southern and black diaspora studies. To explain the field's growth and to consider what literary studies in particular may yet be able to bring to it, one can look to the South as an especially interesting location to think about the connections between food, history, memory, and identity—for two reasons.

First, one might think of the American South this way because of its distinctive culinary history. In *Southern Food: At Home, on the Road, in History* (1987), Egerton points out that the everyday reality of the experience of hunger, across nearly all classes of people in the South during the Civil War and Great Depression eras, as well as its failing but still predominantly agrarian economy, set it apart from much of the nation, especially the iconic American Northeast. The antebellum system of race-based slavery in the American South, followed by generations of poverty, resulted in a unique combination of Native American, African, and European culinary traditions and cooking styles. For Egerton, Taylor, and others, southern food is not only a way of thinking about and understanding the region's checkered history, but it also may arguably be what Egerton calls "the most positive element of our collective character, an inspiring symbol of reconciliation, healing, and union" (viii). "It is," he writes at the outset of *Side Orders: Small Helpings of Southern Cookery and Culture* (1990), "our oldest and most persistent cultural asset—and perhaps our most important one" (np).

A second reason to tell about the South as an especially interesting location to consider food as living history is the emergence of interest in southern foodways amidst the region's anxiety about its disappearing distinctiveness, or what Cobb calls the "cultural nakedness" of the late twentieth-century South. Substantial changes in southern food habits since WWII mean that, as Egerton confirms, "[O]ld-fashioned southern cooking no longer dominates the daily diet of people in this region as it once did" (*Side Orders* np). As in many places in the United States, issues of time, expense, mass production, and shifting ideas about nutrition, among other factors, are reducing access to traditional cooking in daily life (*Southern Food* 48). Because of the centuries of food's distinctive importance in southern society, however, those changes seem "especially noticeable" in the South, and, as the editors of *The Sociology of Food* suggest, there is a special anxiety attached to the perceived loss of food traditions because of the ways shared meals identify communities. Southern writers since the mid-twentieth century have drawn on the imagery of foodways to talk about memory and identity, to bridge the gap between the historical South and the present, and to clothe its diminishing distinctiveness, reflecting Egerton's argument that, where "remnants of the genuine old cookery remain, . . . you will find food that offers comfort and satisfaction and even identity, food for thought and conversation as well as nourishment" (*Side Orders* np). Unlike the diseased race consciousness around which so much of the white South was once united, and unlike the debunked romantic mythology of a genteel plantation South and an (ig)noble Lost Cause, southern foodways remain a safe location in which to perform southernness. It is possible to find community at the table across divisions of race, class, and gender, and to make peace with the past without submerging the darkest truths of southern history. As Yusef Komunyakaa writes in his essay "An Ode to Raccoon" for *Oxford American*'s 2005 food issue, when he shows his dubious grandmother that he still remembers how to cook game, he feels: "My grandmother was in her world. I was almost back inside my skin. And I knew that the sweet, peppery, wild taste of this delicacy of the poor would bring me the full distance. In that moment, I believed there was a basic truth in this taste" (53). At the table, then, past and present still meet, and taste and the memory of taste become a special place to explore regional identity.

One unusual aspect of the issue of the *Oxford American* that I just quoted was that, despite containing only a few poems, the brief essays that dominated the issue were predominantly constructed around the idea of "odes"—ode to raccoon, ode to chicken-fried steak, ode to boiled peanuts, and so on. Similarly, the preface to *Southern Quarterly*'s 2007 "Southern Food and Drink in History, Literature, and Film" issue quotes blues lyrics, but then largely disregards poetry as a place for talking about foodways and regional identity. The "Literature" entry in John T. Edge's food volume of *The New Encyclopedia of Southern Culture* (2007) does not mention a single poet—despite, among other things, the visibility of poetry in *Cornbread Nation*. Yet, what other contemporary literary mode is more dependent on the relationship of sense impressions to memory than is poetry? Egerton observes, "Food is the only element in our culture that reaches our consciousness through all five of the senses. . . . Such a powerful force is bound to linger in the memory" (*Southern Food* 49). It remains for scholars of southern literature and southern studies as a group to explore poetry as a special place for talking about food, memory, and identity, but, I hope, having demonstrated that the South is a special location for talking about food and culture, that I may offer a few persuasive examples of poetry about the literal and figurative southern kitchen table that suggest just how rich the untapped possibilities are for finding "basic truth in . . . taste."

The notion of the southern table as a happy meeting place for multiple versions of the regional experience is one that has appealed to a range of poets. A notable example is Roy Blount, Jr., a well-known southwatcher, sports writer, humorist, and regular contributor most recently to *Oxford American* and NPR's "Wait, Wait, Don't Tell Me." He is also the author of a series of occasional food poems—inflected, not incidentally, by his growing up in Georgia. Though his poems are light verse, they also speak directly to the idea of taste as cultural marker and site of memory. Blount's "Song to Barbecue Sauce," first published by *Sports Illustrated* in 1975 and later revised and reprinted in *One Fell Soup, or, I'm Just a Bug on the Windshield of Life* (1982), performs southernness on the palate, saying, "Brush it on chicken, slosh it on pork, / Eat it with fingers, not with a fork, / Serve it in Georgia, not in New York" (11). Despite the regional associations with the sauce being celebrated, the speaker also unhooks its southernness from history, as he offers the testimonial:

Hear this from Evelyn Billiken Husky,
Formerly Evelyn B. of Sandusky:
Ever since locating down in the South,
I have had barbecue sauce on my mouth.

Though the speaker asserts, "Nothing can gloss / Over barbecue sauce," the sauce is offered up as a taste that itself can gloss over regional prejudice. Blount's "Song to Grits" takes a similar approach, stating,

When my mind's unsettled,
When I don't feel spruce,
When my nerves get frazzled,
When my flesh gets loose—

What knits
Me back together's grits. (11)

As the poem continues, it participates in the symbolism of southern food as a healing force, not just for the individual taking refuge in the food habits of childhood, but also as a larger cultural meeting place:

Rich and poor, black and white,
Lutheran and Campbellite,
Jews and Southern Jesuits,
All acknowledge buttered grits.

That acknowledgment provides a basis for a shared community life across race, class, and religious difference. If indeed "[l]ife is good where grits are swallered," the implication is that the grits are where that possibility begins.

North Carolina poet Michael McFee's poetic mode also deploys tongue-in-cheek humor in its consideration of southern tastes, but it complicates the notion of foodways as cultural or nostalgic meeting places where "life is good." Rather, McFee's humor moves in the background of semiautobiographical poems such as his meditations in poems such as "Gravy" and "Saltine" that engage an array of feelings about the foods of his childhood in a working class community of southern Appalachia. The grown-up speakers of these poems and others reclaim inexpensive foods that may have embarrassed their adolescent selves—their nostalgia thereby reconsidering cheap eats as totems for accessing ways of taking pride in their background. In "Saltine," the speaker admits to an abiding craving for the crackers, how "well its square / fit my palm, my mouth...," especially with peanut butter or cheese sandwiched on it, "the closest we ever got / to serving hors d'oeuvres" (16). Each bite of memory is leavened with the consciousness that he is not supposed to like this food now that he does not have to eat it, and the poem closes calling his favorite snack a guilty pleasure, a way of performing southernness and class memory: "the redneck's hardtack, / the cracker's cracker." In "Gravy," the speaker recalls how his working mother would sometimes make gravy to "moisten and darken and quicken / the bowls of bland white rice or mashed potatoes" that were staples of their diet (129). "Good gravy's not an afterthought, a dressing," he realizes as an adult, "a murky cloud masking a dish's dull prospect: . . . / it's the meal's essence, where flesh meets spirit, / where fat becomes faith, where juice conveys grace. . . ." In the mixture of "meat grease, flour and water, stirred till smooth," the speaker connects his forebears, his mother, and his own childhood, as well as his adulthood as a poet—finding in gravy an apt symbol for class mobility, and yet at the same time a reproduction of the experience of hunger. He concludes, "whenever I think of those savory names / and the times I've poured or ladled or spooned / . . . / not wanting to waste a single filling drop, / my mouth starts making its own thin gravy again."

As much or more than any other living southern poet over the past decade, McFee has made the nuanced connection of food, memory, and class essential to the evolution of how his poetic mode evokes place and time. "Pork Skins" and "Salt," which appeared in *Cornbread Nation 4: The Best of Southern Food Writing* (2008), explicitly connect the cravings of his and his ancestors' "country tongues" to the poet's sense of regional and class dislocation as adult. There is a literal foodstuff in "Pork Skins," but the memory of this particular taste is also a kind of figurative skin to chew over: "there's this pesky question of skin / to be gotten past somehow, / a greasy rind that must be dealt with" (214). The memory brines the speaker's exalted body with the "hint of pig ... / ... / dusting / my chest and fingers with pale gold, / the apotheosis of the epidermis" (214–15). Further, to the extent we are to take this poem as autobiographical, the description of the pork skins as "salty parchments" ties the taste his body is literally bathed with directly to the speaker's adult life as an artist. "Salt" makes this connection even more explicitly, as the speaker admits that, even though he "watch[es his] sodium intake / as the doctors instruct...," he "crave[s] it" (212), and confirms, "One day, like my parents and all their parents, / I'll become the salt of the earth, pale seasoning / waking the hidden flavor of the family plot." (213)

James Applewhite, a contemporary of McFee's—though a poet whose artistic vision evokes instead the tastes and spaces of eastern North Carolina of the same era—also has written evocatively of the piedmont foodways of his childhood in semiautobiographical verse that includes meditations on collards, tobacco, blackberries, and barbecue, among other things. For Applewhite, to smell, eat, and remember regional foods through poetry is a way of accessing a seemingly lost South, though, like McFee, he accesses that South with complex attitudes towards it, especially as embedded in the racial and socioeconomic history of those foods. In "Earth Lust," Applewhite celebrates blackberry picking, though his alter ego closes reflecting, "We southerners must survive an embrace / Of briars, a thirst for a touch of earth / Too rough for love" (10). In "Barbecue Service," Applewhite's persona admits to stalking "the elusive aroma" across the countryside, and compares slow-cooked pork to a religious sacrifice in which "the pig / Flesh [is] purified by far atmosphere. . . . / This smolder draws the soul of our longing" (4). Just as Komunyakaa's exchange with his grandmother in "Ode to Raccoon" puts him back inside his own skin, the speaker of "Barbecue Service" becomes a part of a community of men from whom he otherwise is entirely cut off. "We barbecue pigs," he writes. "The tin-roofed sheds with embers / Are smoking their blue sacrifice / Across Carolina." One of Applewhite's best-known poems, "Some Words for Fall," turns on the poet's wish when he smells barbecue "shine blue on the wind" or "whiffs" of curing tobacco to return not just home, but to "step through the horizon's frame" to an earlier, simpler time. He writes, "People down-home in Eastern N.C., / When they have that unlimited longing, / ... / No words they have are enough" (50). These smells render the poet wordless, even "lonesome for something more," though in Applewhite's speaker's case, as for McFee's, his longing reaches toward the ever-present past. "The language they speak," writes Applewhite in a signature line, "is things to eat."

Indeed, McFee drew on this line as the title for his 1994 anthology of North Carolina poets, *The Language They Speak Is Things to Eat: Poems by Fifteen Contemporary North Carolina Poets*, underscoring his sense of the interconnection between foodways and southern poetic modes.

Alabama native Honorée Jeffers's title poem for her award-winning first collection *The Gospel of Barbecue* (2000) also deploys sacrificial religious language to consider pork barbecue as a problematic symbol for class mobility in the South and, in her case, for race consciousness. In the story of Uncle Vess's reluctance to give up pork and eventual death from heart disease, Jeffers embeds the cultural memory of African American foodways—the roots of Vess's longing for barbecue, and his appreciation of even hog leavings, in the conditions of slavery. For Vess, it is a connection to his past. "Perfectly good food," he says, "can't be no sin. / ... / ... survival ain't never been / no crime against nature / or Maker" (15). For the poem's speaker, presumably Jeffers's alter ego, there is a mixture of shame and pride in Vess's hunger that is not unlike McFee's dubbing of his speaker's reluctantly beloved saltines as the "cracker's cracker." For both, the old-fashioned food prepared in the present is a living memory of a distinctive southernness that is performed with every bite. "Go on," Jeffers's poem admonishes, "and gnaw that bone clean." Rather than symbolizing the cross-racial healing power of food in Blount's mode, Jeffers's "Gospel of Barbecue" suggests that the ritual of eating reinscribes racial memory. Indeed, Jeffers's poetry, like contemporary studies in African American foodways, resists eliding some of the problematic complexities of thinking about food as a commensal symbol of the New South. Beth Latshaw's recent study in *Southern Cultures* suggests that though data points from Southern Focus Polls support the position that southerners continue to share "taste for and pride in" regional cuisine, that taste and pride come from different understandings of what these foods symbolize (125). Stanonis takes Egerton and his colleagues to task, too, in much the way Jeffers's version of southern foodways rebukes Blount and to some extent Applewhite on the subject of barbecue, while at the same time sharing their sense of taste as an important, indeed inexorable location for cultural memory—a sensory place in which southerners work through their attitudes towards where they came from and where they are going.

In Jeffers's third collection, *Red Clay Suite* (2007), food memories continue to be the most palatable link or "way back" to the poet's alter ego's regional past. Uncle Vess's ghost reappears behind a grill in "What Grief Is," as "the sizzling of good pigmeat, / ... / sings a hymn that rises / from beneath Alvester's fingers" (63). In "Eatonton (One)," a dislocated child isn't frightened by squalid new surroundings because "There's cobbler every evening after supper," and she can "hold onto the funk / of neckbones and greens" (58). Another poem, "Suddenly in Grace" calls on the poet to "Again, look at the table," her mother laid, and remember "how she plunged the greens over and over / watched the water run free of dirt / and tried to teach me this way back, / though I had no interest then" (53). The repetitive washing of the collards becomes a type of the poet's art, a version of how each of these poems deploys specific regional food memories as points of access to the speaker's vexed relationship with her past; as in McFee's reconsideration of the "cracker's cracker," a mediated nostalgia exists alongside the remembered pain of poverty, violence, or displacement. In "Days Are Plain," Jeffers writes, "Rage has its moments and sympathies, / but some days are plain, if not uncomplicated." The southern expatriate's writing day is tensed by the sudden and less-than-welcome longing for ". . . the hot arms of the South, / the old men who sell fresh produce // from their roadside stands" (55). Driven by "hunger for the fruit of my youth," the speaker buys bags of inadequate grocery store peaches and "walks through my small rooms with stingy / bits of home on my tongue and I give praise. / You know I just give praise" (55–56). Praise for home, but for surviving and achieving not-home too.

Kevin Young's award-winning autobiographical sixth collection of poetry, *Dear Darkness*, turns substantially on poems in which meditations on familiar tastes become ways of coming to terms with unimaginable loss. In his introduction to *The Hungry Ear: Poems of Food and Drink* (2012), Young writes, "Nothing is as necessary yet as taken for granted these days as food—except maybe poetry" (1). Neither eliding the problematic claim of the commensal southern table nor entirely rejecting it in *Dear Darkness*, Young's alter ego speaker returns South through foodways by remembering special tables whose settings inevitably link a collective experience of blackness in the South with his personal experience. In "Ode to the South," Young writes, "I want to be soused, / doused / in gasoline / & fried" (81). This darkly humorous play on Blount's light verse claims the poet's family's southern past for better and worse—that is to say, coming South may be coming home, but laying hold of that family history is also a kind of figurative lynching. Woven through with images of coming reluctantly to the table after the funerals of the speaker's father and grandmother, the collection's series of odes to regional foods in fact becomes a feast of elegies as childhood foods are presented to the adult mourner. In a section of "Pallbearing" titled "Victuals," Young writes, "He is dead so we eat. / In his heaven he must be / hungry—so we fill / ourselves, stomachs, // for him . . ." (36). The display of meats and pies presents a stunning, initially almost grotesque orgy of excess in which the mourners "[b]ury // our faces in food / to forget, in vain, the rain / falling, fallen, water standing /

like he never again" (36–37). Later, in "Eulogy," the speaker commands the listener after weeping to

. . . eat till

your stomach spills over
No more! You'll cry

too full for your eyes
to leak. (161)

By the end of the collection, however, in "Ode to Turtle Soup," the poet's representation of the table shifts from desperate excess to a solemn ritual, reflecting, "I come now / with my plate / again empty // I come with arms full / of pleas, terrapin-slow // & steady, hoping / your cast iron will feed me" (184–85). Rather than burying the mourner's face in food to stop tears, the feast becomes itself a living elegy in daily life, a way to experience grief and honor the dead through nourishment rather than starving, as familiar foods become points of access to remembering the lives of lost loved ones—a legacy in taste. "Such meals and drink," Young writes in *The Hungry Ear*, "remind us we're alive, while also making us realize: what else can we do but provide some sustenance for those whose only meal otherwise may be sorrow?" (3) As the speaker faces a "plate full of bones / I'm scared to swallow," in "Ode to Catfish," he knows, "No matter / the pain it takes / to hold you," the taste and smell of the fried fish breakfast will always resurrect the memory of sitting at the table with his living family one morning when his father "declared it / perfect" (167). Belatedly, the speaker tells his father's shade, "Sweet Jesus / you were right."

In poems like "Ode to the South" with its evocation of the lynching bee, as well as "Field Trip" and "Ode to Okra," among others, the central conscious-ness of *Dear Darkness* acknowledges ways foods link to issues of class mobil-ity and even the slaveholding legacy of the South. The speaker of "Ode to Pork" reminds one of Jeffers's Uncle Vess as well as the salt-craving of McFee's "country tongues," as he asserts, "Without you / I'd be umpteen / pounds lighter & a lot / less alive" (87). Yet, Young's poetic mode renovates these con-nections into a necessary rememory of his family's long legacy in Louisiana. In his version of Blount's "Ode to Barbecue Sauce," Young's speaker discovers a last bottle of his father's special sauce in the refrigerator after his funeral, "a manna none // but you could make / & I can only // hope to copy" (177). In the same way that there "never is / enough" of "that sauce / darkening your fallow fridge" (178), the father did not have time to get to the promised land in this life—his dream to see his small farm become fertile. In "Ode to Okra," the speaker addresses the garden plant as a relative or neighbor that "weep[s] when stirred, / make[s] a gumbo worth / fasting for" (95), and, in "Ode to Gumbo," the poet describes a great-grandmother's recipe, saying, "I know Gumbo / starts with sorrow / ... / Done right, it will feed // you and not let go" (171). The soup becomes a satisfying grief that "fills / this house like silence / & tells me everything // has an afterlife ..." (173). Preparing his grandmother's last cushaw using an old recipe, the speaker of "Ode to Cushaw" pronounces it

> ... what the past
> tastes like—
>   like promise,
> or promises, something
> unspoken & never seen
> again, but known
> by heart. (194)

The preparation and consumption of food here transcends loss to underscore how the the kitchen and the tabletop are special locations where living memories can link past to future. In the final poem of *Dear Darkness*, "Ode to Boudin," boudin, too, becomes a taste of pastness, a "[h]omemade saviour/ [who] fed me the day / my father sat under flowers / white as the gloves of pallbearers / tossed on his bier" (195). The food eaten that day becomes "root of all / remembrance."

The root of remembrance in Nikky Finney's poetry has also often been linked to regional foods whose historical importance gives rise to the more intimate links that inspire her work—rice in her collection by the same name and fresh fish in *Head Off and Split* (2011). In her prose introduction to *Rice* (1995), Finney writes, "I call South Carolina land that Black folks made because it was on the backs and knees, the minds and muscles of Africans, that acres of timber dense South Carolina were transformed into rich rice fields.... From the early 1700's and for years beyond, in South Carolina, Black people were the major import, and rice, its most favored export." Just as these two are "intimately linked" historically, Finney describes how that history and her family's food habits are also intimately linked, writing, "In the 1960's, as a girl growing up in the Palmetto state, there was always a punch bowl of rice on the dinner table. In my own house today, we eat rice daily.... I hold this tradition of rice culture and diet to be sacred" (11–12). Just as Young suggests in his equation of poetry and food in *The Hungry Ear*, the central metaphor of

Finney's collection equates plain rice to the life-sustaining words in which she describes family and community stories of suffering, struggle, and strength over time. The poet's family history becomes a type of the larger narrative of black American history as family heroes and heroines with what she calls "country fried beginnings" in "He Never Had It Made" (117) are juxtaposed with black icons from the pages of history throughout the collection. "Slavery was no opera / soaped or staged / was no historical moment," the poet writes in "Pluck" (83), and the book's opening poem, "The Blackened Alphabet," asserts, "I am pencilfrying / sweet Black alphabets / in an allnight oil" (16). In the closing poem, "The Rice," the narrator admonishes, "It is the sweet rice you throw away / but food for the hungry that will return" (175). That is to say, as is true for the "country tongues" seasoning the poet's art in McFee's food poems, country-fried family beginnings become a nourishing legacy in Finney's *Rice*, just as the poet seems to hope her words, too, may fall on fallow ground.

In Finney's most recent collection of poems, *Head Off and Split* (2011), the poet sets aside the rice bowl as a controlling metaphor for her sense of place and picks up Young's scary "plate full of bones" from "Ode to Catfish" to parse the literal and figurative possibilities of fresh catch at her alter ego's home-coming. Three of the poems that seem to frame the larger narrative of the book turn on the metaphor of the butchering and tasting of the fish's body for trying to access the legacy of home and family celebrated in *Rice* but denied in some ways to the speaker of *Head Off and Split* because of ways in which her choices as an adult have cut her off from her family. In Finney's prose poem "Resurrection of the Errand Girl: An Introduction," an adult woman returning home to visit her parents reprises a frequent childhood errand to the fishmonger. She remembers, "Head off and split? Translation: Do away with the watery gray eyes, the impolite razor-sharp fins, the succulent heart, tender roe, delicate sweet bones? Polite, dutiful, training to be mother, bride, kitchen frau. Her answer, Yes" (3). Though the child would always accept a prebutchered fish, the adult hears in the question a kind of metaphor for her own coming of age and insists on the whole fish. She thinks, "This time she wants what she was once sent for left whole, just as it was pulled from the sea, everything born to it still in place. Not a girl any longer, she is capable of her own knife-work now.... She would rather be the one deciding what she keeps and what she throws away."

In "Penguin, Mullet, Bread," the poet's alter ego sees in the memory of her mother premasticating her first taste of fish a metaphor for a kind of mother's love: "*This is why you / have a mama . . . / . . . Why you must never talk back. Why you must love, honor, obey. My job . . . // is to feed and tell you the stories, & keep / you away from sharp things that might / slip into your throat and never completely / disappear"* (83). Yet, part of adulthood is rejecting the kind of love that requires the daughter's body to be "head off and split" to fit her mother's expectations, and, a few pages later, in the title poem, the fishmonger becomes a kind of "crossing guard of her goodbye" after "everyone gathered for the morning goodbye / smells   of fried fish and grits   sacred   Sunday morning goodbye / food   made especially for only daughters w h o have perfected // the art of leaving" (89). As the poem closes and the adult poet leaves home once again, the fishmonger forgets to finish his fillet, and the speaker dreams of being accepted as that whole fish, "tossed into / the icy silver bowl   A lifetime of waiting   Hungering / to be called Delicious" (94). In the book's final poem, the speaker merges the fish/body metaphor of *Head Off and Split* with the rice/words metaphor of *Rice* as she cautions readers to "[b]e careful to the very end what you deny, dismiss, and cut away," and to "Look up the word *southing* before you use it in a sentence" (97). Referring to a southerly shift in latitude, or a general southward movement, Finney's invocation of a "southing" near the close of her collection as not a verb, but a concrete noun and unit of measurement, reinscribes the reality of regional experience in shaping her poetry and her life in the world. As do each of the poets discussed above, Finney acknowledges the real geography of her regional experience as the underground springs of her art, and the sense impressions of the kitchen table as essential points of access for considering what that can mean moving forward. Her award-winning collection of poems, then, is itself a southing.

All of these poets and their southings, from Blount's light verse to McFee's and Applewhite's meditations on class and childhood to Jeffers's reconsideration of her uncle's unruly desire for self-destructive foods and Young's family rapprochement across a funeral table, share the premise of the sensory experience of food as a way of confronting and gnawing on the bone of southern identity. Though each of the six poets I have considered (and there are many more) find different "basic truths" in taste, they share the representation of food habits as powerful compulsions that refract into questions of identity and history that belie Cobb's image of the New South as naked with no clothes on. One of the closing poems of Finney's *Rice*, "Rule Number One," reflects on how "the love cover we always find to throw / no matter how wide the waters roll // how we hide our heavy hearts / and laugh with our soup bone boney selves // and boil some water and offer even you some / supper has always been on us " (168). Though Finney, like Jeffers and to some extent Young, explores how southern history inflects black American food habits, her metaphor of laying the table for supper as like a quilt, or love cover, over the heavy heart, is not that far away from McFee's thin gravy, Applewhite's embrace of briars, or even Blount's soul-knitting grits that have the Lutherans and Campbellites lying down together. Each, like Egerton, suggests that not just the best of southernness, but the very hope of a workable regional identity in the new century, survives, more than anywhere else these days, at the kitchen table.

Works Cited

Applewhite, James. "Barbecue Service." *Ode to the Chinaberry Tree and Other Poems*. Baton Rouge: Louisiana State UP, 1986. 4.

———. "Earth Lust." *Ode to the Chinaberry Tree and Other Poems*. Baton Rouge: Louisiana State UP, 1986. 10.

———. "Some Words for Fall." *Following Gravity: Poems*. Charlottesville: UP of Virginia, 1980. 50.

Blount, Roy, Jr. "Grits." *Sports Illustrated*, July 1975: 11.

———. *One Fell Soup, or, I'm Just a Bug on the Windshield of Life*. New York: Little, Brown and Co., 1982.

———. "Song to Barbecue Sauce." *Sports Illustrated*, July 1975: 11.

Chambers, Douglas B. "Editor's Introduction." *The Southern Quarterly: Southern Food & Drink in History, Literature and Film* 44.2 (2007): 5–8.

Cobb, James. *Redefining Southern Culture: Mind and Identity in the Modern South*. Athens: U of Georgia P, 1999.

Egerton, John. *Side Orders: Small Helpings of Southern Cookery and Culture*. Atlanta: Peachtree Publishers, 1990.

———. *Southern Food: At Home, on the Road, in History*. 1987; Chapel Hill: U of North Carolina P, 1993.

Finney, Nikky. *Head Off and Split*. Evanston, IL: Northwestern UP, 2011.

———. *Rice*. Toronto: Sister Women, Black Women and Women of Color P, 1995.

Head, Thomas. "Literature, Food in." *Foodways: The New Encyclopedia of Southern Culture*, Vol. 7. Ed. John T. Edge. Chapel Hill: U of North Carolina P, 2007. 70–73.

Jeffers, Honorée Fanonne. *The Gospel of Barbecue*. Kent, Ohio: Kent State UP, 2000.

———. *Red Clay Suite*. Carbondale: Southern Illinois UP, 2007.

Komunyakaa, Yusef. "An Ode to Raccoon." *Oxford American* 49 (2005): 52–53.

Latshaw, Beth A. "Race, Region, Identity, and Foodways in the American South." *Southern Cultures: The Edible South* (Winter 2009): 106–28.

McFee, Michael. "Gravy." *Southern Cultures: The Edible South* (Winter 2009): 129.

———, ed. *The Language They Speak Is Things to Eat: Poems by Fifteen Contemporary North Carolina Poets*. Chapel Hill: U of North Carolina P, 1994.

———. "Pork Skins." *Cornbread Nation 4: The Best of Southern Food Writing*. Eds. Dale Volberg Reed and John Shelton Reed. Athens: U of Georgia P, 2008. 214–15.

———. "Salt." *Cornbread Nation 4: The Best of Southern Food Writing*. Eds. Dale Volberg Reed and John Shelton Reed. Athens: U of Georgia P, 2008. 212–13.

———. "Saltine." *Threepenny Review* 27.3 (2006): 16.

Mennell, Stephen. *The Sociology of Food: Eating, Diet and Culture*. London: SAGE Publications, 1992.

Reed, John Shelton. "The South's Mid-Life Crisis." *My Tears Spoiled My Aim and Other Reflections on Southern Culture*. Columbia: U of Missouri P, 1993. 42–53.

Stanonis, Anthony. "Just Like Mammy Used to Make: Foodways in the Jim Crow South." *Dixie Emporium: Tourism, Foodways, and Consumer Culture in the American South*. Ed. Anthony Stanonis. Athens: U of Georgia P, 2008. 208–33.

Taylor, Joe Gray. *Eating, Drinking, and Visiting in the South: An Informal History*. Baton Rouge: Louisiana State UP, 1982.

Young, Kevin. *Dear Darkness: Poems*. New York: Alfred A. Knopf, 2008.

———, ed. "Introduction." *The Hungry Ear: Poems of Food and Drink*. New York: Bloomsbury, 2012. 1–6.

CONTRIBUTORS

David A. Davis is an assistant professor of English and Southern Studies at Mercer University. He is the author of several essays on southern literature and culture, and he is currently writing a book on World War I and southern modernism.

Elizabeth S. D. Engelhardt is a professor of American Studies and Women's and Gender Studies at the University of Texas at Austin. She is author of *A Mess of Greens: Southern Gender and Southern Food* and lead author of *Republic of Barbecue*, among others. Her next project is a coedited volume on southern food methodologies. She helped found Foodways Texas and currently serves on the board of Southern Foodways Alliance, organizations dedicated to preserving, documenting, and analyzing diverse food stories.

Marcie Cohen Ferris is an associate professor in the Department of American Studies at the University of North Carolina at Chapel Hill, where she directs the Southern Studies concentration. Her research and teaching interests include the history of the Jewish South and the foodways and material culture of the American South. From 2006 to 2008, she served as president of the board of directors of the Southern Foodways Alliance. She has served as editor for two special issues on food for UNC's Center for the Study of the American South's journal, *Southern Cultures*. Her book *Matzoh Ball Gumbo: Culinary Tales of the Jewish South* was nominated for a 2006 James Beard Foundation Award. Her current work, "The Edible South: Food and History in an American Region," examines the expressive power of food in narrative and material culture from the plantation South to the struggles of the Civil Rights Movement.

Lisa Hinrichsen is an assistant professor of English at the University of Arkansas. She has contributed essays to *The Southern Literary Journal, Journal of Modern Literature, The Robert Frost Review, The Southern Quarterly*, and *Etudes Faulknériennes*, among other publications. She is currently revising a manuscript on the roles trauma, fantasy, and misrecognition play in modern and contemporary southern literature. This book manuscript, entitled *The Fantasy of Mastery: Memory, Identity and Alterity in the Post-Plantation Southern Imagination*, draws on the interdisciplinary relationship between literature, history, and psychoanalytic theory to focus on the multiple ways in which the literature of the U.S. South both stages and displaces critical confrontation with its traumatic history through complex systems of historical remembrance and aesthetic erasure.

Erica Abrams Locklear is an assistant professor in the Department of Literature and Language at the University of North Carolina at Asheville. She is author of *Negotiating a Perilous Empowerment: Appalachian Women's Literacies*, and she has published in *The Southern Literary Journal, Appalachian Heritage, Community Literacy Journal, Crossroads: A Southern Culture Annual, North Carolina Folklore Journal*, and others. A native of western Carolina, she focuses much of her scholarship on the region.

Tara Powell is an associate professor of English at the University of South Carolina. She is the author of *The Intellectual in Twentieth-Century Southern Literature* and also of *Physical Science*, a chapbook of poems. Her current research project explores tropes of regional identity in New South verse memoirs.

Ann Romines is a professor of English at George Washington University. She is author of the books *The Home Plot: Women, Writing, and Domestic Ritual* and *Constructing the Little House: Gender, Culture, and Laura Ingalls Wilder*, and of numerous essays on Willa Cather. She also wrote "Baking the Cake: My Recipe for Mashula's Coconut Cake," which reconstructs a recipe from Eudora Welty's *Delta Wedding*.

Ruth Salvaggio is a professor of English and American Studies at the University of North Carolina at Chapel Hill. She is author of the book *Hearing Sappho in New Orleans: The Call of Poetry from Congo Square to the Ninth Ward* and of several other books and essays on poetry and feminist studies. She is a native of New Orleans and has eaten every poetic creation described in her essay for this volume.

David S. Shields is the McClintock Professor of Southern Letters at the University of South Carolina and the chairman of the Carolina Gold Rice Foundation. His most recent book is *Still, American Silent Motion Picture Photography*. His history of Lowcountry foodways, *Southern Provisions: The Creation and Revival of a Cuisine*, is forthcoming.

Melanie Benson Taylor is an associate professor of Native American Studies at Dartmouth College. She is the author of *Disturbing Calculations: The Economics of Identity in Postcolonial Southern Literature, 1912–2002* and *Reconstructing the Native South: American Indian Literature and the Lost Cause*. She has published articles on Barry Hannah, William Faulkner, Louis Owens, and others, and continues to work at the intersections of Native, southern, and American studies.

Sarah Walden is a temporary full-time lecturer in the English Department and Honors College at Baylor University. Her research interests include studies of gender, domesticity, and taste development in nineteenth- and early twentieth-century American literature and culture. She recently completed her dissertation, "Reforming Tastes: Taste as a Print Aesthetic in American Cookery Writing," which examines the rhetorical role of the American cookbook in the creation of national standards of taste.

Psyche Williams-Forson is an associate professor of American Studies at the University of Maryland, College Park and an affiliate faculty member of the Women's Studies and African American Studies departments and the Consortium on Race, Gender, and Ethnicity. She is coeditor with Carole Counihan of *Taking Food Public: Redefining Foodways in a Changing World* and author of the award-winning *Building Houses Out of Chicken Legs: Black Women, Food, and Power*. Her new research explores the role of the value market as an immediate site of food acquisition and women, food, and the underground economy. Williams-Forson's work has received support from, among others, the Smithsonian Institution and the Ford Foundation.

INDEX

CPSIA information can be obtained
at www.ICGtesting.com
Printed in the USA
LVHW041628101218
599930LV00003B/504